ngol
Chinese
nese
Thai
Khmer
Vietnamese
Korean
Ainu
Japanese
Spanish
English
Tagalog
Malay
Balinese

Poetry of Asia

Poetry of Asia

Five Millenniums of Verse from Thirty-three Languages

General Editor:
KEITH BOSLEY

New York · WEATHERHILL · *Tokyo*

First edition, 1979

Published by John Weatherhill, Inc., of New York and Tokyo, with editorial offices at 7–6–13 Roppongi, Minato-ku, Tokyo 106, Japan; by arrangement with Paul Elek Limited, London. Printed and first published, under the title *The Elek Book of Oriental Verse*, in Great Britain.

ISBN 0–8348–0139–6

Printed in Great Britain by
Latimer Trend & Company Ltd Plymouth

To the Reader

This book presents English translations of poetry from thirty-three languages, ranging in space from Japan to Egypt and medieval Spain, from Indonesia to Siberia—a vast area that may be called the Orient with more cultural than geographical accuracy—and in time from the third millennium BC to the present day. It is arranged by language, moving roughly from east to west—the opposite direction to most empire-builders: thus individual traditions are illustrated, and the reader can discover cross-currents for himself. Selections from the 'great' Oriental literatures—Chinese, Japanese, Indian, Persian, Arab, Hebrew—have been kept to a decent minimum to allow many other literatures to make a rare (or even first) appearance in English: thus the presence of only four out of some twenty literary languages in the Indian subcontinent makes possible the introduction of—say—Abkhaz, which in turn is but one of at least seven Northern Caucasian languages sharing the Nart oral tradition.

Each language section has been edited by a specialist, who briefly introduces his choice of material; in a few cases where an appropriate specialist was not available, the general editor took on the task. Since limitations of space ruled out any hope of being comprehensive, it was left to section editors to decide the manner of representation, bearing in mind that literary quality should have precedence over cultural significance: thus some sections concentrate on lyric poetry, some on an outstanding period, and one on a particular verse-form. Where further guide-lines were sought, they were given: that poems should embody what was felt to be a language's own contribution to human culture; that they should be more about this world than any other; that they should be chosen for their quality in the original language rather than because a good translation exists.

'No nation has its own culture; only its own barbarism,' said the Finnish Academician Kustaa Vilkuna; and it is certainly true that those nations which have had contact with others have produced the richest heritage. Some readers of this anthology may scan its pages for the lotus, that great emblem of self-contemplation; but they will find a Thai poet responding to England, a Bengali exploring a Greek myth, an Armenian celebrating a Turkish bath. On the other hand, there has been no editorial whoring after a spurious internationalism: the poets have no doubts about where they belong.

The concern throughout has been to produce (or reproduce) translations with a poetic life of their own in English. For this reason poets whose native language is English, usually working with the specialists and often also advising on the choice, have specially translated over half the material in this book; existing translations have been used where the book was unthinkable without them.

Where in the list of contents two translators are credited for a poem, the names are in chronological order of work done: the first made a literal version (not always in English, not always for this book), the second made an English poem. In the case of Abkhaz, where there are three translators, the first made a literal version in Georgian, the second translated that into English and the third made the English poem.

Some editors discuss, and some translators reflect, the prosody of the original poems; but this was thought to be too complex a subject for fuller treatment in the space available. The demands of translation have sometimes meant abandoning with a sigh a favourite poem so deeply embedded in its culture that commentary would outweigh text: the essay in 'deep translation' on pages 43–44 is a memorial to such casualties. Where the choice was between accuracy and liveliness, preference has been given to the latter: hence, in the Chinese and Japanese sections there is more Pound than Waley—but the latter has the Ainu to himself; in the Tibetan the cavalier versions of Sir Humphrey Clarke and Peter Whigham have been preferred to the more scrupulous renderings of Antoinette K. Gordon and Alexandra David-Neel; and the Hebrew editor finds the tone of his Scriptures better matched by King James than by many more accurate later translations. Much of the time, however, there was no such dilemma, thanks largely to the collaborations which it is hoped will continue beyond this book.

Romanisation in the translations follows the practice of the translators, but diacritics have been kept to a minimum to make for economy of printing and ease of reading; where translators offered alternative romanisations, the more readable was adopted—for example, the amorous Dalai Lama is Tsangyang Gyatso rather than Ts'angs-dbyangs Rgya-mts'o. In the list of sources, where information is more important than readability, romanisation is more precise.

The first people it is a pleasure to thank are those contributors who gave help beyond their assignments. Texts, advice and moral support were generously lent by Mr Peter J. Bee, Professor David Marshall Lang, Mr Nigel Phillips and Dr W. E. Skillend of the School of Oriental and African Studies, and by Dr G. F. Cushing of the School of Slavonic and East European Studies, London University; by Mr George Campbell and Mr Colin Wild of the BBC External Services; by Mrs Seta Arrowsmith, Mr Arthur Cooper, Mrs Bonnie R. Crown of the Asian Literature Program, New York, Mr A. C. Jacobs, Mr Anthony Rudolf of the Menard Press, London, and Miss N. K. Sandars; by the staffs of the School of Oriental and African Studies Library, of the BBC External Services Library and of the Robert Taylor Library, Slough; by Miss Christine Muirhead of Paul Elek Ltd, and by her colleague Mr Antony Wood, whose 'pipe dream' this anthology was. In the face of so much goodwill, remaining imperfections must be laid at the door of the general editor.

Keith Bosley

Contents

CHINESE

edited by Shui Chien-tung and Keith Bosley

CHOU DYNASTY

from THE BOOK OF ODES (10th–7th cents. BC)
11. Ware, ware, snares for hares (*Arthur Cooper*) 28
26. Pine boat a-shift (*Ezra Pound*) 28
55. Dry in the sun by corner of K'i (*Ezra Pound*) 29
from SONGS OF THE SOUTH (4th–3rd cents. BC)
THE SPIRITS OF THE FALLEN (*David Hawkes*) 30

HAN DYNASTY

from NINETEEN OLD POEMS (3rd cent. BC–3rd cent. AD)
Green, green (*Shui Chien-tung/Keith Bosley*) 31

PERIOD OF THE SIX KINGDOMS

T'ao Ch'ien (372–427)
WRITTEN ON THE NINTH DAY OF THE NINTH MONTH OF THE YEAR YI-YÜ (*William Acker*) 31
Hsieh Ling-yün (385–433)
TUNG-YANG VALLEY (*William McNaughton*) 32
Shen Yüeh (441–513)
AN INTERRUPTED EMBOSOMING (*William McNaughton*) 33

T'ANG DYNASTY

Wang Wei (699–761)
SEEING MASTER YÜAN OFF ON HIS MISSION TO KUCHA (*C. H. Kwôck/Vincent McHugh*) 34
Li Po (701–762)
THE RIVER MERCHANT'S WIFE: A LETTER (*Ernest Fenollosa/Ezra Pound*) 34
A SONG OF ADIEU TO THE QUEEN OF THE SKIES, AFTER A DREAM VOYAGE TO HER (*Arthur Cooper*) 35
Tu Fu (712–770)
THE BALLAD OF THE ARMY WAGGONS (*Arthur Cooper*) 37
BALLAD ON SEEING A PUPIL OF THE LADY KUNG-SUN DANCE THE SWORD MIME (*Arthur Cooper*) 38

Han-shan (late 8th–?early 9th cents.)
from COLD MOUNTAIN POEMS (*Gary Snyder*) 40
Han Yü (768–824)
A WITHERED TREE (*A. C. Graham*) 40
Po Chü-i (772–846)
THE RED COCKATOO (*Arthur Waley*) 40
Yüan Chen (779–831)
THE PITCHER (*Arthur Waley*) 41
Li Ho (791–817)
ANCIENT ARROWHEAD (*C. J. Chen/Michael Bullock*) 42
Li Shang-yin (813–858)
THE BRIGHT LUTE (*Shui Chien-tung/Keith Bosley*) 43

SUNG DYNASTY

Li Yü (937–978)
CLEPSYDRA SONG (*Lenore Mayhew*) 45
Li Ch'ing-chao (1081–?1149)
TUNE: 'MAGNOLIA BLOSSOM' (*C. H. Kwôck/Vincent McHugh*) 45
Hsin Ch'i-chi (1140–1207)
WHEN I WAS GREEN (*Arthur Cooper*) 46

YÜAN DYNASTY

Wang Shih-fu (?1250–?) *and* Kuan Han-ch'ing (?–?)
from ROMANCE OF THE WEST CHAMBER (*Henry H. Hart*) 46

MING DYNASTY

T'ang Yin (1470–1523)
INSCRIPTION FOR A PORTRAIT (*John Scott/Graham Martin*) 47

REPUBLIC

Mao Tse-tung (1893–1976)
SNOW (*Alan Ayling/Duncan Mackintosh*) 47
Wen I-to (1899–1946)
from SCARLET BEADS (*Tao Tao Sanders*) 48
Sun Yü-t'ang (?1905–)
from THE RARE HORSES (*Shui Chien-tung/Keith Bosley*) 49

JAPANESE
edited by Harry Guest

ANCIENT PERIOD

from the KO-FUDOKI (early 8th cent.) *William I. Elliott/Noah S. Brannen*
THE COVE 52

Wind and tide 52
In the midst 52
She held the grass 52
from the KINKAFU (date unknown) *William I. Elliott/Noah S. Brannen*
Under a clear 52
Before the shrine 53
Upon the slope 53
Though cow and boar 53
I pray you, rooster 53
See how supply 54
Kakinomoto no Hitomaro (c. 700)
Your hair has turned white (*Kenneth Rexroth*) 54
A strange old man (*Kenneth Rexroth*) 54
The colored leaves (*Kenneth Rexroth*) 54
Night's centre (*Harry Guest*) 54
Yamabe no Akahito (?–736)
I wish I were close (*Kenneth Rexroth*) 55
Ôtomo no Yakamochi (718–785)
A garden. In the spring (*Harry Guest*) 55
Sarumaru (c. 750)
Depth of the mountains (*Harry Guest*) 55
Mononobe Hirotari (before 760)
By my gate camellias (*Harry Guest*) 55

HEIAN PERIOD

Ôe no Chisato (c. 825)
As I watch the moon (*Kenneth Rexroth*) 55
Lady Ono no Komachi (834–880) *Donald Keene*
Thinking about him 56
The flowers withered 56
Lady Ise (late 9th cent.) *Donald Keene*
Not even in dreams 56
If I consider 56
Fujiwara no Toshiyuki (880–907)
Autumn has come invisibly (*Kenneth Rexroth*) 56
Ki no Tsurayuki (882–946)
Out in the marsh reeds (*Kenneth Rexroth*) 56
Ki no Tomonori (early 10th cent.)
This perfectly still (*Donald Keene*) 57
Ôshikôchi no Mitsune (859–907)
The white chrysanthemum (*Kenneth Rexroth*) 57
Anonymous (before 905)
If only, when one heard (*Arthur Waley*) 57
Nôin (11th cent.)
As I approach (*Kenneth Rexroth*) 57

Jakuren (?–1202)
The hanging raindrops (*Kenneth Rexroth*) 57
Saigyô (1118–90)
In a tree standing (*Donald Keene*) 58
Princess Shikushi (?–1201)
The blossoms have fallen (*Donald Keene*) 58

MUROMACHI PERIOD

Zeami Motokiyo (1363–1443)
from the Nô play THE SPIRIT OF THE IRIS (*Ernest Fenollosa/Ezra Pound*) 58

TOKUGAWA PERIOD (*mostly translated by Harry Guest*)

Chikamatsu Monzaemon (1653–1725)
from the puppet play THE LOVE SUICIDES AT SONEZAKI (*Donald Keene*) 60
Bashô (1644–94)
AT TAKADATE 63
A lightning-flash 63
Plum-branch on the mirror's back 63
Crow settling 63
When drinking all alone 63
Autumn has started 64
Purple hibiscus by the road 64
An/old/pond 64
Sea raging 64
I hate crows as a rule 64
A cuckoo winging out of sight 64
LAST POEM 64
Kyoroku (1656–1715)
Now's the time 65
Bonchô (?–1714)
. . . the sound made 65
Onitsura (1660–1738)
Daybreak
THE ANNIVERSARY OF BASHÔ'S DEATH 65
Kikaku (1661–1707)
Flashes of lightning 65
Red hint of dawn 65
And now 66
Chiyo (1703–75)
MY WELL-BUCKET 66
Buson (1715–83)
Spring sunset 66
They left 66
Sunset 66

I leave, you stay 66
A summer thicket 66
Letting its petals 67
WIDOWER 67
Ryôta (1718–87)
This is the world 67
There is no speech 67
Chora (1729–81)
Tarnished alas 67
Issa (1762–1826)
ON THE DEATH OF HIS CHILD 67
Swaying 68
My birthplace 68
The cat 68
STEPMOTHER 68
These mushrooms kill 68
The high grass rustles 68
THE NEXT-TO-LAST POEM 69
HIS MIDWINTER DEATH 69

MODERN PERIOD (*translated by Harry Guest*)

Shiki (1867–1902)
One backward glance 69
Late March 69
Wide moorland spring 69
Shimazaki Tôson (1872–1943)
KOMORO CASTLE 69
Hagiwara Sakutarô (1886–1942)
NIGHT TRAIN 70
WHITE MOON 71
Katô Shûson (1905–)
A winter seagull 71

AINU

SONG (*Arthur Waley*) 72

KOREAN

edited and translated by Peter H. Lee

Master Wŏlmyŏng (c. 742–765)
REQUIEM 75
Master Ch'ungdam (c. 742–765)
ODE TO KNIGHT KILBO 75
Great Master Kyunyŏ (917–973)
from ELEVEN DEVOTIONAL POEMS 76

Unknown *kisaeng* (c. 13th cent.)
THE TURKISH BAKERY 76
WINTER NIGHT 77
SPRING OVERFLOWS THE PAVILION 77
Yi Cho-nyŏn (1269–1343)
White moon 78
Sŏng Sam-mun (1418–56)
Were you to ask me 78
Kim Chŏng-gu (c. 1495/1506)
Who says I am old 78
Hwang Chin-i (c. 1506–44)
I cut in two 79
Sŏng Hon (1535–98)
The mountain is silent 79
Kim Sang-yong (1561–1637)
Fierce beats the rain 79
Yun Sŏn-do (1587–1671)
from SONGS OF FIVE FRIENDS 79
TO MY FRIEND 80
from THE ANGLER'S CALENDAR 80
Prince Inp'yŏng (1622–68)
Don't mock a pine 80
Yi T'aek (1651–1719)
O roc, don't ridicule the small black birds 80
Anonymous
In the wind that blew last night 81
Deep among green valley grasses 81
Pak Tu-jin (1916–)
A MESSAGE FROM THE CRANE 81
APRIL 82
Pak Mogwŏl (1916–78)
UNTITLED 82
A METEORITE 83
Shin Kyŏng-nim (1936–)
TODAY 84

VIETNAMESE

edited and translated by Nguyen Thi Chan Quynh and Keith Bosley

Dang Tran Con (c. 1710–45) *and* Doan Thi Diem (1705–46)
from ODE OF THE WAR WIFE 85
On Nhu Hau (1741–98)
from ODE OF THE RESENTFUL COURTESAN 87
Nguyen Du (1765–1820)
from KIEU 89
Ho Xuan Huong (1768–1839)
SWINGS 90

Folk poems
Plum to peach 91
Remember when you looked green 91
Rain fell in torrents last night 91
In the sky a cloud of blue 91
To Huu (1920–)
LUOM 92

KHMER

edited and translated by Judith Jacob and Edwin Morgan

from the REAMKER (c. 17th cent.) 94
from THE CODE OF BEHAVIOUR FOR THE YOUNG (c. 1700) 95

PHILIPPINE (TAGALOG, SPANISH, ENGLISH)

HOUSEWARMING SONG (*A. Z. de la Cruz/Keith Bosley*) 97
José Rizal (1861–96)
POEM BEFORE EXECUTION (*Keith Bosley*) 98
José García Villa (1914–)
Inviting a tiger for a weekend 100

MALAY

edited and translated by Harry Aveling

Pantuns
They wear/bangles on their arms 101
Ouch!/pricked my foot 101
A thousand doves/fly past 102
Be careful when you choose/a place to bathe 102
Amir Hamzah (1911–46)
TO YOU AGAIN 103
Chairil Anwar (1922–49)
FUTILE 104
FOR RASID 104
Sitor Situmorang (1924–)
TWILIGHT 105
Rendra (1936–)
A WORLDLY SONG 105
Taufiq Ismail (1937–)
GIVE INDONESIA BACK TO ME 106
Sutardji Calzoum Bachri (1942–)
CAT 107
A. Ghafar Ibrahim (1943–)
CROWS 108

BALINESE

from THE SONG OF BAGUS DIARSA (*J. H. Hooykaas-van Leeuwen Boomkamp/Keith Bosley*) 109

THAI

edited and mostly translated by Usa Kanchanavatee and Alan Marshfield

Anonymous (c. 14th–17th cents.)
from THE EPIC OF EXCELLENCY LŎ 112
Si Prat (17th cent.)
REPARTEE 113
Sunthŏn Phu (1786–1855)
from LINES WRITTEN NEAR THE STATUE OF THE BUDDHA AT PRATHOM 114
Phra Maha Montree Sub (fl. 1809–51)
from POOR PRINCE 114
Mŏm Rachothai
from LONDON JOURNEY (1857; *Usa Kanchanavatee/Keith Bosley*) 115
Sujit Wongtes (1945–)
LITTLE STAR (1973) 116
Wat Wanlayangkoon
LOST BANANAS (1975) 117
Nowarat Pongpaiboon (1940–)
INTERCONTINENTAL QUESTION (1975) 118

BURMESE

edited and translated by John Okell and Keith Bosley

Padei-tha-ya-za (c. 1684–1754)
THE FARMER'S FAMILY 120
Sein-dakyaw-thu (1736–71)
SOLDIER'S LETTER 121
Nu Yin (1916–)
TWO STRINGS OF BEADS 122
Thamein Thaung (1932–)
A FORTNIGHT LATER 123
Tin Mo (1939–)
THE SKY IS THE LIMIT 124

TIBETAN

Milarepa (1039–1122)
When the tiger-year was ending (*Sir Humphrey Clarke*) 126

Tsangyang Gyatso, Sixth Dalai Lama (1683–1706) *Peter Whigham*
The old dog/at the west postern 128
Frost/lacing 129

SANSKRIT

edited and translated by Edwin Gerow and Peter Dent

from the RIGVEDA (c. 15th–10th cents. BC)
HYMN TO NIGHT 131
from the RAMAYANA (2nd cent. BC–2nd cent. AD)
I yearn to see the streams 131
Hala (?2nd cent. AD)
To reach my love 132
This flake of moon 132
Thinking you would come 132
How she scolded him 132
Shudraka (?3rd cent.)
from THE LITTLE CLAY CART 132
Kalidasa (4th cent.)
from THE CLOUD-MESSENGER 133
Bhartrihari (early 7th cent.)
The clear lamp of wisdom 134
Woman is the hook 134
Firelight I have 134
Cloud-draped the sky above 134
Amaru (late 7th cent.)
Hurrying to your lover 134
Explain the passion 135
Pouting, in bed 135
from Vidyakara's Treasury (11th cent.)
Bracelets jingle 135
The luck is yours 135
Jayadeva (fl. 12th cent.)
from THE SONG OF THE COWHERD 136

BENGALI

edited by Syed Shamsul Haq

Three Vaishnava poets (15th–16th cents.)
MILAN (*Edward C. Dimock Jr/Denise Levertov*) 137
Rabindranath Tagore (1861–1941) *Syed Shamsul Haq/Keith Bosley*
from BIRTHDAY 139
from ON A SICKBED 139
LAST POEM 140

Jibanananda Das (1899–1954)
SAILOR (*Syed Shamsul Haq/Keith Bosley*) 141
Sudhindranath Datta (1900–64)
OSTRICH (*author*) 141
Buddhadev Bose (1908–)
ICARUS (*Syed Shamsul Haq/Keith Bosley*) 143
Shamsur Rahman (1929–)
THE MEMORY OF YOU (*Syed Shamsul Haq/Keith Bosley*) 144
Syed Shamsul Haq (1935–)
CHAMELEONS (*author*) 145

URDU

edited and translated by David Matthews and Peter Dent

Dard (1721–85)
Charges we've heaped against ourselves 149
Mir (1722–1810)
My plans all overturned 150
Insha (1756–1818)
We're dressed and ready 151
Ghalib (1797–1869)
Desires in thousands fill my mind 152
My foolish heart, what's wrong with you 153
Momin (1800–52)
That understanding we both came to 153
Zafar (1775–1862)
No light in any eye is me 154
Iqbal (1877–1938)
That song, my shaken nightingale 155

TAMIL

edited and mostly translated by A. K. Ramanujan

from the Eight Anthologies (c. 1st–3rd cents.)
'interior' poems
WHAT HER FRIEND SAID *by Kollan Aṛici* 156
WHAT HE SAID *by Cempulappeyanirar* 157
WHAT HE SAID *by Kapilar* 157
WHAT SHE SAID *by Kapilar* 157
WHAT SHE SAID *by Maturai Eṛuttalan Centamputan* 158
WHAT SHE SAID *by Milaipperun Kantan* 158
WHAT HE SAID *by Auvaiyar* 159

'exterior' poems
RELATIONS *by Oreruṛavanar* 159
ELEGY ON A YOUNG WARRIOR *by Ponmutiyar* 160
Nammaṛvar (?9th cent.)
POSSESSION 160
Kampan (11th/12th cents.)
A RIVER 161
Subramanya Bharati (1882–1921)
A NEW HYMN TO THE SUN 162
N. Piccamurti (1900–76)
NATIONAL BIRD (*R. Parthasarathy*) 163

MONGOL

ERINDZEN MERGEN (*G. J. Ramstedt/Keith Bosley*) 165
Pajai (1902–)
BIRTH OF THE HERO (*G. Kara/Keith Bosley*) 167

KIRGHIZ

from MANAS (*Pertev Boratav/Keith Bosley*) 169

KAMASSIAN

edited by Peter Sherwood

LAMENT (*Peter Sherwood/Keith Bosley*) 171

VOGUL

edited and translated by Peter Sherwood and Keith Bosley

SONG MADE BY TUR MY GRANDFATHER 172
SONG OF CONVERSION 173
SONG ABOUT MY VILLAGE 175

ABKHAZ

edited by Zaira Khiba and George Hewitt

MOTHER OF HEROES (*Zaira Khiba/George Hewitt/Keith Bosley*) 176

GEORGIAN

edited and translated by Donald Rayfield

THE YOUTH AND THE LEOPARD 182
Shota Rustaveli (c. 1200)
from THE KNIGHT IN THE PANTHER SKIN 184
Vazha Pshavela (1860–1915)
from THE SNAKE EATER 186
Galaktion Tabidze (1893–1958)
THE WIND BLOWS 189
Titsian Tabidze (1895–?1938)
POEM-LANDSLIDE 190

ARMENIAN

edited and translated by Garbis Yessayan and Keith Bosley

BIRTH OF THE FIRE-GOD (pre-Christian) 191
St Gregory of Narek (c. 945–c. 1003)
SPEAKING WITH GOD FROM THE DEPTHS OF THE HEART 192
Nahabed Kouchag (c. 1500–92)
I've never made a confession to a priest 193
I'm young, you're young 193
Vahan Tekeyan (1877–1944)
MY ONLY ONE 193
Siamanto (1878–1915)
THE DANCE 194
Daniel Varouzhan (1884–1915)
ORIENTAL BATH 196
Yeghishe Charents (1897–1937)
INTO THE FUTURE (1920) 198

PERSIAN

edited by Peter Avery

Rudaki (?–940/1)
All the teeth ever I had (*Basil Bunting*) 202
Your cruel heart is never satisfied (*L. P. Elwell-Sutton*) 203
You have stolen colour and fragrance (*L. P. Elwell-Sutton*) 204
Firdawsi (?934–1020/1 or 1025/6)
from THE BOOK OF KINGS (*Peter Avery/John Heath-Stubbs*) 204
Farrokhi (?–1037/8)
from QASIDA OF THE AMIR'S BRANDING-GROUND (*Peter Avery/John Heath-Stubbs*) 207
'Unsuri (?–1039/40)
Three things have modelled themselves (*L. P. Elwell-Sutton*) 209

Minuchihri (?–c. 1040/1)
AUTUMN WINE (*Peter Avery/John Heath-Stubbs*) 209
Abu Sa'id ibn Abi'l-Khair (967–1048)
Love flowed like blood (*L. P. Elwell-Sutton*) 212
Mu'izzi (1048–1124)
O King, the morning drink's a splendid thing (*L. P. Elwell-Sutton*) 212
Omar Khayyam (1048–1131)
QUATRAINS (*Peter Avery/John Heath-Stubbs*) 212
Rumi (?–1273) *Peter Avery/John Heath-Stubbs*
from THE GREAT COLLECTION 214
from THE MASNAVI 215
Amir Khusrow Dehlavi (1253–1325)
Last night I dreamt you brought me wine (*Omar S. Pound*) 216
Hafiz (c. 1325/6–90) *Peter Avery/John Heath-Stubbs*
Boy, set the bowl on fire 216
Come, hope's palace 217
Now that the cup of clear wine 217
Tresses dishevelled 218
When God formed the shape 219
I saw last night how angels knocked 219
Abu Talib Kalim (?–1651/2)
. . . Half my life spent attaching my heart (*Omar S. Pound*) 220
Hatif of Isfahan (?–1783/4)
THE MESSAGE (*Peter Avery/John Heath-Stubbs*) 220
Iraj (1874–1924)
A VEILED GIRL (*Omar S. Pound*) 221

ANCIENT EGYPTIAN

edited by Francis Landy

Pyramid texts (*Miriam Lichtheim*)
THE KING PRAYS TO THE SKY-GODDESS (c. 2250 BC) 222
THE KING HUNTS AND EATS THE GODS (c. 2300 BC latest) 222
Wisdom literature of the Old and Middle Kingdoms (*Miriam Lichtheim*)
from THE INSTRUCTION ADDRESSED TO KAGEMNI (c. 2200 BC) 224
from THE INSTRUCTION OF PTAHHOTEP (c. 2200 BC) 224
from THE INSTRUCTION ADDRESSED TO KING MERIKARE (c. 2100 BC) 225
from THE COMPLAINTS OF KHAKHEPERRE-SONB (c. 1900 BC) 225
from THE DISPUTE BETWEEN A MAN AND HIS *BA* (c. 1800 BC) 226
Religious poetry (*Miriam Lichtheim*)
from THE INSTRUCTION ADDRESSED TO KING MERIKARE (c. 2100 BC) 226

from THE GREAT HYMN TO THE ATEN (c. 1350 BC) 227
from A HARPER'S SONG (c. 1310 BC) 229
from THE BOOK OF THE DEAD (1500–700 BC): JUDGEMENT 229
Wisdom literature of the New Kingdom (1550–1080 BC) *Miriam Lichtheim*
from THE INSTRUCTION OF ANY 230
from THE INSTRUCTION OF AMENEMOPE 231
from THE IMMORTALITY OF WRITERS 231
Love songs (c. 1400–1200 BC) *John L. Foster*
Aim him straight at the house of your reticent lady 232
How clever my love with a lasso 232
I strip you of your tangled garlands 232
Astray or captured, all bear witness 233
When the fig feels called to speak its mind 233
My heart remembers how I once loved you 233

UGARITIC

edited and translated by Francis Landy

from THE TALE OF AQHAT (recorded c. 1380 BC) 234

MESOPOTAMIAN (SUMERIAN, AKKADIAN)

edited by Francis Landy

from THE EPIC OF GILGAMESH (Akkadian, early 2nd millennium BC; *N. K. Sandars*) 237
from THE BABYLONIAN CREATION EPIC (Akkadian, mid-2nd millennium BC; *N. K. Sandars*) 239
from INANNA'S JOURNEY TO HELL (Sumerian, 3rd millennium BC; *N. K. Sandars*) 240
from THE MESSAGE OF LUDINGIRA TO HIS MOTHER (Sumerian; *Jerrold S. Cooper*) 242
from A LATE BABYLONIAN RELIGIOUS TEXT (Akkadian; *W. G. Lambert*) 243
from A LAMENT (Sumerian, c. 1900 BC; *Raphael Kutscher*) 243
PROVERBS (Sumerian; *E. I. Gordon*) 244

TURKISH

edited by Taner Baybars

from THE BOOK OF DEDE KORKUT (compiled c. 13th cent.)
My lord Kazan (*Geoffrey Lewis*) 245

Yunus Emre (?1238–?1320)
Knowledge is to understand (*Taner Baybars*) 247
Eşrefoğlu (?–1469)
O my God do not part me from thee (*Taner Baybars*) 247
Nedim (?1681–1730)
SONG (*Talat Sait Halman*) 248
Ahmet Haşim (1884–1933)
PROMISED LAND (*Talat Sait Halman*) 249
Nazım Hikmet (1902–63) *Taner Baybars*
A SAD STATE OF FREEDOM 250
DON QUIXOTE 251
Cahit Sıtkı Tarancı (1910–56)
ROBINSON CRUSOE (*Mesut Önen/Richard McKane*) 252
Fazıl Hüsnü Dağlarca (1914–)
ECHO (*Talat Sait Halman*) 253
HEADACHE (*Talat Sait Halman*) 253
HALİM THE THIRD (*Feyyaz Kayacan Fergar*) 253
Orhan Veli Kanık (1914–50)
FOR THIS COUNTRY (*Taner Baybars*) 254
TWEEZERS (*Anıl Meriçelli*) 254
Oktay Rifat (1914–) *Taner Baybars*
ONCE UPON A TIME 254
STARS 255
Melih Cevdet Anday (1915–)
OUR TABLE (*Nermin Menemencioğlu*) 255
İlhan Berk (1916–)
THE GATE OF AHMET THE FIRST (*Talat Sait Halman*) 255
Cahit Külebi (1917–)
IN THE WAR (*Nermin Menemencioğlu*) 256
Behçet Necatigil (1917–)
HARBOUR (*Nermin Menemencioğlu*) 256
Attilâ İlhan (1925–)
ISTANBUL GATE OF FELICITY (*Nermin Menemencioğlu*) 256
Can Yücel (1926–)
ALEA IACTA EST (*Murat Nemet-Nejat*) 257
Cemal Süreya (1931–)
SONG ABOUT EXECUTIONERS (*Nermin Menemencioğlu*) 258

ARABIC

edited and translated by Abdullah al-Udhari and G. B. H. Wightman

PRE-ISLAMIC PERIOD

Find al-Zimmani (?–530)
We forgave the Banu Duhl 260
Munakhal al-Yashkuri (?–597)
It was raining 260

Urwa ibn al-Ward (?–615)
When a man fails to provide for himself 260
I must go and make money 260

POST-ISLAMIC PERIOD

Abu Mihjan (?–652)
I know what the Merciful said of drink 261
When I die bury me by a vine tree 261

UMAYYAD PERIOD

Majnun Laila (?–682)
When Laila was a small tomboy 261
My soul clung to her soul 261
I saw a gazelle 261
How can a pain in the chest be softened 262
Jamil (?–701)
Let us live till we grow old 262
Waddah al-Yaman (?–709)
She said: Don't come to my door 262
Umar Ibn Abi Rabi'a (644–711)
I'm obsessed with a girl who suspects me 263
They told her I married 263
Arji (?–738)
My people forgot me 263

ABBASID PERIOD

Abu al-Shamaqmaq (?–796)
If I sailed a ship 263
When I sat in that empty house 264
Abbas ibn al-Ahnaf (750–809)
Love has trees in my heart 265
When I visit you 265
Abbas I wish you were the shirt 265
Zalum said 265
Abu Nuwas (762–813)
When she left me 265
Ibn al-Rumi (835–896)
When a baby is born 266
I have a country I'd never sell 266
Buhturi (821–897)
Cheerful Spring 266
Abdullah ibn al-Mu'tazz (861–908)
The cavalry of dew 267
Watch now the beauty of the crescent moon 267
I don't want to drink in ruins 267

Mutanabbi (915–965)
Our forebears stayed in the world 267
Abu al-Ala al-Ma'arri (973–1058)
Needles have stitched a death shroud 268
The comet, has it nerves 268
Sin and crime, Raven 268

ANDALUSIAN PERIOD

Hafsa bint Hamdun (10th cent.)
I've a lover who checks his feelings 269
Wallada (?–1091)
Good God, I was born to live a noble life 269
If you were loyal to our union 269
Nazhun (?–1155)
The nights are great 269
Mariam bint Abu Ya'qub (11th cent.)
What does one expect from a woman 270
Hafsa bint al-Haj (?–1189)
The garden didn't smile 270
Shall I join you 270
I send my poems 270
Ask the lightning 270

MODERN PERIOD (translated by Abdullah al-Udhari)

Yusuf al-Khal (1917–)
PRAYERS IN A TEMPLE 271
Nizar Qabbani (1923–)
A PERSONAL LETTER TO THE MONTH OF JUNE 273
Abdul Wahab al-Bayati (1926–)
THE SINGER AND THE MOON 274
Buland al-Haidari (1926–)
CONVERSATION AT THE BEND IN THE ROAD 274
Mouin Besseiso (1926–)
TO RIMBAUD 275
Adonis (1930–)
THE MARTYR 276
A MIRROR FOR THE TWENTIETH CENTURY 276
Muhammad al-Maghut (1934–)
THE POSTMAN'S FEAR 276
Shauqi Abu Shaqra (1935–)
THE FAN AND THE OBSERVATORY DOME 277
Unsi al-Haj (1937–)
GIRL BUTTERFLY GIRL 278
Samih al-Qasim (1939–)
THE CLOCK ON THE WALL 278

HEBREW

edited by Hyam Maccoby

ANCIENT PERIOD

THE BLESSING OF BALAAM 280
(10th cent. BC; Numbers 24: 1–9; *Authorised Version*)
THE LAMENT OF DAVID FOR SAUL AND JONATHAN 281
(8th cent. BC; 2 Samuel 1: 19–27; *Authorised Version*)
NOW I WILL SING TO MY WELLBELOVED 282
(8th cent. BC; Isaiah 5: 1–7; *Authorised Version*)
COMFORT YE, COMFORT YE MY PEOPLE 283
(6th cent. BC; Isaiah 40: 1–8, 10–11; *Authorised Version*)
THE HEAVENS AND THE LAW 284
(?7th cent. BC; Psalm 19; *Authorised Version*)
HOW MANIFOLD ARE THY WORKS! 284
(?7th cent. BC; Psalm 104; *Authorised Version*)
A PILGRIM'S SONG. FOR DAVID 286
(?6th cent. BC; Psalm 122; *Francis Landy*)
LOVE SONG 287
(?5th cent. BC; Song of Songs 7: 1–9; *Keith Bosley*)
OUT OF THE WHIRLWIND 288
(?5th cent. BC; Job 38: 1–14, 16–18; *Stephen Mitchell*)
OLD AGE 289
(3rd cent. BC; Ecclesiastes 12: 1–7; *Authorised Version*)
from THE PRAYER-BOOK (*Hyam Maccoby*)
from the EIGHTEEN BLESSINGS (1st cent. AD) 290
from the BLESSINGS OF 'HEAR, O ISRAEL' (1st cent. AD) 290

MEDIEVAL PERIOD

Amittai ben Shephatiah (8th-9th cent.)
from THE DAY OF ATONEMENT SERVICE (*Nina Salaman*) 291
Solomon ibn Gabirol (1020–c. 1057)
from THE ROYAL CROWN (*Israel Zangwill*) 291
Moses ibn Ezra (c. 1055–1135)
from TARSHISH (*S. Solis-Cohen*) 292
A man should remember (*A. C. Jacobs*) 293
Judah ha-Levi (c. 1075–c. 1141) *David Goldstein*
ISRAEL'S COMPLAINT 293
DIALOGUE BETWEEN ISRAEL AND GOD 294
Abraham ibn Ezra (1089–1164)
OUT OF LUCK (*S. Solis-Cohen*) 295
Anonymous (12th cent.)
ADON OLAM (*George Borrow*) 295
Immanuel Frances (1618–1710)
EPITAPH ON A DWARF (*Hyam Maccoby*) 296

MODERN PERIOD

Chaim Nachman Bialik (1873–1934)
WHEN THE DAYS GROW LONG (*A. C. Jacobs*) 296
David Vogel (1891–1944)
TO HIS DAUGHTER (*A. C. Jacobs*) 298
Uri Zvi Greenberg (1894–)
WITH MY GOD THE BLACKSMITH (*Dom Moraes*) 298
S. Shalom (1904–)
Guard me, O God, from hating (*Ruth Finer Mintz*) 298
Leah Goldberg (1911–)
Will there yet come days of forgiveness (*Ruth Finer Mintz*) 299
Yehuda Amichai (1924–)
from THREE SYNAGOGUES (*A. C. Jacobs*) 299
Haim Be'er (1945–)
THE ORDER OF THE GENERATIONS (*Hyam Maccoby*) 300

CONTRIBUTORS 302

SOURCES 306

Chinese

To speak of Chinese poetry, both terms demand definition. Behind the vast range of virtually separate languages spoken today by a quarter of mankind lie the classical literary language and the script which, being ideographic rather than phonetic, can be read irrespective of speech variations. Much Chinese literature is written in verse without being regarded as poetry—philosophy, criticism, the descriptive essay: the present selection concentrates on the lyric.

The earliest surviving Chinese literature is *The Book of Odes*, a collection of 305 anonymous lyrics compiled—according to tradition—by Confucius, who taught with them, using their rhymed four-character lines and pentatonic tunes as a model of order in language and hence in human affairs—and conferring on poetry a prestige it has enjoyed ever since. Loyalty to the Emperor is a primary Chinese virtue demonstrated in 'The Spirits of the Fallen' from *Songs of the South*, a poem which contrasts strongly with 'The Ballad of the Army Waggons', written a thousand years later by Tu Fu: the humanity of this poem reflects the universal sympathy of the Tao, the Way which is the great counterweight to Confucius, the *yin* to his *yang*. Such a rigidly stratified society had a high drop-out rate among the educated, and there is a lively tradition of hermit poets communing with humbler creatures: Li Shang-yin's famous poem contrasts an Emperor who built a city with a philosopher who achieved enlightenment on dreaming of a butterfly and wondering whether the butterfly was dreaming of him instead. Li Shang-yin lived in the twilight of China's golden age, the T'ang Dynasty, with its twin luminaries Li Po and Tu Fu. By this time the *shih* with its regular five-character line, which had been in use since the Han Dynasty, had acquired tonal patterning in addition to rhyme; a further refinement of syntactic patterning culminated in the eight-line poem which has been dubbed the 'Chinese sonnet'. This is the form of—among others—'A Withered Tree' by the stylist Han Yü, a poem asserting native values against the imported Buddhism of hermits like Han-shan; it is also the form of 'The Bright Lute', which uses the later seven-character line. Meanwhile, the introduction of more complex musical styles from Western Asia led to the development of a new type of poem, the *tz'u*, combining lines of varying length, which reached its peak under the Sung Dynasty: the *shih*, with its regular lines, and the more colloquial *tz'u* remain the two basic types of Chinese lyric poetry.

When the invading Mongols established themselves as the Yüan Dynasty, cultural life suffered such a reverse that the 'mixed entertainment' became respectable: its modern descendant, known as Chinese opera, still combines drama, mime, music and dance. The *Romance of the West Chamber*, which has been described as a Chinese *Romeo and Juliet*, is one of the most popular works of the period; the speech given here illustrates the directness of idiom which characterises the genre and sets it apart from most Chinese poetry. The expulsion of the Mongols and the founding of the Ming Dynasty saw the rise of the novel but did little to revive the lyric, which went into a decline until modern times.

Of the modern masters represented here, Mao Tse-tung—revolutionary leader though he was—was a deeply conservative poet, while Wen I-to abandoned the classical language and introduced Western forms. It was to Wen I-to that Sun Yü-t'ang dedicated his most ambitious work, *The Rare Horses*, which attempts a synthesis of East and West in both subject and form. It tells the story of a Han emperor's expedition in the 2nd century BC to the steppes of Bactria (modern Turkestan) in search of thoroughbred horses; it is itself a rare beast, a Chinese epic whose bounding rhythms recall Homer. The selection ends with the opening lines of this neglected masterpiece.

from 'The Book of Odes' (10th–7th cents. BC)

11

Ware, ware, snares for hares,
Peg 'em down, ding, ding:

Fair, fair, the Warriors,
My Lord's
Bucklers and Bastions!

Ware, ware, snares for hares,
Spread 'em in the tracks:

Fair, fair, the Warriors,
My Lord's
Dearest Companions!

Ware, ware, snares for hares,
Spread 'em in the woods:

Fair, fair, the Warriors,
My Lord's
Soul and Opinions!

26

Pine boat a-shift
on drift of tide,

for flame in the ear, sleep riven,
driven; rift of the heart in dark
no wine will clear,
nor have I will to playe.

Mind that's no mirror to gulp down all's seen,
brothers I have, on whom I dare not lean,
angered to hear a fact, ready to scold.

My heart no turning-stone, mat to be rolled,
right being right, not whim nor matter of count,
true as a tree on mount.

Mob's hate, chance evils many, gone through,
aimed barbs not few;
at bite of the jest in heart
start up as to beat my breast.

O'ersoaring sun, moon malleable
alternately
lifting a-sky to wane;
sorrow about the heart like an unwashed shirt, I
clutch here at words,
having no force to fly.

55

Dry in the sun by corner of K'i
green bamboo, bole over bole:
Such subtle prince is ours
to grind and file his powers
as jade is ground by wheel;
he careth his people's weal,
stern in attent,
steady as sun's turn bent
on his folk's betterment
nor will he fail.

Look ye here on the coves of the K'i:
green bamboo glitteringly!
Of as fine grain our prince appears
as the jasper plugs in his ears

ground bright as the stars in his cap of state;
his acumen in debate
splendid, steadfast in judgement-hall
he cannot fail us
nor fall.

In coves of K'i,
bamboo in leaf abundantly.
As metal tried is fine
or as sceptre of jade is clean;
stern in his amplitude,
magnanimous to enforce true laws, or lean
over chariot rail in humour
as he were a tiger
with velvet paws.

from 'Songs of the South' (4th–3rd cents. BC)

THE SPIRITS OF THE FALLEN

Grasping our great shields and wearing our hide armour,
Wheel-hub to wheel-hub locked, we battle hand to hand.
Our banners darken the sky; the enemy teem like clouds:
Through the hail of arrows the warriors press forward.
They dash on our lines; they trample our ranks down.
The left horse has fallen, the right one is wounded.
Bury the wheels in; tie up the horses!
Seize the jade drumstick and beat the sounding drum!
The time is against us: the gods are angry.
Now all lie dead, left on the field of battle.
They went out never more to return:
Far, far away they lie, on the level plain,
Their long swords at their belts, clasping their elmwood bows.
Head from body sundered: but their hearts could not be vanquished.
Both truly brave, and also truly noble;
Strong to the last, they could not be dishonoured.
Their bodies may have died, but their souls are living:
Heroes among the shades their valiant souls will be.

from 'Nineteen Old Poems' (3rd cent. BC–3rd cent. AD)

Green, green
the grass by the river
sad, sad
the willow in the park
come, come
smiles the girl in the pavilion
pale, pale
idling at the window
flutter, flutter
eyebrows
made up like moths' wings
slender, slender
white hand
stretched out naked

O once I was a good-time girl
then I married a ne'er-do-well
but now my ne'er-do-well has gone:
how can I lie in bed alone?

T'ao Ch'ien (372–427)

WRITTEN ON THE NINTH DAY OF THE NINTH MONTH OF THE YEAR *YI-YÜ* (409)

Slowly, slowly,
the autumn draws to its close.
Cruelly cold
the wind congeals the dew.
Vines and grasses
will not be green again—
The trees in my garden
are withering forlorn.
The pure air
is cleansed of lingering lees
And mysteriously,
Heaven's realms are high.

green, green: the colour associated with immorality—a 'green pavilion' is a brothel. The lady's behaviour is therefore to be deplored.

Nothing is left
of the spent cicada's song,
A flock of geese
goes crying down the sky.
The myriad transformations
unravel one another
And human life
how should it not be hard?
From ancient times
there was none but had to die,
Remembering this
scorches my very heart.
What is there I can do
to assuage this mood?
Only enjoy myself
drinking my unstrained wine.
I do not know
about a thousand years,
Rather let me make
this morning last forever.

Hsieh Ling-yün (385–433)

TUNG-YANG VALLEY

I

This I regret—
a woman
I do not know

washes her white
feet
in the dark water.

The bright moon
shines
in the clouds

so far, far away
no one
shall reach it.

II

This I regret—
a man
I do not know

rides a white
boat
on the dark water.

Just as I
would ask
what he is

up to, the moon
sinks
into the clouds.

Shen Yüeh (441–513)

AN INTERRUPTED EMBOSOMING

Shadows, carried
on the slanting
moon, fall by.

Perfumes, set on
by the distant
wind, move near.

She says, 'It is'
and sees
at once, it is not.

She almost laughs
but the laugh
comes out as tears.

Wang Wei (699–761)

SEEING MASTER YÜAN OFF ON HIS MISSION TO KUCHA

City on Wei
        the morning rain
                wet
                on light dust
Around the inn
        green willows
        fresh
I summon you:
        Drink one more cup
No old friends, my friend
When you speed westward
                past Yang Kuan

Li Po (701–762)

THE RIVER MERCHANT'S WIFE: A LETTER

While my hair was still cut straight across my forehead
I played about the front gate, pulling flowers.
You came by on bamboo stilts, playing horse,
You walked about my seat, playing with blue plums.
And we went on living in the village of Chokan:
Two small people, without dislike or suspicion.

At fourteen I married My Lord you.
I never laughed, being bashful.
Lowering my head, I looked at the wall.
Called to, a thousand times, I never looked back.

At fifteen I stopped scowling,
I desired my dust to be mingled with yours
Forever and forever and forever.
Why should I climb the look out?

At sixteen you departed,
You went into far Ku-to-yen, by the river of swirling eddies,

And you have been gone five months.
The monkeys make sorrowful noise overhead.

You dragged your feet when you went out.
By the gate now, the moss is grown, the different mosses,
Too deep to clear them away!
The leaves fall early this autumn, in wind.
The paired butterflies are already yellow with August
Over the grass in the West garden;
They hurt me. I grow older.
If you are coming down through the narrows of the river Kiang,
Please let me know beforehand,
And I will come out to meet you
As far as Cho-fu-Sa.

A SONG OF ADIEU TO THE QUEEN OF THE SKIES, AFTER A DREAM VOYAGE TO HER

Seafarers tell of the Fairy Isles
Hid in sprays of great seas, not easily sought;
Yüeh people say the Queen of the Skies
Can for moments be seen in a rainbow's light,
Risen high in the air beneath Heaven's Yoke,
Overawing Red Rampart, above the Five Peaks;
Where Heaven's Terrace, forty-eight thousand feet,
Faces, as if it would fall, towards the South-East:

To dream my way to Wu and Yüeh
I flew the other night over Mirror Lake;
Mirror Lake's moon, chasing my shadow,
Saw me as far as the Darting Brook;
And the Mansion still stood of the good Duke Hsieh,
Where his green waters rushed and his gibbons wailed;

There the Duke's climbing clogs I took for my feet
For I too would ascend his blue cloud ladder;
And I saw, from half-way, Sun spring from the sea,
Heard Heaven's Cock himself crow down from Heaven!
But in a thousand crags my way was unclear
Till, lost in wild flowers in those scars and ghylls,
I reclined on a rock: suddenly dark fell
And bears growled, dragons howled, waterfalls thundered,

Affrighting the forests,
aye,
And the piled-up peaks!

The clouds were black, black,
aye,
And the rain would come!

The waters still, still,
aye,
And making mists!

Then lightning flashed,
Thunder rolled,
And peaks collapsed!
And, guarding Heaven's Grotto,
The rock split in two
On a great blue cavern: I could see no ground,
Sun *and* Moon on the roofs of silver and gold!

Rainbows their raiment,
aye,
The winds for their steeds!

Her Cloud Princesses,
aye,
Came riding in train!

Her Lutenists tigresses,
aye,
Phoenix drawing her Car!

And all her Fairy Folk,
aye,
Were like fields of flax!

My spirit was startled,
my senses were stirred,
With such awe upon me
that I sighed aloud;

Then woke to find nothing
but pillow and quilt,

And lost was that Vision
of Vapour and Cloud
(And so Joys go for ever, where here below
The waters in the rivers all Eastward flow!)

O Queen, I must leave you,
aye,
But when to return?

Upon this green hillside
I'll keep a white deer
To ride, when the time comes,
to your Glorious Peaks!

For how can I drop my glance, bow my waist to the Great,
Who will never let me show my true heart or true face?

Tu Fu (712–770)

THE BALLAD OF THE ARMY WAGGONS

The din of waggons! Whinnying horses!
Each marcher at his waist has bow and quiver;
Old people, children, wives, running alongside,
Who cannot see, for dust, bridge over river:

They clutch clothes, stamp their feet, bar the way weeping,
Weeping their voices rise to darkening Heaven;
And when the passers-by question the marchers,
The marchers but reply, 'Levies come often:

'They take us at fifteen for up the river,
To garrison the West, they'll take at forty,
Your Headman has at first to tie your turban,
Grey-headed you come home, then back to duty—

'The blood that's flowed out there would make a sea, Sir!
Our Lord, his lust for land knows no degree, Sir!
But have you not heard
Of House of Han, its East two hundred regions
Where villages and farms are growing brambles?

'That though a sturdy wife may take the plough, Sir,
You can't see where the fields begin and end, Sir?
That Highlanders fare worst, they're hardy fighters
And so they're driven first, like dogs and chickens?

'Although you, Sir, ask such kind questions,
Dare the conscripts tell their wretchedness?
How, for instance, only last winter
The Highland troops were still in the line
When their Prefect sent urgent demands,
Demands for tax, I ask you, from where?
So now we know, no good having sons,
Always better to have a daughter:
For daughters will be wed to our good neighbours
When sons are lying dead on Steppes unburied!

'But have you not seen
On the Black Lake's shore
The white bones there of old no one has gathered,
Where new ghosts cry aloud, old ghosts are bitter,
Rain drenching from dark clouds their ghostly chatter?'

BALLAD ON SEEING A PUPIL OF THE LADY KUNG-SUN DANCE THE SWORD MIME

A Great Dancer there was,
the Lady Kung-sun,
And her 'Mime of the Sword'
made the World marvel!

Those, many as the hills,
who had watched breathless
Thought sky and earth themselves
moved to her rhythms:

As she flashed, the Nine Suns
fell to the Archer;
She flew, was a Sky God
on saddled dragon;

She came on, the pent storm
before it thunders;

And she ceased, the cold light
off frozen rivers!

Her red lips and pearl sleeves
are long since resting,
But a dancer revives
of late their fragrance:

The Lady of Lin-ying
in White King city
Did the piece with such grace
and lively spirit

That I asked! Her reply
gave the good reason
And we thought of those times
with deepening sadness:

There had waited at Court
eight thousand Ladies
(With Kung-sun, from the first,
chief at the Sword Dance);

And fifty years had passed
(a palm turned downward)
While the winds, bringing dust,
darkened the Palace

And they scattered like mist
those in Pear Garden,
On whose visages still
its sun shines bleakly!

But now trees had clasped hands
at Golden Granary
And grass played its sad tunes
on Ch'ü-t'ang's Ramparts,

For the swift pipes had ceased
playing to tortoiseshell;
The moon rose in the East,
joy brought great sorrow:

An old man knows no more
  where he is going;
On these wild hills, footsore,
  he will not hurry!

Han-shan (late 8th–?early 9th cents.)

from COLD MOUNTAIN POEMS

Clambering up the Cold Mountain path,
The Cold Mountain trail goes on and on:
The long gorge choked with scree and boulders,
The wide creek, the mist-blurred grass.
The moss is slippery, though there's been no rain
The pine sings, but there's no wind.
Who can leap the world's ties
And sit with me among the white clouds?

Han Yü (768–824)

A WITHERED TREE

Not a twig or a leaf on the old tree,
Wind and frost harm it no more.
A man could pass through the hole in its belly,
Ants crawl searching under its peeling bark.
Its only lodger, the toadstool which dies in a morning,
The birds no longer visit in the twilight.
But its wood can still spark tinder.
It does not care yet to be only the void at its heart.

Po Chü-i (772–846)

THE RED COCKATOO

Sent as a present from Annam—
A red cockatoo.

Han-shan **(Cold Mountain): the name both of the poet and of his place of retreat.**

Coloured like the peach-tree blossom,
Speaking with the speech of men.
And they did to it what is always done
To the learned and eloquent.
They took a cage with stout bars
And shut it up inside.

Yüan Chen (779–831)

THE PITCHER

I dreamt I climbed to a high, high plain;
And on the plain I found a deep well.
My throat was dry with climbing and I longed to drink,
And my eyes were eager to look into the cool shaft.
I walked round it, I looked right down;
I saw my image mirrored on the face of the pool.
An earthen pitcher was sinking into the black depths;
There was no rope to pull it to the well-head.
I was strangely troubled lest the pitcher should be lost,
And started wildly running to look for help.
From village to village I scoured that high plain;
The men were gone; fierce dogs snarled.
I came back and walked weeping round the well;
Faster and faster the blinding tears flowed—
Till my own sobbing suddenly woke me up;
My room was silent, no one in the house stirred.
The flame of my candle flickered with a green smoke;
The tears I had shed glittered in the candle-light.
A bell sounded; I knew it was the midnight-chime;
I sat up in bed and tried to arrange my thoughts;
The plain in my dream was the graveyard at Ch'ang-an,
Those hundred acres of untilled land.
The soil heavv and the mounds heaped high;
And the dead below them laid in deep troughs.
Deep are the troughs, yet sometimes dead men
Find their way to the world above the grave.
And tonight my love who died long ago
Came into my dream as the pitcher sunk in the well.
That was why the tears suddenly streamed from my eyes,
Streamed from my eyes and fell on the collar of my dress.

Li Ho (791–817)

ANCIENT ARROWHEAD

Lacquer flakes, bone-dust and water
    made this vermilion colour;
And fearful, ancient stains
    bloomed on this bronze arrowhead.
Its white feathers and gold rings
    have now gone with the rain,
Leaving only this angular wolf's tooth.

Riding the plain with a pair of horses,
I found it, east of the courier station,
    among the weeds.
The long wind shortened the day,
    while a few stars shivered,
And damp clouds like black banners
    were hoisted in the night.

Thin devils and ghosts sang
    to the left and right.
I offered them pressed mutton and cream,
And crickets were silent, wild geese sick and reeds turned
red.
The spirit of the whirlwind spat emerald fire
    to bid me farewell.

I stowed it away with my tears.
Its point, crimson and crooked,
    once bit into flesh.
In various districts, young riders ask me
Why I don't sell it to buy firewood.

Li Shang-yin (813–858)

THE BRIGHT LUTE

theme and variations

The bright lute—to what end?—
has fifty strings:
each string, each bridge
recalls a flowering year.

Chuang-tzŭ dawned, dreamed
of turning butterfly.
Wang-ti in spring
loved, wept and was a rose.
The vast sea, the moon full:
a pearl sheds tears!
The Blue Field, the sun warm:
jade gives off mist!

Did this scene wait
to hound the memory?
Well, it is past and gone:
now all is vague.

1

Play the lute!
and she did, the god's daughter
so well the god's eyes swelled with tears, and he
smashed it in two.
How many years
double with sorrow, halve with tears?

2

To see the
light, to know
all is one:

theme and variations: the *theme* is a translation of the highly allusive original; the *variations* expand on some of the allusions, but 'bright lute' must still serve for a zither-like instrument adorned with varnished layers of brocade, 'rose' and 'nightingale' for a rhododendron and a nightjar associated with adultery like the Western cuckoo.

butterfly
    do I dream
        you or you
me?

3

They named the city after me because
I turned spring floods away: but I had turned
a minister away to build canals
so that his wife and I
could flood each other. Now the nightingale
sobs blood into the rose: listen, they say
the Emperor is singing to his love!

4

The mind is on the water:
the fingers on the lute
            strum empty chords
            but the lute's belly
fills as the oyster fills with pearls at full
moon
    as the mermaids in the south sea spill
    pearls from their weeping eyes.

The mind is in the mountains:
the fingers on the lute
            pluck high, far notes
            but the lute's belly
fetches them back and warms them as the sun
warms
    jade, the cold virgin from the hills.
    Likewise the poem: STAND WELL BACK!

5

I stand. I sit. I dream. Or do I lie?

Li Yü (937–978)

CLEPSYDRA SONG

Gold sparrows held your hair
and for a moment
            among flowers
your face colored
            under its powder.

I knew my mind
I guessed your heart
            but love must answer Heaven.

The incense cones its ash
the candle piles its tears
as tears and ash, our thought.

The mountains on my pillow shine,
my worked silk quilt is cold,
and time's fragmented by the water-clock.

Li Ch'ing-chao (1081–?1149)

TUNE: 'MAGNOLIA BLOSSOM'

Bought
            from the flower-peddler's tray
one spring branch
                        just open
                        in bloom
Droplets
                  fleck it evenly
still clouded red
                        with a mist of dew
I'm afraid he'll
                        take it into his head
that my face is not
                  so fair!
                  so fair!

In high-
combed hair

I fasten
a gold pin
aslant
There!
let him look
Let him compare the two

Hsin Ch'i-chi (1140–1207)

WHEN I WAS GREEN

When I was green, and hadn't seen
The bitterness of sorrows,
And upper floors
I loved to gain:
And upper floors
I loved to gain,
To put in odes, très à la mode,
My sorrows, I sought 'em!

Now all there's been, so that I've seen
The bitterness of sorrows,
I long to tell,
But I refrain:
I long to tell,
But I refrain,
And only say: 'Cooler today,
Quite a nip of autumn!'

Wang Shih-fu (?1250–?) and Kuan Han-ch'ing (?–?)

from ROMANCE OF THE WEST CHAMBER

Spring is astir in her milk-white breast,
And the beauty of the springtime gleams upon her broad fair brow.
She scorns the jades and riches that other men may give.
Her face as lovely as the blossom of the apricot
And her cheeks so like the flower of the peach
Are illumined by the brilliant moon above,
Making even more resplendent
The crimson and pure white of her fair skin.

She descends the fragrant stair
And walks daintily upon the bright-green moss
With slippers tiny as the phoenix-head.
Ah, how I regret my own unworthiness,
And how I thank you, my beloved one,
For this, the supreme gift of love that you have brought.
If you can, come back,
Come back early to me, again, this very night!

T'ang Yin (1470–1523)

INSCRIPTION FOR A PORTRAIT

Last night the cherry-apple
  deflowered by the first rain-drops
Its fallen petals slight and frail
  their beauty almost articulate.
My mistress rising early
  leaves her bedroom
In her hand a mirror
  to admire her painted cheeks.
She asks me 'Which is prettier
  the petals or my complexion?'
To her question I reply
  'They win by innocence.'
At hearing this my mistress
  displays a charming anger
Refusing to believe dead petals
  surpass a real live person.
She crumbles a handful of blossom
  to throw in my face—
'Tonight, my dear' she says
  'sleep with the flowers!'

Mao Tse-tung (1893–1976)

SNOW

The North country;
A thousand miles sealed with ice,
Ten thousand miles of whirling snow;

On either side of the Great Wall
Endless waste and wilderness;
Up and down, the Great River
Lost without its swirling flow.
Mountains, dancing silver snakes;
Massifs, humped white elephants—
As if they wished to rival heaven in height!
And when the day shines clear
A sun-red robe colours the mantling white;
Supreme delight!

Country of overpowering beauty such as this
Has led unnumbered heroes to concede their homages.
A pity the First Ch'in and Wu of Han
Lacked somewhat in refinement;
That T'ang Tsung and Sung Tsu
In literary merit fell away;
That he, the pride of heaven in his day,
Genghiz Khan,
Who bent his bow at mighty eagles, learned no other lesson.
All these are past and gone.
To make a record of Heroic Man
Look to the Present!

Wen I-to (1899–1946)

from SCARLET BEADS

We are one body!
Our union
Is as round and perfect as the globe.
But you are the Eastern hemisphere,
And I the Western,
The tears that we ourselves have shed
Made this vast Pacific,
Cutting us in two.

*

I send these poems to you,
Even if you do not know all the words,
It doesn't matter.
With your fingers you can

Gently caress them,
Like a doctor feeling a patient's pulse,
Perhaps you can detect in
Their excited pulsations
The same rhythm as your own heart-beats.

*

Do you understand?
We are a pair of red candles
Shining on a wedding feast for guests;
We stand at opposite corners
Of the table,
Quietly burning away our lives,
Companions to their pleasure.
When they have eaten,
Our lives will have burnt away.

Sun Yü-t'ang (?1905–)

from THE RARE HORSES

West from Chang-an ten thousand miles, thorny desert road.
On the roof of the world the thousand peaks of the Hindu Kush
rise: layer on layer of ageless drifting snows
melting to glaciers, streams tumbling, roaring down
under cliff, through ravine, west beyond an ancient kingdom
set in a ring of mountains. Seventy-odd walled cities,
three hundred thousand people: larks hovering
over barley fields that billowed in the wind,
innumerable sheep grazing on hills, and in mid-autumn
vines shedding fragrance hundreds of miles around,
orchards heavy with all manner of golden fruit,
songs floating down from the vineyards, echoing from the western
to the eastern hills, bearing peace, bearing dreams.
When the vines were ripe, girls lugged bamboo baskets,
whole families with mule-carts piled high with luscious grapes
purple and scarlet, the temples a riot of lanterns,
each household busy with the wine harvest:
the tables of the rich were heaped with opium
and winking glasses slowly filled, silently drained.

King Urgua had a thick red beard, a gorgeous palace
in Kushan, a turquoise crown green as his eyes,
a park of peonies scarlet as his desires:
he loved wise men from Antioch, great pearls from India,
maidens from Oxiana, peacocks from Persia,
he loved jade from Khotan, purple yet translucent,
carved bows from the Uzun that shot barbed arrows whistling,
he loved naked women covered with sand and snow-white gauze
stretched out on Kapisan carpets, smiling like stranded fish,
he loved to drink fine wines from gold goblets, to open
his blood-red lips and sing to a moon hazy with sand.
The precious wine spilled sweetness on the sleeves that danced
across the lutes, stained the bare breasts, the royal robes.
But above all he loved rare horses (was this not his fate?),
he loved their bodies eight feet long, red manes, black tails,
he loved their noble height as they reared up, their sheer
power that would drive them a thousand miles at full gallop:
and he commanded all his keepers, all his trainers
to breed them in his stables, in his parks, to fit them
with stirrups of gold, with saddles splendidly inlaid,
and he named them—Kilin, Chaoa, Valiu, Lüer.
He was well pleased: his sharp forked tongue flickered with a smile
out of the evil depths of his heart, a smile of red flame
mocking all neighbouring states, claiming to be supreme. . . .

Japanese

Although the Japanese had no written language until Buddhist missionaries arrived from China in the 5th century there seems to have been a considerable body of poetry created and preserved orally—folk songs, love poems, statements of national pride and rituals associated with Shintô ceremonies. These, together with various myths and facts, were compiled by court order when it had—laboriously—become possible to write the native language down using Chinese characters and syllabaries derived from them.

In the 8th century the first anthology devoted only to poetry was begun—the *Manyôshû*—which contains some of the most beautiful lyrics ever written. The range and control of a poet like Hitomaro is as sophisticated as that of any comparable Chinese poet but the tone is uniquely and splendidly Japanese. In the *Manyôshû* many of the poems are in *tanka* form—31 syllables arranged 5–7–5–7–7, a form that remained the first method of expression for Japanese poets for about 800 years. Indeed, the *haiku* which perhaps replaced it is really a conciser *tanka* being 17 syllables arranged 5–7–5, a *tanka* in fact without the final couplet.

Japanese poets—both male and female—show an intense awareness of the beauty of their landscape, a keen often heartbroken response to the passage of the seasons, a poignant sensuality and above all in a land of earthquakes and typhoons a fatalistic understanding of the shortness and vulnerability of human life.

All these qualities are to be found in maybe the most perfect poetic drama ever written. In the 15th century the greatest Nô plays appeared, in which ghosts of lost passions return to haunt the scenes of their distress, or heroes and heroines while realising the fleeting quality of all happiness still go seeking it in all the knowledge of despair. Two centuries later, in the more bustling world of Ôsaka and Edo (later Tokyo), a robuster form of theatre arose, Kabuki, and its puppet counterpart, Bunraku.

During the 17th and 18th centuries the masterpieces of *haiku* were written. In essence a *haiku* must bring together two unlikely themes and let them interplay, though the process is lyrical rather than intellectual. *Haiku* particularly include many untranslatable 'words' that are similar to interjections or pauses: these have been rendered where possible in the present work by the arrangement of words on the page.

In the 19th century Japan—half-willingly—was brought into contact with the outside world from which she had isolated herself since the early 17th century. Many poets responded with a wild and untrammelled tastelessness but Shimazaki and Hagiwara are good examples of poets who combined the spirit of classical forms with a flowing colloquial idiom that is still the basis for much of the best poetry being written in Japan today.

from the 'Ko-fudoki'
(topographical records, compiled early 8th cent.)

THE COVE

Close to pines
purified by sun and wind,
waters peel off
into tides that
bubble over white sand.

*

Three poems reflecting perhaps a Shintô rite in connection with spring rice-planting and autumn rice-harvesting, in which young men and women would meet on a mountain top and, as a climax to the various festivities, spend the night together.

Wind and tide
have never devastated
so deliciously
as here,
last night.

*

In the midst of
all these celebrants
I should have been anonymous
and still I blushed,
feeling your eyes upon me.

*

She held the grass
for help
uphill,
but found my hand
dependable.

from the 'Kinkafu'
(a single scroll of twenty-one ancient songs, date unknown)

Under a clear
incomparable sky,
Yamato awaits me—

Yamato, whose rocks and trees,
streams and mountains, house the gods.
O Isle of the Dragonfly,
unspeakable your grandeur,
and my longing.

(The emperor is homesick for the capital.)

*

Before the shrine
rice grows green
plenteous and plain.

*

Upon the slope
that shades the spring
of this far mountain,
bamboo brought from Awaji
is languishing,
as slender as an arrow,
frail and forlorn.

(The emperor has sent for a girl who has to wait in an outbuilding until domestic troubles are smoothed over.)

*

Though cow and boar
are free to roam the sedge field
at the mountain's foot,
mere commoners will kindly
refrain from all trespassing.

*

I pray you, rooster,
if at dawn you find
my love and me still locked
beyond the light's awakening,
stand tall in the garden,
rooster—rear back
and crow us lustily awake.

(According to etiquette a man must depart stealthily before dawn.)

*

See how supply
side-by-side beside the road
oak and hazel sway
away the lazy hours,
oh, wagging their long, loose tongues!

(Scolding two wayside whores.)

Kakinomoto no Hitomaro (c. 700)

Your hair has turned white
While your heart stayed
Knotted against me.
I shall never
Loosen it now.

*

A strange old man
Stops me,
Looking out of my deep mirror.

*

The colored leaves
Have hidden the paths
On the autumn mountain.
How can I find my girl,
Wandering on ways I do not know?

attributed to Hitomaro

Night's centre
deepening.
Cry of wild geese.

I watch the moon along the sky.

Yamabe no Akahito (d. 736)

I wish I were close
To you as the wet skirt of
A salt girl to her body.
I think of you always.

Ôtomo no Yakamochi (718–785)

A garden. In the spring.
Deep red and fragrant the peach-flowers
    shedding their glow
    on the path
    she leaves by.

Sarumaru (c. 750)

Depth of the mountains
The red leaves beneath my feet
            A deer calls

Autumn sadness

Mononobe Hirotari (before 760)

By my gate camellias
hang above the slope
and should my hand brush you
flowers may
fall to the ground.

Ôe no Chisato (c. 825)

As I watch the moon
Shining on pain's myriad paths,
I know I am not
Alone involved in autumn.

Lady Ono no Komachi (834–880)

Thinking about him
I slept, only to have him
Appear before me—
Had I known it was a dream,
I should never have wakened.

*

The flowers withered,
Their colour faded away,
While meaninglessly
I spent my days in the world
And the long rains were falling.

Lady Ise (late 9th cent.)

Not even in dreams
Can I meet him any more—
My glass each morning
Reveals a face so wasted
I turn away in shame.

*

If I consider
My body like the fields
Withered by winter,
Can I hope, though I am burnt,
That spring will come again?

Fujiwara no Toshiyuki (880–907)

Autumn has come invisibly.
Only the wind's voice is ominous.

Ki no Tsurayuki (882–946)

Out in the marsh reeds
A bird cries out in sorrow,
As though it had recalled
Something better forgotten.

Ki no Tomonori (early 10th cent.)

This perfectly still
Spring day bathed in the soft light
From the spread-out sky,
Why do the cherry blossoms
So restlessly scatter down?

Ôshikôchi no Mitsune (859–907)

The white chrysanthemum
Is disguised by the first frost.
If I wanted to pick one
I could find it only by chance.

Anonymous (before 905)

If only, when one heard
That Old Age was coming
One could bolt the door
Answer 'not at home'
And refuse to meet him!

Nôin (11th cent.)

As I approach
The mountain village
Through the spring twilight
I hear the sunset bell
Ring through drifting petals.

Jakuren (?–1202)

The hanging raindrops
Have not dried from the needles
Of the fir forest
Before the evening mist
Of Autumn rises.

Saigyô (1118–90)

In a tree standing
Beside a desolate field,
The voice of a dove
Calling to its companions—
Lonely, terrible evening.

Princess Shikushi (?–1201)

The blossoms have fallen.
I stare blankly at a world
Bereft of colour:
In the wide vacant sky
The spring rains are falling.

Zeami Motokiyo (1363–1443)

from the Nô play

THE SPIRIT OF THE IRIS (*KAKITSUBATA*)

The play is based on an episode in the 9th-century *Tales of Ise* (*Ise Monogatari*) in which the nobleman and poet Narihira and his companions visit a marsh full of irises. The priest in the play makes a pilgrimage to the marsh, where he meets the spirit of the poet's beloved.

CHORUS

. . . The world's glory is only for once,
Comes once, blows once, and soon fades,
So also to him: he went out
To seek his luck in Adzuma,
Wandering like a piece of cloud, at last
After years he came
And looking upon the waves at Ise and Owari,
He longed for his brief year of glory:
        The waves, the breakers return,
        But my glory comes not again,
            Narihira, Narihira,
        My glory comes not again.

He stood at the foot of Asama of Shinano, and saw the smoke curling upwards.

LADY

The smoke is now curling up
From the peak of Asama.

Narihira, Narihira,
My glory comes not again.

CHORUS

Strangers from afar and afar,
Will they not wonder at this?
He went on afar and afar
And came to Mikawa, the province,
To the flowers Kakitsubata
That flare and flaunt in their marsh
By the many-bridged cobweb of waters.

'She whom I left in the city?' thought Narihira. But in the long tale, Monogatari, there is many a page full of travels . . . and yet at the place of eight bridges the stream-bed is never dry.

He was pledged with many a lady.
The fire-flies drift away
From the jewelled blind,
Scattering their little lights
And then flying and flying:

Souls of fine ladies
Going up into heaven.

And here in the under-world
The autumn winds come blowing and blowing,
And the wild ducks cry: 'Kari! . . . Kari!'
I who speak, an unsteady wraith,
A form impermanent, drifting after this fashion,
Am come to enlighten these people.
Whether they know me I know not.

SPIRIT

A light that does not lead on to darkness.

CHORUS
(*singing the poem of Narihira's*)

No moon!
The spring
Is not the spring of the old days,

My body
Is not my body,
But only a body grown old.
Narihira, Narihira,
My glory comes not again.

Chikamatsu Monzaemon (1653–1725)

from the puppet play

THE LOVE SUICIDES AT SONEZAKI

A domestic tragedy based on a real event involving Tokubei, employee of a dealer in soy sauce, and Ohatsu, a courtesan. The opening of the final scene, given here, portrays the lovers' journey to the shrine of Tenjin at Sonezaki.

NARRATOR

Farewell to this world, and to the night farewell.
We who walk the road to death, to what should we be likened?
To the frost by the road that leads to the graveyard,
Vanishing with each step we take ahead:
How sad is this dream of a dream!

TOKUBEI

Ah, did you count the bell? Of the seven strokes
That mark the dawn, six have sounded.
The remaining one will be the last echo
We shall hear in this life.

OHATSU

It will echo the bliss of nirvana.

NARRATOR

Farewell, and not to the bell alone—
They look a last time on the grass, the trees, the sky.
The clouds, the river go by unmindful of them;
The Dipper's bright reflection shines in the water.

TOKUBEI

Let's pretend that Umeda Bridge

Is the bridge the magpies built
Across the Milky Way, and make a vow
To be husband and wife for eternity.

OHATSU

I promise. I'll be your wife forever.

NARRATOR

They cling together—the river waters
Will surely swell with the tears they shed.
Across the river, in a teahouse upstairs,
Some revelers, still not gone to bed,
Are loudly talking under blazing lamps—
No doubt gossiping about the good or bad
Of this year's crop of lovers' suicides;
Their hearts sink to hear these voices.

TOKUBEI

How strange! but yesterday, even today,
We spoke as if such things did not concern us.
Tomorrow we shall figure in their gossip.
If the world will sing about us, let it sing.

NARRATOR

This is the song that now they hear.
'I'm sure you'll never have me for your wife,
I know my love means nothing to you . . .'
Yes, for all our love, for all our grieving,
Our lives, our lots, have not been as we wished.
Never, until this very day, have we known
A single night of heart's relaxation—
Instead, the tortures of an ill-starred love.
'What is this bond between us?
I cannot forget you.
But you would shake me off and go—
I'll never let you!
Kill me with your hands, then go.

the bridge the magpies built: an allusion to the Chinese legend, familiar also in Japan, which tells of two stars (known as the Herd Boy and the Weaver Girl) that meet once a year, crossing over a bridge in the sky built by magpies.
I'm sure you'll never have me: from a popular ballad of the time which describes a love suicide.

I'll never release you!'
So she said in tears.

OHATSU

Of all the many songs, that one, tonight!

TOKUBEI

Who is it singing? We who listen

BOTH

Suffer the ordeal of those before us.

NARRATOR

They cling to each other, weeping bitterly.
Any other night would not matter
If tonight were only a little longer,
But the heartless summer night, as is its wont,
Breaks as cockcrows hasten their last hour.

TOKUBEI

It will be worse if we wait for dawn.
Let us die in the wood of Tenjin.

NARRATOR

He leads her by the hand.
At Umeda Embankment, the night ravens.

TOKUBEI

Tomorrow our bodies may be their meal.

OHATSU

It's strange, this is your unlucky year
Of twenty-five, and mine of nineteen.
It's surely proof how deep are our ties
That we who love each other are cursed alike.
All the prayers I have made for this world
To the gods and to the Buddha, I here and now
Direct to the future: in the world to come
May we be reborn on the same lotus!

unlucky year: according to yin-yang divination, a man's 25th, 42nd and 60th years were dangerous; for a woman her 19th and 33rd years.

NARRATOR

One hundred and eight the beads her fingers tell
On her rosary; tears increase the sum.
No end to her grief, but the road has an end:
Their minds are numbed, the sky is dark, the wind still,
They have reached the thick wood of Sonezaki. . . .

Bashô (1644–94)

AT TAKADATE

(site of the castle where the popular hero Yoshitsune was killed in 1189)

Where once
those bright warriors . . .

Where their dreams . . .

. . . the summer grass now waves

*

A lightning-flash—
and, slanting through the dark,
night-heron's cry.

*

Plum-branch on the mirror's back—
a spring no-one has seen.

*

Crow settling
on the dead branch.
Autumn dusk.

*

When drinking all alone
no moon—
no flowers.

*

rosary: the Buddhist rosary has 108 beads, one for each of the sufferings occasioned by the passions; cf. the poem by Nu Yin (p. 122).

Autumn has started—
sea and rice-fields make
a single green.

*

Purple hibiscus by the road—
but my horse
cropped it.

*

An
old
pond
and then a frog jumps in making a splash

*

Sea raging
while above
the island slanting spreads
the Milky Way

*

I hate crows as a rule
but somehow
this morning
on the snow . . .

*

A cuckoo winging out of sight
towards a lone
island

LAST POEM

Falling ill on a journey
with dreams still
moving over the empty fields

Kyoroku (1656–1715)

Now's the time
to settle round the fire
and talk of earthquakes
safe in the past.

Bonchô (?–1714)

. . . the sound made
by a scarecrow
falling
all by itself

Onitsura (1660–1738)

Daybreak
and white spring frost
on the barley-leaves.

THE ANNIVERSARY OF BASHÔ'S DEATH

Dreams still moving though
the fields are burned
and the wind sounds

Kikaku (1661–1707)

Flashes of lightning
in the east yesterday
the west to-day

*

Red hint of dawn—
cockcrow
among peach-flowers.

*

And now
the cool.
Plain stretching wide. Streak
of a meteor.

Chiyo (1703–75)

MY WELL-BUCKET

The morning-glory has captured it—
so it means
borrowing water.

Buson (1715–83)

Spring sunset
stamping the pheasant's tail
in the mountain

*

They left—
some yesterday
and some to-day.

To-night
there are no wild geese.

*

Sunset
and the deer moves
grazing the shadow-mountain
by the temple gate

*

I leave, you stay—
two autumns.

*

A summer thicket. No
leaf moves.
Shiver of awe.

*

Letting its petals
fall the peony
drops now two
here three
there

WIDOWER

The scar hurt again
when I trod on her comb
just now in our
bedroom.

Ryôta (1718–87)

This is the world:
three days pass, you look up,
the blossom's out or fallen.

*

There is no speech:
a host, a guest,
one white chrysanthemum.

Chora (1729–81)

Tarnished alas
the gold has gone . . .
. . . old times recalled
among spring leaves

Issa (1762–1826)

ON THE DEATH OF HIS CHILD

Life is as drops of dew
ah yes
as drops of dew
ah yet

*

Swaying
swaying
watch
the spring depart
among the fields of grass

*

My birthplace is
a village I abandoned yet
to-day
the cherries must be out

*

The cat
sleeps
wakes up
gives one vast yawn then
exits for the purposes of love

STEPMOTHER

This was my birthplace, I
draw near,
make contact, no—
—a flower with thorns.

*

These mushrooms kill
and of course
how beautiful they are

*

The high grass rustles
withered.
Once upon a time
there was a witch . . .

THE NEXT-TO-LAST POEM

Man's body moves
from that first washing to the last—
the interim
mere gibberish.

HIS MIDWINTER DEATH

A song of thanksgiving
is called for now because
the snow on my counterpane's
as pure as paradise.

Shiki (1867–1902)

One backward glance
but the man I talked to
is lost in mist.

*

Late March—
in that forgotten pot
a flower blooming.

*

Wide moorland spring
with people going to and fro
to and fro
and why

Shimazaki Tôson (1872–1943)

KOMORO CASTLE

Near the old castle
a traveller grieves among white clouds.
Green chickweed hasn't sprung yet.
There's no young grass.

On the nearby hills a covering of silver:
the light snow is dissolving in the daylight.

Warmer brightness.
No scents float from the fields.
A slight mist hangs over March.
A sparse hint of green shows new wheat.
Groups of wayfarers
scurry along the road between the farms.

It is too dark to see the volcano.
A sad tune is played on a flute.
Reaching an inn by the river
I hear its waves creep by.
Drinking a glass of wine,
opaque, making the mind opaque,
I console myself for a while
as I make my way.

Hagiwara Sakutarô (1886–1942)

NIGHT TRAIN

Near daybreak in the dark
Fingerprints chill on the window
        Like a soft spill of mercury
white glimmer on the mountains

Passengers hang between sleep and waking
        Over them the light-bulbs
sigh with fatigue

There's a sweetish smell of varnish
so the smoke of my cigarette
trickles unconsoling on my tongue
        The woman opposite is married
        When I exhale
she must taste the same sourness

We're nowhere near the station but she still
loosens the nozzle on her air-cushion

watching the way it gently
sags and loses
air

Unexpectedly
we draw close in sadness
and gazing at the eastern clouds
watch light touch
a nameless village in the mountains
where flowers are blooming
white under daybreak

WHITE MOON

One hand was on my swollen cheek
to force back the wild toothache
and I dug holes beneath the palmtree in my garden
intending to sow some grass seeds.

The action dirtied my delicate fingers
but as I kept digging in the cool soil
I forgot the pain.

Twilight fell on the day's chill.
Worms
were wriggling in the brand-new holes I'd made
when
from behind the low house
like the deadwhite curve of a woman's ear
softly
caressingly
the moon rose, the moon
rose.

Katô Shûson (1905–)

A winter seagull
    in life no home
    in death no grave

Ainu

'It is not perhaps necessary to remind you that the Ainus were a primitive people living in the northern island of Japan, in the adjacent promontory of Sakhalin and in the Kurile Islands, a people that has now been almost entirely assimilated or died out. You probably know too that the Ainu language is apparently unrelated (apart from the borrowing of culture-words from Gilyak and Japanese) with any other speech. Two facts about the Ainus struck Japanese observers from the eighteenth century onwards—the richness of their oral literature and the length of their beards. This literature includes prose stories, songs, ballads and various kinds of long narrative poem.'

Arthur Waley

SONG

I with my brother
In anger we left our home
And on the western borders
Of another land we lived.
But our village on the Sara,
Our old home, we could not forget;
Food would not pass our throats
And when we lay down to rest
All the time our tears flowed.
Over new-served food
The white mildew spread and spread;
Over old-served food
The black mildew spread and spread.
Then on a day
That in weeping, in weeping only,
We two had passed,
'Oh terrible, my sister,'
Said my brother to me,
'That you should have come to this.
See, of our old home an image,
A form have I carved.
Come here and look.'
So he said to me;
And when under my raised sleeve I looked,
Indeed it was so.
In the middle of the embers

Was the form, the image,
Of the home we had lived in,
And thus was it carved:
There, just as it had always been,
Was our village, and above it
Blue sky coming, blue sky going—
Oh the happiness, the joy!
And the long stretch
Of our village river,
No other can it be,
The river mouth high,
Looking high above;
The river source looking low,
Deep sunken and low.
As it goes by,
How even, how smooth!
The tips of the willow-trees
So thick on the shore,
The tips of the hazel-bushes
So thick on the bank,
The reed-clumps growing
So thick on the bank,
The rushes all growing
So thick on the shore.
And the men starting
For the morning-hunt, young men
Bow in hand, arrows in hand,
Some this way, some that,
Setting out along the mountain paths:
The young girls,
Sickle in hand,
Going out to cut the grass,
Following along the mountain paths . . .
To see it all before me,
Oh the happiness, the joy!
But in a little while,
For it was only embers,
It died away, and there was nothing left.
And since then, always,
No food have we eaten,
No morsel of food eaten,
But wept and wept only;
So has it been with us.

Korean

Korean poetry has maintained an unbroken tradition for almost 2,000 years, from the earliest songs originating in religious and agricultural festivals to the present. Although Korean literature encompasses as wide a variety of genres as may be found in any other literature, the Koreans have been happiest in their poetry, which has always been an essential part of their culture.

In Korea all poetry was meant to be sung. The forms and styles of Korean poetry therefore reflect their melodic origins. Its prosody, the basis of which is a line consisting of alternating groups of three and four syllables, is probably the rhythm most natural to the language. The association, not to say identification, of the verbal rhythm and musical rhythm can be seen in the refrain in the medieval *changga* (e.g. 'The Turkish Bakery'). Nonsense jingles or onomatopoeic representation of the sounds of musical instruments, such as the drum, attest to the use of refrain long after the disappearance of its musical origin and function.

The *sijo*, the most popular and versatile form in Korean poetry—its use ranges from philosophical reflection to humble mnemonic—is a three-line verse dating from the 15th century. Each line consists of four groups of three or four syllables, with a minor pause occurring at the end of the second, and a major at the end of the fourth. The emphatic syntactic division is usually introduced in the third line, in the form of a countertheme, paradox, resolution, judgment, and the like. It often presents a leap in logic and development, and the skilful poet achieves a pattern of thought within formal limits and a unity in variety. The introduction of a deliberate twist in phrasing or its meaning is often a test of the poet's originality. The *sijo* was sung and orally transmitted until the texts began to be written down from the 18th century. It is an oral art still today for the lettered and the unlettered, and even the shoeshine boys learn the texts without their tunes.

Twenty out of the twenty-five extant Old Korean poems were inspired by Buddhism, the state religion from the early 6th to the end of the 14th century. The topics of poetry since the 15th century, when Confucianism was an official political ideology and society placed such a premium on public service, include the nature of fame, the relative merits of city and country and of engagement and withdrawal, the act of retirement as a show of moral protest or a search for contemplation and self-fulfilment. Whether the figure evoked is the pine of the Confucian paedeutic tradition (Master Ch'ungdam), the moonlit autumn field of Buddhist epistemology (Kyunyŏ), or the priceless moon and ownerless wind of the Confucian-Taoist double vision (Sŏng Hon), or the unity of the cuckoo, willow, fish and man (Yun Sŏn-do), each is an attempt to understand life in relation to the patterns of nature, a revelation of man to himself, and the final acceptance of the human condition.

Modern times in Korea have brought a complete break with the past.

The struggle against tradition was a struggle with the language: a greater grammatical precision was demanded of the written language, together with a greater metrical freedom in poetry, to incorporate everyday speech and to express local political and spiritual predicaments. After a long germinative period, major poets have successfully absorbed the new and reanimated the old: the longest way, said Lao-tzŭ, is the way back.

Master Wŏlmyŏng (c. 742–765)

REQUIEM

On the hard road of life and death
That is near our land,
You went, afraid,
Without words.

We know not where we go,
Leaves blown, scattered,
Though fallen from the same tree,
By the first winds of autumn.

Abide, Sister, perfect your ways,
Until we meet in the Pure Land.

Master Ch'ungdam (c. 742–765)

ODE TO KNIGHT KILBO

The moon that pushes her way
Through the thickets of clouds,
Is she not pursuing
The white clouds?

Knight Kilbo once stood by the water,
Reflecting his face in the blue.
Henceforth I shall seek and gather
Among pebbles the depth of his mind.

Knight, you are the towering pine,
That scorns frost, ignores snow.

Great Master Kyunyŏ (917–973)

from ELEVEN DEVOTIONAL POEMS

To the boundless throne of Buddha
In the realm of dharma,
I fervently pray
For the sweet rain of truth.

Dispel the blight of affliction
Rooted deep in the ignorant soil,
And wet the mind's field
Where the good grass struggles to grow.

The mind is a moonlit autumn field
Ripe with the gold fruit of knowledge.

Unknown 'kisaeng' (c. 13th cent.)

THE TURKISH BAKERY

I go to the Turkish shop, buy a bun,
An old Turk grasps me by the hand.
If this story is spread abroad,
You alone are to blame, little doll on the shelf.
I will go, yes, go to his bower;
A narrow place, sultry and dark.

I go to the Samjang Temple, light the lantern,
A chief priest grasps me by the hand.
If this story is spread abroad,
You alone are to blame, little altar boy.
I will go, yes, go to his bower:
A narrow place, sultry and dark.

I go to the village well, draw the water,
A dragon within grasps me by the hand.
If this story is spread abroad,
You alone are to blame, O pitcher.

kisaeng: female entertainers.

I will go, yes, go to his bower:
A narrow place, sultry and dark.

I go to the tavern, buy the wine,
An innkeeper grasps me by the hand.
If this story is spread abroad,
You alone are to blame, O wing jug.
I will go, yes, go to his bower:
A narrow place, sultry and dark.

WINTER NIGHT

The sleet falls thick and fast;
Do you come, false love, who made me
Lie awake for half the night?
Are you crossing the pass
Where the wind cries in the bushes?

Fires of hell or thunderbolts
Will soon consume my body.
Fires of hell or thunderbolts
Will soon consume my body.

On what wild mountain shall I seek you?
I will do anything, anything you say,
This and that, whatever you ask of me.
I will follow you anywhere, I swear.

SPRING OVERFLOWS THE PAVILION

Were I to build a bamboo hut on the ice,
Were I to die of cold with him on the ice,
O night, run slow, till our love is spent.

When I lie alone, restless, vigilant,
Only peach blossoms wave over the west window.
You have no grief, welcome the spring breeze.

I have believed those who vowed to each other:
'My soul will follow yours forever.'
Who, who persuaded me this was true?

'O duck, beautiful duck, why do you come
To the swamp, instead of the shoal?'
'If the swamp freezes, the shoal will do.'

A bed on Mount South, a jade pillow, gold brocade,
And beside me a girl sweeter than musk,
Let us press our hearts together, our magic hearts.

Yi Cho-nyŏn (1269–1343)

White moon, white
Pear blossoms, the Milky Way
White across the sky.
An ignorant bird
Repeats and repeats its song,
Not noticing
The sorrow of spring.
Too much awareness is a sickness;
It keeps me awake all night.

Sŏng Sam-mun (1418–56)

Were you to ask me what I'd wish to be
In the world beyond this world,
I would answer, a pine tree, tall and hardy
On the highest peak of Mount Pongnae,
And to be green, alone, green,
When snow fills heaven and earth.

Kim Chŏng-gu (c. 1495/1506)

Who says I am old?
Is an old man this way?
Heart welcomes sweet flowers,
Laughter floats over fragrant cups:
But what can I do, what can I say?
My hoary hair floats in the spring wind.

Hwang Chin-i (c. 1506–44)

I cut in two
A long November night, and
Place half under the coverlet,
Sweet-scented as a spring breeze.
And when he comes, I shall take it out,
Unroll it inch by inch, to stretch the night.

Sŏng Hon (1535–98)

The mountain is silent,
The water without form.
A clear breeze has no price,
The bright moon no owner.
Here, after their fashion,
I will grow old in peace.

Kim Sang-yong (1561–1637)

Fierce beats the rain
On the paulownia's wide
Majestic leaves.
My grief awakes and twists my heart,
The loud rain beats on my sorrow.
Never again shall I plant
A tree with such broad leaves.

Yun Sŏn-do (1587–1671)

from SONGS OF FIVE FRIENDS

How many friends have I? Count them:
Water and stone, pine and bamboo—
The rising moon on the east mountain,
Welcome, it too is my friend.
What need is there, I say,
To have more friends than five?

TO MY FRIEND (1645)

Heart wants to sing, but cannot sing alone;
Heart wants to dance, but dancing must have music.
 Then lute shall play,
For none but lute can strike the secret tone
 My heart would sing
 So heart and song are one;
 Then lute shall play,
For none but lute knows what is heart's desire
 So heart may spring
 Into the dance
 And beat its rhythm out.
Welcome, sweet lute, my dear, my dearest friend,
There is no hurt your music cannot mend.

from THE ANGLER'S CALENDAR (1651)

Is it a cuckoo that cries?
Is it the willow that is blue?
Several roofs in a far fishing village
Swim in the mist, magnificent.
Boy, fetch an old net!
Fishes are climbing against the stream.

Prince Inp'yŏng (1622–58)

Don't mock a pine
Twisted and bent by the winds.
Flowers in the spring wind,
Can they keep their brilliance?
When wind blows and snow whirls,
You'll call for me.

Yi T'aek (1651–1719)

O roc, don't ridicule the small black birds:
You and the little birds both fly way up in the clouds,
You're a bird,
And they're birds.
Really, I can't see much difference between you!

Anonymous

In the wind that blew last night
Peach blossoms fell, scattered in the garden.
A boy came out with a broom,
Intending to sweep them away.
No, do not sweep them away, no, no.
Are fallen flowers not flowers?

*

Deep among green valley grasses
A stream runs crying.
Where is the terrace of songs,
Where the hall of dancing?
Do you know, swallow,
Cutting the sunset water?

Pak Tu-jin (1916–)

A MESSAGE FROM THE CRANE

On a deserted islet in the ocean
Stay even if the sun sets and the moon
Stay even if winds howl and rain.

During the day chitchat with waves
At night repeat the names of stars
Memorize the names of countless stars

Eat grass berries
Wet your throat with dewdrops

Weave your dress with flowers
Inscribe your syllables on the sand

Wait there
On that lonely island.

Don't say my words are foolish
The words I send to the winds.

Flying over the six oceans
I'll bring you back

The joy
Of wings growing in my armpits
Of my flesh and bones

Till that day that morning
Wait.

APRIL

Even if you're a dagger pointed at me,
A cup of poison to be drained,
I must embrace you.
I'll open the burning heart to huddle you,
Digest you till my stomach turns,
And walk to the heaven at the earth's end.
One sun one moon
Inextinguishable
The timeless flow of water unending
Till my soles hardened into paws,
This naked body will endure your lashes
Till flowers bloom in profusion.

Pak Mogwŏl (1916–78)

UNTITLED

Where I sit is my place,
A field of gravel, a plain of sand.

On that rock
A gull perches,
Trying its wings, letting out cries.

Yesterday
I gazed on the rushing tide
And longed for men.

Today
I want to pack and go,
Looking at the floating clouds.

For everything
Where it sits is its place.

From a crack in a cliff
A grassblade sprouts,

On a steep slope
A tree strikes root.

No place
Leaves any trace, once gone—
Grasses, flowers, and all.

There
Where waves wash the rock,
The gull cries in the sky,

Here
Where I shook off the sand and rose,
Winds stroke and erase my trace.

A METEORITE

To bed.
When I turn to the wall,
A caress of forgetfulness.
That's the way it is.
A pleasant meteorite,
A burnt remainder is bound to be light.
My poems lighter than sponge,
Can they be called poetry?
I've no complaint about
My common days and nights—
My liberal predilections!
Let me sleep.
When I turn to the wall,
Clouds and mist delight me,
Round my head a wind blows.
That's the way it is.
An inventory of conflagration,
A burnt remainder is always clean—
A light meteoric stone!

My poetry of tomorrow,
Flavorless but free,
Evening of my life.

Shin Kyŏng-nim (1936–)

TODAY

Our bellies full of rice wine
On top of a half-bowl of noodles.
'The farmer, foundation of society!'
County chief in the lead,
We raise the farmers' banner,
Take a turn round the village head's house.
'We feel the nation's bounty in our hearts.'
Gongs and cymbals sound,
The county chief dances a hunchback dance,
As the farm adviser beats the drum.
'Grain production up 13 to 14 percent!'
The expressway's seventy miles away.
Trying to filch dried squid,
Village kids in rags
Knock over a wine jar.
The death of the old man at Dragon Rock
Is no match for soap operas on the radio.
Wives are drunk,
Croaking out their old tunes in the yard,
Girls, within the back fence,
Hoarse from learning the latest pop-songs.
The whole village drunk and dizzy,
Ah, today, what day is this?
What day?

Vietnamese

Until the 19th century, Vietnamese was written in characters derived from Chinese, a system known as *chu nom* ('popular writing'). The great age of *chu nom* literature—which in Vietnamese is virtually synonymous with poetry—was the 18th and early 19th centuries: the first great poem, the *Ode of the War Wife*, exists in six versions based on the original in Chinese: the extract given here is translated from the version of the woman poet Doan Thi Diem. Another woman poet of distinction is Ho Xuan Huong, whose artistry, outspoken humour and celebration of everyday life have earned her the title 'queen of *chu nom* poetry'. During the 19th century, *chu nom* gave way to *quoc ngu* ('national script'), the system of romanisation in use today. French rule introduced Western ideas to an already highly sophisticated culture: a synthesis is achieved in the racy yet moving narrative of the poem given here by the Communist poet To Huu, prompted by an episode in the war of independence.

Verse is organised by syllable, tone and rhyme. The two great odes use a four-line stanza of seven, seven, six and eight syllables; *Kieu* is in couplets of six and eight syllables only, where sixth syllables rhyme and each eighth syllable introduces the rhyme for the next couplet: these are the two principal metres of Vietnamese poetry. The form of 'Swings', however, is that of the 'Chinese sonnet' (see p. 27).

Dang Tran Con (c. 1710–45) and Doan Thi Diem (1705–46)

from ODE OF THE WAR WIFE

When in the world wild dust blows
fair of face has many woes:
Lord of the far blue kingdom
on whose account has this come?
Moonlight trembles to the thuds
        of Trang-an's drum:
Cam-tuyen's fire reaches the clouds.
The Emperor at midnight
bares his jewelled sword to fight:
        a proclamation
        and the war is on.
Past three hundred years of peace:
soldiers are called to service.
Imperial envoys travel:

duty now is all their will.
Though in arrows apparelled
the soldier's heart
is fixed on his wife and child.
Shadow of flag, distant drum:
sorrow runs to the frontier
resentment fills the room.
Young men of heroic rank
put away their pen and ink
take up their sword to conquer
cities for the Emperor.
A man's will is do or die
to toss great mountains lightly:
in battledress
he bids his family farewell
whips his horse, crosses
Vi Bridge, the autumn winds howl.
The brook runs clear, seems filtered,
grass is still young by the road:
see him off with heavy heart
its road unlike his horse
its water unlike his boat.
Water flows, grief is turbid:
grass smells sweet
the heart is not comforted.
Goodbyes, more goodbyes and walk
hold hands
at each step tug his tunic.

My heart follows like the moon:
your heart has far wars to win.
You fling
the last cup down, point your spear
at the cave of the tiger.
You set out to fight the foe
in the steps of a hero
your horse snow-white, uniform
red as sun before a storm.
Harness bell blends with drum beat.
Together, the next minute
apart: you must be away.
At the roadside
the flag waves sadly, sadly.

Chariots already press north:
horses still paw western earth.
Horses, chariots go with you:
does the willow
facing north-west know such woe?
The flute of war blows, echoes:
the flags move forward in rows.
Into far clouds
I watch your footsteps vanish:
returning home
I watch the mountains and wish.
You go forth to wild and wet:
I back to mat and blanket.
Each looks round, and is alone
in floods
of blue cloud and green mountain.

On Nhu Hau (1741–98)

from ODE OF THE RESENTFUL COURTESAN

The lovely girl
in the picture charms no more:
sad eyes turn to his locked door
alone to stand, sad to sit
weep with flowers, cry with moonlight.
Sad all things, this heart is sad
sick of all things, distracted:
that he should fly past this flower
leaving her red
frayed and her yellow meagre!
All night grope the fragrant wall:
who made such sorrow to kill?
A sword kills with more kindness
than this murderous distress.
The old moonman respects none
his thread wrecking lives: here's one
who'd gladly hack his fabric
gave this room a parting kick!

courtesan: not quite: one of the Emperor's wives, she is neither empress nor concubine.

Walking in the flower gardens
plucking young peach blossoms once
        with Phoenix on high
        with Oriole below:
there still where they used to lie
        the magic pillow.
Now disregarded, this hair
spun like fine silk spins finer:
why is the spring sun so cool?
        Flower stem, faded moon
are angry and resentful.

Pausing once by the palace
breaking young willow branches
        by fine drapery
        by ivory screen:
shift still bears testimony
        to where he has been.
Now neglected, this body
floats like a limp flower away:
why does the Creator tease?
        Lamplight, faded moon
are bored with this life's odours.

The scene: flower fallen, moon blurred—
burning hearts the dusk glows red.
Sunset, then again sunset
        moon and flower
then moon and flower sadder yet!
Who cares for a moon gone dim
looks at a flower stripped of bloom?
Such a sad scene is tiresome:
such a sad love is the same.

When the wind is in the trees
there comes a faint creaking noise:
perhaps his chariot draws up!
        Kindle sandalwood
        to air the wardrobe . . .
No: a lonely cricket chirps
through the autumn where one weeps
abandoned, beyond rumour.
Fireflies dance through chill, sad air.

When moonlight slants on the house
ears crane at a calling noise:
perhaps a pageboy will speak!
        Dab some stale powder
        on a wrinkled cheek . . .
No: a lonely cuckoo sings
to a widow of no springs
in the cold, beyond solace.
Fallen flowers perfume the place.

Laughter has hollow echoes
glamour has its day and goes:
when laughter and glamour pall
quietly, quietly end it all.

Nguyen Du (1765–1820)

from KIEU

This 3,254-line verse novel, based on a Chinese legend and considered the greatest work of Vietnamese literature, is a moral tale of trials and eventual triumph. At one point Kieu, the heroine, secretly becomes a man's second wife—to the disgust of his first wife who, while he is at a wake for his mother, kidnaps Kieu and compels her to be his wife's servant. On the husband's return, the first wife orders Kieu to attend to the master.

Scared of her she must obey:
bows her head, makes a curtsy.
He has nearly fainted: 'No!
Can this be Kieu? O sorrow!
This situation—how come?
So I have fallen victim.'
He fears lest his looks reveal:
cannot stop sob, check trickle.
The wife sees his face, inquires:
        'Just back,
what so disturbs those features?'
He says: 'Mother's memory
will remain always with me.'
'Commendable devotion!
We will drink to your return
        to ease your spirit

this autumn night.'
Wife and husband—down it goes:
she must stand at their elbows
do this, that and the other
kneel before him, press and pour.
He looks dazed, about to fall:
tears drip, drop, cup full, half-full.
Turning his head
feigning drunk he speaks, bursts out
laughing, plans an escape route.
The Mistress calls: 'Little Flower!
Bid him
drink up, or you will suffer.'
His heart breaks, his soul dissolves:
he just join bitter revels.
The Mistress, drunk with success
announces songs and dances:
Little Flower is talented
will play what is requested.
The distracted girl must tune
her instrument
before the silk partition.
Four strings break the husband's heart
with their comfortless concert:
from the quiver of a string
outer mirth, inner weeping.

Ho Xuan Huong (1768–1839)

SWINGS

Eight poles: praise to him who put them up!
Some folk rise and swing, some sit and watch.
Boy contracts his knees, bends, bends his loins:
girl flexes her wasp waist, leans, leans back.
Four individual pink trousers flap:
two pairs of legs stretch out parallel.
Sweet spring! Now tell truly what it is:
the props gone, nothing is left at all.

Folk poems

Plum to peach: Has anyone
come into the rose garden?

Plum of peach makes inquiry
therefore peach will make reply:

The rose garden has a gate
but no one has come in yet.

*

Remember when you looked green
the hand which brought your medicine
with a quarter of lemon:

now you're fine—hale and hearty
some girl's driving you crazy
and you've got no time for me.

I'm better off down the well.

*

Rain fell in torrents last night
lightning flashed far out to sea.
Is milord sorry or not?

If he is he will not speak.
The marriage is destiny
punishment or a mistake.

*

In the sky a cloud of blue:
inside white, all round yellow.
I should like to marry her:
buy best bricks, be a builder
dig a hole, lay bricks in it
build a pond to wash her feet.
LOVE is the name of this pond:
most girls come to be freshened.
She may wash
feet, hands, but (please) not eyebrows:

their sharp points are dangerous
and my fish
would perish!

To Huu (1920–)

LUOM

Back in blood-hot Hue
uncle from Hanoi
stumbles across his
nephew in the street:

nephew tiny, tiny
bag little, little
feet nimble, nimble
head cocked to one side

cap at an angle
mouth whistles loudly
sings like a bird, hops
on the yellow road.

'I'm a runner now—
very smart, uncle.
I'd much rather be
in camp than at home.'

Nephew laughs two slits
cheeks red as date plums:
'Right. Goodbye, comrade!'
Nephew goes away.

He goes his own way:
his uncle goes back.
Now in the sixth month
there is news from home.

That's how it is, Luom.

One of these fine days
like any other

little comrade puts
letters in his bag

crosses battlefield
shells wow-wowing by
letters marked URGENT
fearless of danger

empty country road
the paddy in bloom
the little lad's cap
bobs above the field.

A sudden red flash
and there it is, Luom:
the little comrade
a stream of fresh blood.

On rice nephew lies
hand tight round a stem
of sweet-smelling rice.
Soul flits over fields.

Luom, what is there left?

Nephew tiny, tiny
bag little, little
feet nimble, nimble
head cocked to one side

cap at an angle
mouth whistles loudly
sings like a bird, hops
on the yellow road.

Khmer

Among the oldest Khmer poetry must be counted the *Reamker*, of which an extract is given here. This epic, based on the Indian *Ramayana* but changed and adapted by the Khmers, has had a profound influence on Khmer culture. It was the subject of sculptures at Angkor in the 12th century when Cambodia was a major power in South-East Asia, of paintings on monastery walls, of dances performed by the royal ballet and of scenes played by the shadow theatre. It is impossible to date old Khmer poetry with any precision: manuscripts perished quickly in the hot, damp climate, and were changed by copyists, so that a single text often presents features of several periods. Another old and well-loved genre of Khmer poetry is the body of didactic Buddhist poems, the *Chbap* or Code of Behaviour, which gives advice on social as well as moral conduct. These poems are much more charming than the description might suggest. The short extract given here is from a serious passage; the reference to light and sunshine is very typical of Khmer poetry.

from the REAMKER (*c. 17th cent.*)

In this extract from the Cambodian *Ramayana*, the exiled Prince Rama (really an incarnation of the god Vishnu) journeys through the forest with his wife and brother.

It was the season of heat and sun,
the sun-rays focused on
the broken wood that strewed their track.

The earth was dried up into cracks;
the light was a blinding flash.
Flames ran sizzling through the air,

melting the forest everywhere.
Death to fruit and flower:
leaf and blossom dropped, shrivelled.

Some leaves were charred, and some were red.
The forest fire spread
till straw and grass and reed were blighted.

Rama, meditation-strengthened,
one of the Enlightened,
guided his wife along the way.

And the great forest canopy
of branches began to play
gentle and fresh on either side.

Flowers sprang up far and wide
suddenly, richly displayed,
as if by an arranger's art.

Huge, bone-dry trees stood dead and silent,
coiled with leaves that bent
shaking and waving into the wind.

The flowers fluttered out their fund
of perfume, which unwound
sweetness pervading all the scene.

Buzzing, honey-bearing bees
murmured as they breathed
the nectar; busy were their wings.

Their hum strummed out like plucked strings
into the silence, stirring
the royal wanderers in the wood.

The sunlight, bright as it was, glowed
in the sky as glad and bland
as brilliance sent from a full moon,

and could not burn one royal person
in that trio—the sign
of Rama's virtue in that journey.

from THE CODE OF BEHAVIOUR FOR THE YOUNG (*c. 1700*)

It is said that fire is bright,
but surely the sun is brighter.
It is said that the brilliance of the sun

(so bright, so clear in the sky)
is surely not as bright
as the divine Dharma
of the Buddha.

The bright fire loses desire,
the bright fire ends its time,
it is lost, extinguished, extinct.
The brilliant sun sails high
in its sky and as surely sinks
and as it sets grows dull,
its rays pale.

But consider the precious Dharma:
bright and more than bright
in this world and no less bright
in the next world it goes through to:
it shines into huge distance, its
virtue is exemplary, inextinguishable
its glory.

Philippine (Tagalog, Spanish, English)

Little remains of the great oral literature the Malayo-Polynesian languages of the Philippines are said to have possessed before the Spanish conquest of 1565. After that date Spanish-style romance and Christian drama were written in Tagalog, but by the 19th century most writers were using Spanish, which became the language of Philippine nationalism: the foremost writer and nationalist was José Rizal, who became the movement's martyr. American rule from 1898 until the Second World War brought another change of language, and modern literature, though vigorous mainly in the short story, has produced one poet of international reputation—José García Villa, who now lives in New York.

Tagalog

HOUSEWARMING SONG

Old comb, old comb
tease out the tangled thoughts
of those who will live here
as you have combed my hair
when it was dirty, caked
with mud and grass.

May those who cross
this threshold think no ill
their faces wear no frown
may they always agree
smooth as a deep river
calm as a night in May.

Water in the pitcher
be cool as forest springs
be still as old mountains
be soft as the east wind
that those under this roof
may be considerate
ready to hear reason.

Wash the foul tongue
cleanse the mind of all stain
that speech from dawn till dusk
may bring quiet content
today and for ever.

Burn brightly, lamp
bless this house with your flame
keep the shadows at bay
that dark thoughts may not plague
those seeking shelter here.

Light the faces, the minds
of those who will live here
that they and their children's
children may live in peace.

Spanish: José Rizal (*1861–96*)

POEM BEFORE EXECUTION

Farewell, beloved country, sun-kissed land,
pearl of the eastern sea, lost paradise!
Gladly I yield my sad, my withered life:
if it were brighter, fresher and more fair,
still I would yield it for your happiness.

On battlefields, struggling with wild delight,
others for your sake selfless met their doom.
No matter where—be it cypress, laurel, iris,
scaffold or plain, combat or martyrdom,
if it was for their country and their home.

I die when I behold the sky turn red,
the last day breaking after gloomy night:
if you need cochineal to stain your dawn
then shed my blood, pour it while there is time,
gild it with tints of its emergent light!

My dreams when I was scarcely a child, a youth,
my dreams when I was young, still in my prime,
were to see you, jewel of the eastern sea,

one day with dark eyes dry, with smooth brow raised,
no frown, no wrinkles, tainted with no crime.

Dream of my life, my burning bright desire,
hail! shouts my soul, now ready to go forth.
Hail! O how sweet to fall to give you flight,
to die to give you life, beneath your sky,
to sleep eternally in your charmed earth.

If on my tomb one day you see a flower,
simple and lowly, pushing through the grass,
lift it towards your lips and kiss my soul,
and on my brow I'll feel, in the cold grave,
the touch, the warm breath of your tenderness.

Let the moon see me with its calm, soft beams,
let the dawn send its rays, so briefly splendid,
let the wind moan, earnestly murmuring;
and if upon my cross a bird should light,
let the bird tune its song of troubles ended.

Let the hot sun evaporate the rains,
and my cries drive them back to their abode;
let one who loves weep for my early end,
and if in the cool dusk one prays for me,
pray, too, my country, for my rest in God.

Pray for all those who perish unfulfilled,
for those who suffer torments unrelieved,
for our poor mothers groaning bitterly,
for orphans, widows, tortured prisoners,
pray for yourself, that you may be reprieved.

And when the dark enfolds the graveyard, leaving
only the dead to watch the long night through,
do not disturb their rest, their mystery:
if you hear strains of harp or psaltery,
dear country, it is I, singing for you.

And if my grave, forgotten by the world,
has neither cross nor headstone left to mark it,
let it be tilled by man, tended and sown,

and let my ashes, while there still is time,
become the very dust upon your carpet.

No matter then that I should be forgotten.
Your air, your space, your values, will know my wraith.
I'll be a throbbing, pure note in your ear;
with scents, lights, colours, whispers, songs and groans
repeating still the essence of my faith.

Country I worship, grief of all my griefs,
dear Philippines, hear now the last farewell!
I leave you all—my fathers, those I love;
I go where neither slaves nor tyrants are;
where God is king, where faith makes no man kill.

Fathers, brothers, parts of my soul, farewell!
friends of my childhood home for ever lost!
Give thanks that I rest from the weary day!
Farewell, fair stranger, happiness, my friend!
To die—farewell, my loved ones!—is to rest!

English: José García Villa (1914–)

Inviting a tiger for a weekend.
The gesture is not heroics but discipline.
The memoirs will be splendid.

Proceed to dazzlement, Augustine.
Banish little birds, graduate to tiger.
Proceed to dazzlement, Augustine.

Any tiger of whatever colour
The same as jewels any stone
Flames always essential morn.

The guest is luminous, peer of Blake.
The host is gallant, eye of Death.
If you will do this you will break

The little religions for my sake.
Invite a tiger for a weekend,
Proceed to dazzlement, Augustine.

Malay

Malay is the national language of both Malaysia and Indonesia. The earliest records we have date from the 7th century, but virtually all records of the Hindu-Buddhist period in the Archipelago have been lost. Some 19th-century copies survive of manuscripts dating back to the beginnings of the Muslim influence on South-East Asian culture, in the 13th century.

The present selection begins with translations of the traditional four-line *pantun* (which the French did much to popularise in Europe); the rest of the verse is from the modern period. Amir Hamzah, a mystic and a prince, marks the break between the old and the new, with his taut poem on frustrated love and the hopeless desire for God. Amir Hamzah was killed during the early stages of the Indonesian Revolution; in Jakarta, the radical anarchist poet Chairil Anwar was turning towards a much freer, more sombre, despairing kind of interior verse. Chairil Anwar opened the way for a private, interior tradition to develop in Indonesia. Sitor Situmorang deepened many of the directions Chairil Anwar had begun, but also allowed for a greater emphasis on local settings which writers like Rendra and Taufiq Ismail were to put to good use.

The current generation of writers—such as Sutardji Calzoum Bachri in Indonesia and A. Ghafar Ibrahim in Malaysia—have moved towards a more aggressive, concrete verse, which again demands a public audience. Sutardji claims to be going back to the 'source' of Indonesian/Malay poetry, the spell. Certainly verse in Malay is moving increasingly away from poetry written elsewhere to more regional, subconscious and mythological concerns.

Pantuns

They wear
    bangles on their arms
I wear
    bracelets on my ankles.
They say
    Mustn't do that!
I do
    as I damn well please.

*

Ouch!
    pricked my foot

on a thorn
    in the swamp!
Ouch!
    hurt my eyes
watching her breasts bounce
    under her blouse.

*

A thousand doves
    fly past
one lands
    in my yard.
I want to die
    on her fingertips
and be buried
    in the palms of her hands.

*

Be careful when you choose
    a place to bathe:
one—a bay
    two—a beach.

Be careful when you choose
    someone to marry:
one—beauty
    two—brains.

One—a bay
    two—a beach
three—well downstream
    from your neighbour's loo.

One—beauty
    two—brains
three—well born
    from a chieftain's line.

Amir Hamzah (1911–46)

TO YOU AGAIN

Lost, purged
My love gone
I return to you
Again

You are a flickering candle
A light in a window on a dark night
Waving me home, slowly
Faithfully, patiently

You are One
I am man
I want to feel
I want to touch

Where are you
I can't see
And a barely audible voice
Words form

You are jealous
You are cruel
I am prey in your claws
Alternately released and caught

I am dazed, wild
Love returns
You are a beautiful jewel
A maid hiding behind a curtain

A solitary love
Waiting alone
Time passes—it is not my turn
Day dies—but not my friend . . .

Chairil Anwar (1922–49)

FUTILE

The last time you came
Bringing flowers
Red roses and white jasmine
Blood and purity
You spread them before me
With a look that insisted: for you.

We both wondered
What is this?
Love? Neither knew.

A day together. Apart.

I would not give in to you
And now my heart crumbles in the silence

FOR RASID

Between
green leaves
vast open fields
small innocent children learning to run
singing birds and
soft fertile rain
a young nation forms
And
a harsh dry wind, a barren plain
swirling sand, deserted towns
We are squeezed, my love
—make yourself small—
Let us free ourselves, search and become doves
Fly
learn the fields, never meeting, never resting
—the only possible non-stop flight—
Never arriving.

Sitor Situmorang (1924–)

TWILIGHT

Poised
between the houses
and the sun
are heavy round pots
of burnt clay
carried
by young girls

From the well
to the village
is a path of sand
Young girls
each with the moon
on her head

Rendra (1935–)

A WORLDLY SONG

As the moon sleeps on an old mattress
I love a maiden in a mango grove.
Her heart is wild and fiery
trampling hunger and thirst underfoot.
In our misery we reach out.
The passion of our rebellion roars
in the dark and the shadows.
And her fierce laughter
makes my heart glad.

Her body shines
in the shadows of the trees
like a golden deer.
Her breasts are like
half-grown fruits.
The sweet smell of her body
is like grass.
I embrace her
as I embrace life and death.

And her fast breathing
whispers in my ears.
She is amazed
at the rainbow
beneath her hooded lids.

Our ancestors
appear from the dark
coming nearer
in their ragged clothing
and squat
watching us.

Taufiq Ismail (1937–)

GIVE INDONESIA BACK TO ME

Indonesia's future is two hundred million gaping mouths.
Indonesia's future is 15-watt light bulbs, some white some black, lighting up alternately.
Indonesia's future is a ping-pong game going on all day and all night with a ball shaped like a goose-egg.
Indonesia's future is the island of Java sinking under its population of a hundred million.
Give
Indonesia
back
to me.

Indonesia's future is a million people playing ping-pong night and day with a goose-egg under the light of 15-watt light bulbs.
Indonesia's future is Java slowly sinking under the weight of its burden and then geese swimming on top of it.
Indonesia's future is two hundred million gaping mouths, with 15-watt light bulbs in them, some white some black, lighting up alternately.
Indonesia's future is white geese swimming as they play ping-pong on top of the sinking island of Java and taking the hundred million 15-watt light bulbs to the bottom of the sea.

Give
Indonesia
back
to me.

Indonesia's future is a ping-pong game going on all day and all night with a ball shaped like a goose-egg.
Indonesia's future is the island of Java sinking under its population of a hundred million.
Indonesia's future is 15-watt light bulbs, some white some black, lighting up alternately.
Indonesia's future is two hundred million gaping mouths.
Give
Indonesia
back
to me.

Sutardji Calzoum Bachri (1942–)

CAT

Meow! There is a cat in my blood he roars he runs
he hurts he flows through my aorta in the forest of my
blood he is enormous but he is not a lion and not a
tiger and not a jaguar and not a leopard but a tabby cat
and not a cat but a cat Meow! he is hungry he
levels the forests of Africa with his claws and madness he
roars he howls don't feed him he doesn't like meat Jesus
don't give him bread he doesn't like bread Meow!

a cat fighting in my blood roaring pushing his way through
the coals in my heart he is hungry very hungry Meow!
he has not eaten for a million days a thousand eons he is never
satisfied very hungry my curious cat perpetually clawing wait
God created the cat I didn't ask Him to he roars in search of
Him he is hungry don't feed him flesh feed him rice
God created him I didn't want Him to he wants God to one day
make him tame so he can live in peace with the world

Meow! he roars how many Gods are there give me one to
keep my cat quiet Meow! shush pussy shush I fix
traps in Africa in the Amazon in Riau in cities who knows

perhaps I'll catch me a God   not bad   a slice for you
and a slice for me   shush pussy shush   Meow!

A. Ghafar Ibrahim (1943–)

CROWS

gak
gak
gak
gak
gak
gak
gak
crows never pretend
that they enjoy singing
the noise helps them survive
the silence
gak
gak
gak   gak
gak   gak
gak   gak
gak   gak   gak
gak   gak   gak
gak
gakkkkk
gakkkkkkk
picking the eyes
out of loneliness
as they melodiously search
for the truth
of hatred
akkk
akkkk   aaaakkkkk
akkkk   aaakkkk
aakkk

Balinese

In a predominantly Muslim area, Hindu Bali is famous for its visual arts and its music. It also has a rich oral tradition: the extract given here from a Shiva legend describes the journey through hell of the impoverished Brahmin Bagus Diarsa to seek the advice of a learned beggar who, unbeknown to him, is the god in disguise.

from THE SONG OF BAGUS DIARSA

He had crossed the seven mountains
    and came to a wide plain
stretching to the west, the east,
to the sea, to the mountains
with barely a single tree
a plain of grass and sword-grass
with not a single mountain
nothing but heaven and earth
as far as the eye could see.

Many souls he met, all wretches
    in burning agony
milling about on the plain:
they were lapping the dewdrops
from the tips of the sword-grass.
And he saw souls of children
that came swarming around him
carrying in their small hands
rough cups of coconut-shells.

And other souls he encountered
    under *manduri*-trees
who were weeping and wailing
their bodies worn out and dry
their eyes sunken, limbs bloated.
With one voice they lamented:
'Why, great lord, is this our lot?
I have long been in torment
I linger in fivefold grief!' . . .

Bagus Diarsa looked and wept
but must think of himself . . .
And he saw other souls too
who bore corpse-towers on their heads
and were hounded by great birds:
these were the souls of people
who had no right to corpse-towers
but had built them with their wealth
aspiring to higher castes . . .

And there were souls he saw hanging
from boughs of kapok-trees
with fires burning under them:
these were the souls of evil men,
blasphemers, loudly crying.
And he saw other souls too
set upon by pigs and dogs
writhing as they were bitten
screaming as they were savaged:

these were people who had not known
the rules of behaviour
regarding decent conduct
heedless of the commandments
comporting themselves badly
altogether like cattle.
He saw souls pecked by great birds—
their blood spouted forth in jets
riddled with wounds like baskets:

these were the souls of the stupid
concerned with just themselves
pursuing their own pleasure.
And he came upon others
who between the Clashing Rocks
roaring, shrieking flung themselves—
their heads, pinched, spattered apart
their blood and their brains gushed out
spurting in all directions:

these were the souls of the fickle
the selfish, unfriendly
the moody who had not worked

for good, who had everywhere
hustled, jostled each other
giving free rein to anger—
this was now their punishment.
Again, he saw other souls
cooking in earthenware pots . . .

He came to the morass of hell
deep, stinking dreadfully:
according to ancient lore
this sprang from rotting bellies
from the leaking of corpses . . .
Many souls floundered in it
amid sharp, bristling sword-grass:
according to ancient lore
this was dead men's living hair.

There again he saw souls that gave
the breast to monstrous beasts
both male and female: these were
the souls of childless women.
And still other souls he met
that were each roasting a child:
according to ancient lore
these had had only one child
and now turned themselves on spits . . .

Souls without issue were hanging
in a bamboo thicket
flapping in the wind, rustling
like the dry leaves of a tree
weeping openly above.
And further on he saw souls
sitting in a parched meadow
thin, nothing but skin and bone
their joints creaking and inflamed:

these were souls who had refused gifts . . .

Thai

As in many countries, the early culture of Thailand centred round the Court and its closed circle. Only princes, monks and courtiers were equipped to write poems. Their works, often long and epic-like, concentrate repeatedly on Buddhist morality on the one hand, and on royal adventures, glorifications of monarchs and courtly love affairs on the other. The first three poems given here bear witness to this tradition. The third of these, by Sunthǒn Phu, comes from a 'journey poem' (*nirat*), perhaps the Thai poetic type best known in the West, as does the extract by Mǒm Rachothai which was prompted by a diplomatic mission to Victorian England.

The 18th and 19th centuries were the transitional period for Thai poetry as the poets, thanks to improved communications, began to venture outside the Court and catch a glimpse of the people's life. *Poor Prince* by Phra Maha Montree Sub is the best known of several mock-epics and a landmark in Thai classical literature, blending royal and popular elements and preparing the way for a more broadly based literature.

Although education in the 20th century has been expanded to cover many areas of the country and made available to many sectors of the population, modern Thai poetry did not really begin till the second half of the century. But it is making up for lost time: especially in the three years from the students' uprising of October 1973 which brought democracy to Thailand—an occasion celebrated by the 'Little Star' of Sujit Wongtes—till the military coup of October 1976, new poems voiced the cry for political freedom, economic equality and social justice.

Anonymous (c. 14th–17th cents.)

from THE EPIC OF EXCELLENCY LǑ

A happily married prince is bewitched and falls in love with the two daughters of a neighbouring ruler with whom he is at war. The death of the lovers leads to the reconciliation of the states.

See three make love who high have reigned:
arms that hold flesh, the body strained
    to press close and admire,
desire, enjoy, raise lips to feed
on crowded tastes of heavenly mead—
    thus one pair squeeze and clutch.

Arms hug, arms cling, support, caress;
flesh, divine flesh, importunes flesh
    and soft young flesh is pleased.
Each visage easeful, bright with youth:
mouth, divine mouth, importunes mouth—
    mouths for each other made.
Male breast to maiden breast is joined;
loins, divine loins, importune loins,
    soft coupling loins that melt.
Oh joy so felt, to newly mate,
oh blended tastes' and odours' weight;
    both mortal lusts devour.
The flower bloats and strains to open,
blossom on blossom crowds on blossom:
    a blossom-clustered pond.
Lo, the bee's fondle, clutch and squeeze
amidst the lotus' rise and tease;
    incessant, they each probe.
Derobed for heaven's pool is not
half such a brave, delightful sport
    as for her smooth-fleshed pool.
'Thy darling pool gives so much joy
for the fish to wallow in, jump, toy:
    thy lotus, open wide.
The pretty side, swept clean and bare
of dust, round thy sweet watery lair!
    Incomparable mound!'
'My lord has found his karma's best
lets him play with my golden breasts.
    Caress me, I implore.'
When Lady Peun the king had cloyed
he then the other nymph enjoyed,
    the noble maid Pang Tong.

Si Prat (17th cent.)

REPARTEE
with the Lady Chulalak

THE LADY: Poor hare jumps at moon? Dotes so!
Does not see how low his place.

Like peacocks who'd know the clouds,
Does not see one ace his place, the rogue.

THE POET: Poor hare dotes, jumps at high glow—
As far as eyes go in sky.
But at times hearts flow; then all beasts mate.
Queen, *do* not berate. My case fits *you.*

Sunthŏn Phu (1786–1855)

from LINES WRITTEN NEAR THE STATUE OF THE BUDDHA OF PRATHOM

Be thou a tree then let me on thee settle;
Let me brood on a branch, bide in the thick.
Be thou a lunar beauty, Passion Petal,
I beg I, as the hero, fly to pick.

Be thou the lotus, let me be the bee,
To court and suck and make much of thy pollen.
Be thou the water, let me dragon be
That I praise and enjoy, once in thee fallen.

Be thou the cooling cave, then, swan of thine,
I'll swirl and dwell and enter in a flood.
Be thou, oh coolest flesh, in fact divine,
Then let me, charmed by thee, be as a god.

Phra Maha Montree Sub (fl. 1809–51)

from POOR PRINCE

So let the tale begin. Poor Prince Lan-dai
alone enjoys his throne, alone goes by—
wandering on tour—that downtown mark, the Swing
before the Brahmin temple; lives in the wing
of Broken Castle whose thin pilasters
are snapped off near the top, where spiky furze
tangles the walls which might have been of glass.
The foe, intending evil, cannot pass,
for night and day a mongrel howls and waits.

On tour he plays a pipe at all the gates
to get rice for his granary and gut.
No one dislikes him, neither man nor slut:
they aim to serve; his karma is their fear.
And then at evening when the shadows near,
mosquitoes congregate. The Prince Lan-dai
makes smoke so he can enter, and can lie
not on a bed of crystal but of reed,
kingly, lethargic, drink on ganjah weed.
Next, when the sun comes up and starts its race
Lan-dai bends to a pan to splash his face,
disrupts his fast with fish-skins and dry dahl
and then completes his bath—in the canal.

Mŏm Rachothai

from LONDON JOURNEY (1857)

And now of fabled England I will tell—
a mighty island doing very well,
its length six hundred miles (I do not lie)
its breadth no one has set down, nor shall I.
Westward it stands and north, so far away
with wooded hills in delicate array,
a hundred cities, thirty thousand ships
that sail the world on ceaseless trading trips.
London, the seat of kings, is capital
protected by a Tower but not a wall.
Several hundred churches are its pride:
from two there are fair vistas far and wide.

Many playhouses of the better kind
are neatly fitted, tastefully designed:
the shows are very different from ours—
not casual, open, but each day, indoors.
Come seven o'clock and dusk each playhouse fills
with lamplight bright as day, and music shrills.
At midnight it is all supposed to end—
and it is yours if you have cash to spend.

Sujit Wongtes (1945–)

LITTLE STAR (1973)

Twinkle twinkle
little star

Through the seven kinds of palm-tree
Jow Kun-thong went out
to live the life of a robber
and has not turned about.

Their rice wrapped in a leaf
his parents hear it said
everywhere they punt in search
that Jow Kun-thong is dead.

From a car they hear cicadas,
parrots they hear from a train,
sawing, jawing and cawing,
calling Kun-thong by name.

You left home at sunrise
—you told your brother and sis—
for rights, dignity, freedom,
as Garibaldi did.

how I wonder
what you are

With his folk-weave shoulder bag
Kun-thong left his veranda,
his moony books blotched with tears
he had wept that night in anger.

Jow Kun-thong, you were weeping
in the house until very late;
your campus flag, blood-soaked,
swam in the Chao-phrya's spate.

up above the world so high
like a diamond in the sky

Your mother is calling, Kun-thong.
Feel what she must have felt.
Your father is waiting: you are no fighter
covered in wounds and welts.

Your body is weak and thin,
bred to soft study from birth.
Your mother knows you are loyal.
Dad knows that you thank the earth.

But who else will know your belief?
They have not Indra's mind.
Men may be able to hear
but authority makes them blind.

You had your way; you sat in;
your parents waited at home.
The Morning Glory opens.
Evening Pride gleams in the gloam.

Your parents stray to the tablets
where democracy is averred.
There is no trace of Jow Kun-thong,
just their grief, their pride, and the word.

Wat Wanlayangkoon

LOST BANANAS (1975)

My house is in a lane:
the 'Lane of Bananas'.
Near me lives a monkey.
Monkey likes bananas.
But monkey lives on lawn
where grow no bananas.
Before I sleep each night
I gorge on bananas.
I have money to spend:
spend it on bananas.
Thus I buy and put by
bunches of bananas.

Each day I go to work:
am paid in bananas.

I came home one evening
and saw no bananas.
Eyes blurred, stomach empty,
I looked for bananas.
I searched, saw a monkey
holding my bananas.
Was angry with monkey,
kicked him, took bananas.
Was angry but I found
just skins of bananas.

Then I learnt the monkey did
not eat my bananas.
Neighbours had seen a man
stealing my bananas.
He was a dirt digger
who disdained bananas
but had a child who ate
rice ground with bananas.
He was a poor man, he
did not have bananas.
His child was so hungry
he stole my bananas.

Nowarat Pongpaiboon (1940–)

INTERCONTINENTAL QUESTION (1975)

Who is dragging what across the mud over there—
that lump of meat ripe for maggots, nearly putrid,
changed from the limbs that cradled, were touched in sleep?

Bloats up now the youthful flesh till it is not flesh;
lies in that muddy graveyard, a painful remembrance.

Its day will be long now, its night long, numbingly cold
in an outer darkness so dark it extends for ever.
That is for you. You can have it for good.

Who humps that soft yielding flesh over there—
brimful with blood its red holes, its soiling craters,
crusted dark, blotchy, unclean, the dirty accused?

His flesh was once white. Clean. Clean! My gorge rises at it.
His quiet eyes, half-closed, afloat, gaze wide up and stare.
They still hold my eyes with their motionless appealing.

Rest now. Go to sleep. You are tired. The pain fades at last.

As for *you*
great American Pal!
What words can I find to make this lucid to you?
What words will command you to see,
will stick in your damned heart until you know?

How much blood do you need? Whose in particular next?
How many more corpses, corpses, of these poor fighters?
How many more sights like this one?
What image will make you
shriek, make you stop, stop,
for pity's sake stop.

Burmese

The earliest known Burmese verse dates from the 14th century. For four centuries poets were monks and scholarly courtiers, writing expositions of Buddhist doctrine, extravagant praises of the Buddha or the king, stylised descriptions of woodland scenes, and expressions of longing for home and loved ones. The classical verse form consists of a four-syllable group whose final syllable rhymes with the third in the group following, then with the second in the group after that, whose final syllable in turn supplies the next rhyme; a verse paragraph—there being no fixed stanza —ends typically with a seven-syllable group which often echoes or rhymes with other end-groups.

The scope of both theme and form widened in the 18th century: of the poems given here, 'Soldier's Letter' is clearly drawn from life, as is 'The Farmer's Family'—which also shows the influence of a song form, adding end-rhyme to the classical form. The latter still holds sway today, and though a poet might write about shipwreck or the after-effects of the Raj, traditional themes, as in 'Two Strings of Beads', continue to flourish.

Padei-tha-ya-za (c. 1684–1754)

THE FARMER'S FAMILY

In the monsoon   when the rain falls
goodman and wife   merrily go
hand tugging hand   their bodies clad
in shirt, sarong   tattered and torn
with red cotton turbans on their heads.

Drenched by the rain   their bodies bare
sons and daughters   are borne along:
while the man ploughs   he grips his pipe
drawing furrows   across the field
and water brims over the rice-beds.

In their baskets   long-legged frogs
water-snails, jute   in a jumble
tender stew-leaves   sweet potatoes
rot-thorn, pumpkin: they lug the lot—
a mass of legs, shells, leaves, flowers and buds.

Tasty? Oh yes— oceans of juice:
moonflower, mouse-ear mixed together.
When they get home they rush to cook:
the rice is hot the stew is hot
with (phew! phew!) chillies cut into shreds.

Crammed on all sides the sturdy brood
gobble and gulp fistfuls of food.

Sein-dakyaw-thu (1736–71)

SOLDIER'S LETTER

In Danubyu
when our shining sceptred lord pitched
his pavilion,
southward, northward still overcast
we tried to moor jammed together
but found nowhere.
Squalls whipped the waves into whirlpools:
to left, to right no oar could steer
no pole could punt nor paddle shift.
The water rose, boat with boat locked
prow pushed, stern pulled, hooks slipped, we thrashed
in the water, sank, choked, got soaked
tugged at ropes' ends, jumped, grabbed reed, rush
to reach the bank all sterns awash:
in wretched state we made our camp—
the night gloomy, dark and dim.

A motley crew
tumbled pell-mell no room to spare
boat to boat jammed grasping the bank
cursing our lot far from supper
the riverbank all mud and slime
no firm ground seen to north or south
only black night:
soldiers, warriors gone to pieces
and dark clouds met merged overhead
the whole sky swirled all night, all day
pouring, drenching.
To homesickness cold was added:

a myriad men miserable—
down South, sticky all the time.

Of present woe
you—who before you bound your breasts
and loosed your hair
loved only me held me captive
my demure one my faultless one—
you know nothing:
'He is having good times abroad
in the army'— do you think that?
I fear you do. But no: at dusk
at dawn we strive in vain to scare
gadflies, midges which bite, suck blood.
Swarming facefuls—
mosquito nets do not stop them.
Troubles pile up—
thickets, bushes, rushes, reeds thick
on the ground, night wind, rain strike, slap:
homesick, I grieve—
they warned us it would be grim.

Nu Yin (1916–)

TWO STRINGS OF BEADS

With skill, with care
striving to be fair, her two cheeks
she tinges rose, serene, smiling
her arching brows she touches black,
serene, content
her forehead fringe she dabs with scent
her scarlet lips she decorates
with lipstick both to make them fair
her glossy black sweet-smelling hair
she knots on top and trails it down
and in that hair
all fragrant kinds of flowers she binds:
thus anointed and thus adorned
striving, scheming to be more fair
around her neck she hangs a string
of splendid pearls and is serene—
such is the way of young girls.

Meditating
meanwhile on the momentary
chance conjunction which is the self
considering
and finding peace in this doctrine
the old lady lowers her head
and lifts off one hundred and eight
beads on a string
which ceaselessly she tells within—
she is filled with quiet joy.

Thamein Thaung (1932–)

A FORTNIGHT LATER

Unexpected
as a lightning stroke, sickening
breaking the heart
an evil fate a sad tale told
from the day the *Progress* sank.

From that day on by night, by day
enough to turn the eyes away
bodies, bodies in piles appeared.

Day followed day
and when a full fortnight had passed
from the sunken *Progress* emerged
a mother's sad tenacity—
a sight to tug at the heart:

though nothing but a skeleton
with arms fast round a smaller one—
her treasure she sought to safeguard—
an only too human pair.

The ripples rocked the waves lapped her
leeches sucked her bugs fed on her:
the wretched plight overwhelmed her
but still she clasped
her child and would not let go.

Mother, mother
you could have swum out of danger
you might have fled to a safe place
but you would not:
you gave up your life instead.

Mother, mother *when all is lost*
my own mother will not know me:
the old adage the hard saying
you have challenged and destroyed.

Mother, mother
one with your child your only joy
before your care your tenderness
your mother-love stronger than death
I for ever bow my head.

Tin Mo (1939–)

THE SKY IS THE LIMIT

Our language is the mere jargon
of fishermen on riverbanks
of small traders:

while his language graces the lips
of officials in tall buildings
administering—
the ambitious are proud of it.

Our writing, our script enables
people to read who's dead, who's born
to make notes of wet crops, dry crops—
it is lowly, unimportant:

while his writing his script is used
in schools, bureaux, books, documents,
for kings, rulers— it carries weight.

What we live by, our religion
is litanies in villages

holy water   at funerals—
a mere solace,   undignified:

what he lives by,   his religion
is bells swinging   in high places
awe-inspiring   ceremonies—
so impressive!

Although this be   our nation, he
with his customs,   his attitudes
his men, his lords,   is still in charge:

although this is   our golden land
his values, his   ideas are those
which we still look   up to, admire.

Let us straighten   our heads, our minds
now we are free   to spread abroad
our religion   our literature
our traditions   to make them ours—
let us found a great people:

let our nation   advance the cause
of its culture,   its many-branched
knowledge and skill,   humanities,
its sciences, its   wealth of knowledge
that they may be learned by all.

Now we are free   at last, our sphere
is the whole earth:
only the sky   is the limit!

Tibetan

Over a millennium of Buddhist monastic culture in Tibet lost its focus in 1959 when the Dalai Lama fled before increasing Chinese domination. The earliest literature consisted largely of translations of Sanskrit religious texts, but by the 13th century an indigenous literature was flourishing. The principal figure is Milarepa, whose poem given here is an account of how he acquired the title *repa* ('cotton-clad'). A very different note is sounded by the quatrains, freely adapted here, of the Sixth Dalai Lama. The Chinese authorities, fearing the effect a brothel-haunting divine ruler might have on political stability, deposed and probably murdered him; his countrymen, however, still revere him as the Merry One who pointed out a spiritual path for ordinary men.

Milarepa (1039–1122)

When the tiger-year was ending
and the hare-year beginning
on the sixth day of the month of the barking of the fox,
I grew weary of the things of this world;
and in my yearning for solitude
I came to the sanctuary wilderness, Mount Everest.
Then heaven and earth took counsel together
and sent forth the whirlwind as messenger.
The elements of wind and water seethed
and the dark clouds of the south rolled up in concert;
the peerless twain, sun and moon, were made prisoner
and the twenty-eight constellations of the moon were fastened together;
the eight planets in their courses were cast into chains
and the faint milky way was delivered into bondage;
the little stars were altogether shrouded in mist
and when all things were covered in the complexion of mist
for nine days and nine nights the snow fell,
steadily throughout the eighteen times of day and night it fell.
When it fell heavily the flakes were as big as the flock of wool,
and fell floating like feathered birds.
When the snow fell lightly the flakes were small as spindles,
and fell circling like bees.
Again, they were as small as peas or mustard-seed,

and fell turning like distaffs.
Moreover the snow surpassed measure in depth,
the peak of white snow above reached to the heavens
and the trees of the forest below were bowed down.
The dark hills were clad in white,
ice formed upon the billowing lakes
and the blue Tsangpo was constrained in its depths.
The earth became like a plain without hill or valley,
and in natural consequence of such a great fall
the lay folk were mewed up;
famine overtook the four-footed cattle,
and the small deer especially found no food;
the feathered birds above lacked nourishment,
and the marmots and field-mice below hid in their burrows;
the jaws of beasts of prey were stiffened together.
In such fearsome circumstances
this strange fate befell me, Milarepa.
There were these three: the snowstorm driving down from on high,
the icy blast of mid-winter,
and the cotton cloth which I, the sage Mila, wore;
and between them rose a contest on that white snow peak.
The falling snow melted into goodly water;
the wind, though rushing mightily, abated of itself,
and the cotton cloth blazed like fire.
Life and death wrestled there after the fashion of champions,
and swords crossed victorious blades.
That I won there the heroic fight
will be an example to all the faithful
and a true example to all great contemplatives;
more especially will it prove the greater excellence
of the single cotton cloth and the inner heat.
For all hidden causes of disorder were balanced
and henceforth, inward and outward conflict past, were reconciled.
The two breaths, both the hot and the cold,
imparted their invigoration
and I utterly overcame the snow-faced demon,
who promised to obey my commands thereafter.
Then I ordered all aright in stillness
and, without seeking to summon the legions of this world,
as sage was victor in the strife that day.
For I am of my grandfather and wear the tiger skin:
when I put on the fox skin there was none to say me nay.
I am my father's son and of the race of champions:

I never suffered defeat from an angry foe.
I am of the breed of the lion the king of beasts:
I never dwelt but in the heart of the snows.
Therefore the foe's preparation proved vanity.

If ye steadfastly obey the words of this old man
the teaching of the practice of conjunction
will spread hereafter and many saints will arise;
and I, Milarepa the sage, shall be most famous
throughout the kingdoms of the world.
Ye, disciples, recollected, will be full of faith
and your good report will be noised abroad.

Tsangyang Gyatso, Sixth Dalai Lama (1683–1706)

The old dog
    at the west postern
has a yellow beard
    and is discreet
as the discreet Mandarin
    whom he resembles,
he does not betray
    my dusk departure
nor my return
    at dawn.

The Lion Throne
    stands empty,
the stiff ceremonial robes
    are hidden
in a clothes closet.
    Here,
I am the best drinking
    comrade,
the consoler
    of fifty young women.

Into the bedroom
    with the first light
comes snow light,
    we look out
and snow has filled the streets.

Though my good Mandarin
opens but one eye
a black snow-snake
clamours
from downtown Lhasa
all the way
to the Potala walls.

*

Frost
lacing
late summer
grass
gives warning
of autumn
winds.
The honeyed
season
is over.
The bee
takes leave
of the flower.
I
bow myself
from your bed.

Sanskrit

The Sanskrit poetry given here spans more than two and a half millennia
—from around 1500 BC to the 12th century AD. From the oldest stratum
of Sanskrit, which is preserved for us only in a collection of Hindu reli-
gious poetry, the *Rigveda*, comes one of the later hymns, to the goddess
Night. Though somewhat uncharacteristic of the whole, the poem is
strongly marked both by lyricism and tightly stanzaic organisation,
qualities that form a unifying thread throughout the long history of
classical poetry, and are equally evident in the last item chosen, from
The Song of the Cowherd (*Gita Govinda*) by the 12th-century Bengal
poet Jayadeva.

Between these temporal extremes, poems have been selected to illus-
trate, albeit briefly, the rich diversity of the Sanskrit lyric. Portions of
the Indian epics, particularly the often quite highly stylised *Ramayana*
are clearly antecedents of the developed classical style which reached its
apogee in the 4th century with *The Cloud-Messenger* (*Meghaduta*) by
Kalidasa. Though longer poems such as this were written, the typica
verse was intended as a stanzaic unit, complete in thought and syntax, an
embellished jewel that had a life of its own. Anthologies of Sanskrit verse
are therefore the standard form of its preservation, either in the famous
'centuries' (collections of a hundred poems) attributed to poets them-
selves (Bhartrihari, Amaru), and written at best on set themes, such as
Love or Success, or merely collected *post hoc* from the large floating
resources of the culture, as Vidyakara's *Treasury*—and even there
grouped into thematic sections.

Lyric poems were an integral part of the Sanskrit drama, which i
really more akin to Western opera than to Western drama: poems, often
twenty or thirty per act, were crucial to the expression of the play's
dominant sentiment, its *rasa*. One example is given here: three poems
from *The Little Clay Cart* (*Mricchakatika*) by Shudraka, probably some-
what earlier than Kalidasa. Such poems were also easily excerpted from
their dramas, and often found their way into the anthologies.

Though the bulk of early Indian writing is preserved in Sanskrit, there
are examples of poetry composed in languages which must have been
akin to the spoken languages of the period: for contrast a few poems from
the 2nd-century anthology of Hala are included, noteworthy for their
unpretentious vividness, qualities sometimes lacking in the elite and often
academic Sanskrit tradition. In this connection too, the earliest and lates
poems, from the *Rigveda* and *The Song of the Cowherd*, show a much
clearer affinity to the popular lyric of a period when Sanskrit—or its
Vedic dialect—was still very much a spoken language; the second is a
rare work whose genius lies precisely in its successful adaptation of the
rich and powerful Sanskrit medium to the demands of a popular religious
devotionalism, a marriage that persists even today in the Sanskri
compositions of many poet-saints.

from the 'Rigveda' (c. 15th–10th cents. BC)

HYMN TO NIGHT

So vast, our Goddess Night, she rises,
star-eyes gazing everywhere;
all her finery of dress displayed.
Space high and low she fills, Eternal Night,
her beauty driving out the dark.
Close on the heels of sister Day
she treads. Let darkness run . . .
As you draw near, we turn for home
like birds that wing to nest.
Life everywhere retreats: man, beast
and bird. Even the soaring hawk
returns to seek out rest.
Night, shield us from the wolf and thief.
Throughout your hours let there be calm.
Pitch dark has brought a shroud for me.
Dawn, drive it, like my debts, away.
Child of Day, to you, as to a calf,
my hymn is offered. Receive it now
as paean to a conqueror.

from the 'Ramayana' (2nd cent. BC–2nd cent. AD)

King Rama courts Sita; she replies.

I yearn to see the streams, the hills and shady groves.
No fears while you, my wise resourceful Lord, are there.

Happily with you I'd look on lotus pools—
flower-ripe, teeming with wild ducks and swans.

There, my wide-eyed one, I'd flirt and play with you
a hundred or a thousand years if you could stay.

Even the endless pleasures found in paradise
would pall for me were I to live that life alone.

None can keep me from the fearsome forest—wild
with monkey, deer and elephant. Your feet alone
I'll clasp, as much at peace as in my father's home.

'Oh take me, please! Apart I'll die. My soul is yours,
my mind will have no other life. Allow me this!
I'll be no burden as your wife.'

But conscious of his duty and despite her words,
the king held firm. He told how grim the forest life
could be, in hope to turn her mind away.

Hala (?2nd cent. AD)

To reach my love I have to penetrate
the darkest night. And don't you know—
my mother, both eyes closed,
can straighten up the house?

*

This flake of moon against the sunset glow.
Love-scratch a bride wears on her breast,
half-glimpsed through fine red silk.

*

Thinking you would come,
for half the night time seemed to fly.
The other half seemed longer than a year,
my eyes downcast in grief.

*

How she scolded him,
the traveller, last night,
handing straw out for his bed.
This morning, picking up the pieces,
how she weeps.

Shudraka (?3rd cent.)

from THE LITTLE CLAY CART

A classical drama of love and political intrigue.

No care derives from loss of wealth.
It's Fate decides how money moves.

But how a poor man's heart must ache
when friends-of-old can't place the name.

*

So long now since
you've lived with me, your friend.
You made yourself a home.
How sad the thought, O Poverty:
where will you go when I am dead?

*

Stormcloud, you know no shame!
Why now? Just when I'm off to meet my love,
as if your fearful thunder's not enough,
you drench me with caressing rain.

Kalidasa (4th cent.)

from THE CLOUD-MESSENGER

A long elegy by the greatest Indian classical poet in which a demigod describes to a cloud the journey it is to make bearing a love-message to his bride.

Seeing the golden-tawny *nipa*,
  stamens yet half-formed,
and plantains showing off new buds
  along the banks,
scenting the fresh earth-fragrance
  lifting clear of bone-dry woods,
the antelope will map a trail
  where you may loose your rain.

*

Your form will swell with incense rising
  from the open windows . . .
  where women dress their hair.
Royal peacocks will dance in your honour,
  come to welcome you as friend.
If your heart is travel-worn, then spend
  the night high on the palace roofs,
where flowers are fragrant and paths printed
  by the red-dyed feet of lovely girls.

*

I see your form in the creeping vine,
your look in a deer's startled eyes;
your cheek gleams with the moon, your hair
there in long peacock plumes.
Those sidelong glances show each time
the river gently purls . . .
Alas my sweet, not one place found
affording you complete.

Bhartrihari (early 7th cent.)

The clear lamp of wisdom shines a while
upon the blessed. A while, no more, unclouded
by the looks of sharp, gazelle-eyed girls.

*

Woman is the hook that Love
casts out on life's wide sea. And fish,
in rising, wild for ruby lips,
are caught and roasted in his fire.

*

Firelight I have and a lamp;
sun, moon and stars for sight.
And yet, without her gaze,
my world is blinding black.

*

Cloud-draped the sky above;
nearby on slopes the peacocks dance;
the earth below pure white with petals.
Where, traveller, will you turn your gaze?

Amaru (late 7th cent.)

Hurrying to your lover
with jingling necklace, bangle,
anklet and girdle . . .
With all this drumming as you go,
why look about so terrified?

*

Explain the passion of your gaze
if seeing ought to be denied.
How can your dear lips tremble so
when utter silence is their aim?
Why does your body thrill and throb
if prayer is what it's fixed upon?
This act of yours—put it aside.
Your torment's clear. Forgive me then,
my love, and rid me of my pain.

*

Pouting, in bed, the pair of them.
Not one word either way
would they allow to pierce
the heavy silence reached.
Faces averted
though their hearts were one.
But glances were more free
and chanced to meet . . .
Only a second's pause before
all bitterness dissolved
in laughter and they fell
into each other's arms.

from Vidyakara's 'Treasury' (*11th cent.*)

Bracelets jingle every time
she lifts her arm, and as her dress
falls open, one can see a line
of nailmarks traced upon her breast.
The pestle lifted once again—
happy in her lotus hands—
her necklace beads go swinging free . . .
How beautiful the threshing girl.

*

The luck is yours that you can talk about
your lover's playful glance, his words and touch.
For me, I swear that once he puts his hand
upon my girdle, I remember nothing.

Jayadeva (fl. 12th cent.)

from THE SONG OF THE COWHERD

A long lyrical poem about the love of Krishna and Radha the milkmaid.

Beautiful, the black cloak, night,
  its kohl dropping on their eyes.
Tapiccha blossom about their ears,
  dark lotuses upon their heads.
  And on the breast, traces of musk . . .
My friend, see how the dark enfolds them:
  sweet rogues, hearts rushing to the tryst.

Darker than *tamala* leaves, the night
  outlined by jewel-clusters;
  cow-girls making for the tryst,
  their bodies yellow with saffron . . .
Darkness the touchstone, to test if love is gold.

Bengali

For better or for worse, the Bengalis are often regarded as the most articulate people of the Indian subcontinent. Certainly theirs is a culture of great vitality, and much of the best Indian poetry of the last two hundred years has been written in Bengali, the language spoken today in Bangladesh (where it is the state language), in West Bengal and in parts of Assam, Bihar and Orissa. Bengali is one of the oldest literary languages of the subcontinent—Sanskrit is a sister- rather than a parent-language—but the present selection concentrates mainly on the unprecedented developments of the last hundred years.

The period from the 14th to the 17th centuries was one of much devotional fervour in northern and eastern India. This *bhakti*, as it is called, found some of its most beautiful expression in the Vaishnava poetry of Bengal, which celebrates the communion of man with the divine in terms of the love between the Lord Krishna and the milkmaid Radha. A typical sequence is given here; the poets, of whom the first wrote in Sanskrit, are identified by their 'signature lines'.

The greatest of all Bengali poets is Rabindranath Tagore. Only a small proportion of his huge *oeuvre* has appeared in English, and that mostly his own rather bland translations of early work; three samples of late work are given here. The generation of the 1930s turned away from Tagore towards Western influences: the Surrealism of Jibanananda Das shows in his poem given here, while the poems of his two most distinguished contemporaries reflect more a concern to make the 'new poetry' acceptable.

Within the few years of its existence, Bangladesh has produced a generation of poets with a strong social and political consciousness. Two of them are represented here.

Three Vaishnava Poets (15th–16th cents.)

MILAN

Radha, reconciled, returns to Krishna, and the lovers are united once again.

He speaks:

My moon-faced one,
I am waiting
        to make our beds ready,

milan: reunion. The arrangement of this sequence is the translators'.

to gather lotus petals—
your body will press them,
hidden from even friendly eyes . . .
Come,
the sweet breeze from the sandalwoods
censes our trysting place . . .

So sings the poet Ramananda Raya,
that pleasure be brought to the heart of the great king Prataparudra.

Her friend speaks:

Her cloud of hair eclipses the lustre of her face, like Rahu greedy for the moon;
the garland glitters in her unbound hair, a wave of the Ganges in the waters of the Yamuna.
How beautiful the deliberate, sensuous union of the two; the girl playing this time the active role,
riding her lover's outstretched body in delight;
her smiling lips shine with drops of sweat; the god of love offering pearls to the moon.
She of beautiful face hotly kisses the mouth of her beloved; the moon, with face bent down, drinks of the lotus.
The garland hanging on her heavy breasts seems like a stream of milk from golden jars.
The tinkling bells which decorate her hips sound the triumphal music of the god of love.

So Vidyapati says.

She speaks:

Beloved, what more shall I say to you?
In life and in death, in birth after birth
you are the lord of my life.
A noose of love binds
my heart to your feet.
My mind fixed on you alone, I have offered you everything;
in truth, I have become your slave.
In this family, in that house, who is really mine?

her cloud of hair . . .: It is said that an eclipse is caused by a demon called Rahu, who eats the moon. The waters of the Ganges are light in colour, while those of the Yamuna are dark.

Whom can I call my own?
It was bitter cold, and I took refuge
at your lotus feet.
While my eyes blink, and I do not see you,
I feel the heart within me die.

A touchstone
I have threaded, and wear upon my throat,
says Chandidasa.

Rabindranath Tagore (1861–1941)

from BIRTHDAY

The *Om* of the ageless sea
booms in my mind:
I do not know what it means,
I am the words, only
the rush, the roar,
the music, the dance, the symphony of pain,
I only swim
sometimes to this shore, sometimes to that
sometimes into the depths
sometimes out to a strange island,
the chiming waves
describe elusive curves and then die out.
Nobody knows
which way this silence flows:
now light, now dark, I can almost
touch it
sometimes far, sometimes near, across
this liquid canvas
eternity assumes two forms
for ever to right and left, speaking and not speaking,
the mystery is mirrored, flowing, breaking,
flowing over for ever.

from ON A SICKBED

Open the door!
Open the blue sky!
Let the scent of flowers tiptoe into my room

let the first sunbeam
come into all my body, my veins
let me hear the rustle of leaf and branch
salute me for being alive!
Let this morning
spread its mantle over my soul
as over new grass in green fields:
I hear the silent speech
of all the love I have ever known
I am baptised
in the sky, in the air
in whose blue I see
the truth of all life as a garland of gems.

LAST POEM

You strewed creation's path
with many wiles
O wanton:
your deft hand laid the snares of a false trust
for the simple soul.
Your falsehood has put greatness to the test:
you have not hid the night from him.
Your star shows him
a path—
his soul's path
for ever clear:
a simple faith
lights him for ever.
Though seeming subtle he is straight at heart—
that is his glory.
He finds the truth
washed by its inner light in every soul.
Nothing can fool him now:
he bears his last reward
off to his inner store.
He who so easily was fooled
receives from you the right none can remove
to peace.

Jibanananda Das (1899–1954)

SAILOR

Ship has drifted away: turning his mind to this,
beaten, weary, the sailor wakes and longs for relief;
sun is sun is sun, up there, beyond a shore,
sounds of a port, a row of pines; yet, naturally enough,

there it is seen as a fabulous egg by a blonde priestess;
seen by a common peasant as a bauble among his corn;
lopped heads throng in the dark under the slant of long
beams by which as by spears their gloomy hovels are torn—

stare at the golden beams, at the atoms colliding and flying,
flying away to a land of wonders beneath his stare.
Sailor, sailor, where are you following the sun? In the mirrors—
those of Babylon, Nineveh, Egypt, China and Ur—

you were caught for a while; then noon, and a change of sea;
winds from Vaishali, from Gethsemane, from Alexandria
drive you as beacons, winking a welcome; for they are also
shores. Yet they will not do. Their wonders urge you away.

So must it be—while bees with wings that sparkle like crystals
score the pink sun and herons with deadlier aim than planes
bring down the virgin blue; so must man seek and for ever
fall; bright hourglass, sailor, endless water remains.

Sudhindranath Datta (1900–64)

OSTRICH

You hear me well: and yet you try
To hide within the desert's fold.
Here shadows shrink until they die,
While dead horizons cannot hold
The quick mirage, and, never near,
The cruel sky is mute and blue.

Vaishali: legendary Hindu city-state.

The hunter stalks no phantom deer;
He loses all by losing you.
The sands are heedless. Why run on,
When tell-tale footprints point your way?
Your prehistoric friends are gone,
And, all alone, you stand at bay.

By brooding on a broken egg
You cannot hatch or make it whole:
The self-consuming hunger's peg,
You play in void a dual role.
Become, instead, my wilful ark
Upon the chartless sea of sand;
For danger you refuse to mark,
Although you know the lie of land.
Come, let us seek a new retreat,
Enclosed in thorn and scorched all through,
Where trickles water, if not sweet;
The earth attracts a date or two.

No wishful creeper shall I grow
To keep your iron cage concealed,
Nor call in hucksters who would know
What price your useless wings would yield.
With moulted feathers I shall make
A fan to suit the anchorite,
But out of fibrils never rake
The dust once raised by steeds in flight.
My apprehensions shall prevail:
Your runic cry will not suborn:
For you are not the nightingale
Who lulls to feed on mortgaged corn.

This ruin is our inheritance:
A line of spendthrifts went before;
They picked the pounds, and left no pence:
Now both of us must pay their score.
And so your self-absorption seems
Inept: can blindness cheat a curse?
The present is not time for dreams:
By shunning me you make bad worse.
Let each of us then seal a bond
To serve the other's interest:

You speed me to the world beyond,
While I propose the human test.

Buddhadev Bose (1908–)

ICARUS

Pure, clear day, no breath upon the sea,
the wind unmoving in the sun-rinsed blue;
so still, so calm—smooth—
    as though with high summer
creation glows after its agony.

The horizon, naked, round, unblinking, kisses
    and the great sky, round, naked, bright, dissolves.

Full, ripe noon, no strife in the lulled sea,
as though this wide horizon is all desire's clear answer,
as though all fortune springs from this transparent blue,
as though the dark veil
will finally be lifted from men's eyes.

A grey dot floats
there: a cargo of passengers, of hopes,
makes for harbour.
No other wound on the sea, light throbs on blue,
pure Mediterranean day, golden wine without end.

Suddenly a wild blow:
like seeds in a flaming stream
gushing from the womb in the fullness of time;
this light—clarity—mystery of high summer
streams down like shooting stars upon the sky,
as though raging at the conjunction of sun and sea.

Head down, feet up, cumbered with useless wings,
faster and faster, swishing in the wind—
'Icarus, O Icarus!'
singing in his ears only till the deep
engulfs his head;
for a moment two legs kicking, molten wax

bites in hot memory—
then silence, stillness.

The sea is calm again, the brief rape over,
the air is drugged again with sunlight,
the sky, adjusted, is itself again.

Meanwhile dinner is served aboard, the harbour near.
Passengers fed on bull's flesh fill their glasses;
some scratch their prickly heat; some think 'Tonight I'll sleep
with my wife.'
In the city
clerks in the secretariat take their break,
excitedly discuss the day's big news:
which minister is out, who bought the job
of Police Commissioner with ten ounces of gold,
which wrestler will win at the next games.

By then
in the cool inner court
ladies are throwing dice with a flourish
or buzzing over the rising cost of honey
or simply dozing off.

At that moment an old rheumatic poet,
defeated, crossed the frontier of despair
realising only failure does not cheat,
choked his dismay, shook off his sterile rage,
upon a pure white sheet
lay down—
thin, dry, silent, wise.

Shamsur Rahman (1929–)

THE MEMORY OF YOU

A bridge collapses inside me, a house burns,
ashes blow, perhaps
the fading melody of an old song.
On the grey rutted road inside me someone calls.
Turning my eyes from the wall
through the dark I glimpse

a torn lonely bat
lying on the cold floor like a dead child.
Memory like a spider's web in moonlight, the memory of you
a kind of elegy in my soul.

A procession of ducks in the street—a tide
of white ripples: people suddenly
make way for them amazed.
The traffic policeman hangs in mid-air, his whistle
between his lips.
The conductor waves his baton through tattered clouds,
the music transforms the street into a flower-market
and a white skull dances madly in the blue sky
with a bird.
Memory like a spider's web in moonlight, the memory of you
a kind of elegy in my soul.

The magician from my childhood far away
turns into a monkey dressed in a billowing skirt
and smiling plays his rattle-drum.
I smoke a few cigarettes, dreaming;
suddenly I see a body
in a pond in Vietnam, muddy water:
in its head, hollow, deaf, arms and legs are flailing.
Memory like a spider's web in moonlight, the memory of you
a kind of elegy in my soul.

Syed Shamsul Haq (1935–)

CHAMELEONS

shouts of triumph are a burning boat   now it
stops   now it glides   cuts through lights   churning
foaming lights bursting all around triumph shouts
and here I am like the Polish Rider   horse galled and
blind in one eye   that could be bearable   but getting
a scent of the city   what made it buck   and turn the
rein   hoofs kicking stones   a storm of dust breathing
preferring another city   and the city crackling with
illuminations down there   not for this horse now

the Polish Rider: painting by Rembrandt.

why ? with heart fluttering I dis-
mounted and walked in and saw laughing procreation
around all around, streets filling with eggs shining
impossible to count eggs countless balls
little balls rolling down the road knocking each
other pushing and rolling pock pick pock pock the air
growing solid with them eggs eggs only a waterfall
of eggs on the road eggs in apartments eggs in offices
in the market place in the schools eggseggseggseggs

incubating the eggs by gently pressing down on them
with breasts they are cracking and heads jutting
out bursting ah burst these are chameleons

delicate near-translucent smooth sleek chameleons
in neatly pressed grey suits only chameleons or chameleons
only in cars walking into offices in every house
on every street I knock on
doors and chameleons open saying who's that knocking
on our door their little tongues flicking like
flags

everywhere only they are

they are staring out with millions of cold
blue ping-pong-ball eyes little grapes
of lust long-necked changing altering metamorphosing
adjusting their colour here
there everywhere in your chair, on the dais of
the conference hall in the throbbing shadows
of all the flags they are on their bellies
staring lying in wait for

now leaves are green again after so long this
is the time now that the sun is shining and it is hoped
now it will stay longer as far as the eye can
see no crevasse or canyon now is the time

the right time gospel time chameleon time

I cannot stay at home I am afraid to come out on the
road I look up and see my body dead
stretched out there I see flowers upside down

eagles swimming in the river   I see fish in the air
in my own land my own body is flaking and scales fall
like dandruff   and   my skin is getting dry   and cracks
in my hands bleed   my hair blows in the wind of my
grief   of what pain   I do not know

I only know   I will   knock from door to door to door
to door   what door will open   and let me stare into
not those chameleon eyes   but man's.

Urdu

Like many other modern languages in the north of the subcontinent, Urdu began to develop after the Muslim conquests of the 11th century. In Delhi and the surrounding areas, Urdu (the name literally means 'army camp') was a medium of communication between the Muslim soldiers and the local people, adding to its vocabulary from Arabic, Persian and Turkish as well as from local languages. The Muslim armies which invaded the Deccan during the 14th century and the preachers of Islam who followed in their wake took Urdu to central and southern India, giving it the rôle, which it has played ever since, of the most widely spoken *lingua franca* of the whole subcontinent.

Urdu literature was first developed in the Muslim courts of the Deccan, which during the 16th and 17th centuries were independent of Delhi, where Persian persisted as the major literary language. From this period we have collections of lyric verse, long narrative poems, laments and a certain amount of religious prose, all showing strong Persian influence. After the annexation of the Deccan by the Moghul emperor Aurangzeb and the subsequent migration of certain poets to Delhi, Urdu, as opposed to Persian, literature became fashionable in the north of India. The politically disturbed period which followed Aurangzeb's death in 1707 gave rise to a number of especially fine Urdu poets, including Mir Taqi Mir and the mystic Khwaja Mir Dard. As the fortunes of Delhi declined, Mir and many of his great contemporaries sought patronage in the newly formed kingdom of Avadh. During the second half of the 18th century, the opulence of the Avadh court and the opportunities afforded to poets by its extravagant rulers made Lucknow one of the major centres of Urdu literature. The great attention paid to language and style is reflected in the works of Insha Allah Khan Insha, who had also migrated there from Delhi as a young man. Delhi reasserted itself during the 19th century and the court of the last Moghul emperor, Bahadur Shah Zafar (an ardent devotee of Urdu poetry) gave shelter to poets like Momin Khan Momin and Ghalib, who along with Muhammad Iqbal is perhaps the best-known name in Urdu literature.

Until the middle of the 19th century, when the novel and other modern forms of prose were developed, much Urdu literature consisted of verse. The poets of India were greatly influenced by Persian models and most of the well-known Persian forms are paralleled in Urdu. From the earliest stages, the dominant poetic genre was the *ghazal*, of which all the poems given here are examples. Formally, the *ghazal* is a short poem consisting of an average of seven to ten couplets with the rhyme scheme aa ba ca etc. The metres, with a few notable exceptions, are those found in the Persian counterparts. One of the most common themes of the Urdu *ghazal* is unrequited love, though the poet is free to express himself on almost any subject within the conventional framework of the poem. There is no obligation to maintain the same theme throughout, and the sentiments expressed in one verse are often quite unconnected or even at variance with those that precede or follow it. The poet is rarely explicit about the nature or identity of his beloved, and many verses in the *ghazal* are capable of mystical interpretation, which may account for the fact that the beloved is always assigned the masculine gender. The poet's attitude to his beloved is to some extent governed by convention, but not entirely so. He may be introspective and submissive like Mir, self-confident and independent like Ghalib or simply facetious like the ebullient Insha, whose taste for elegant language and curious figures of speech characterises his verse. Iqbal is in many ways an exception. His *ghazals*, though formally well within the tradition, are usually written on a unified theme, being a vehicle for the expression of his message to the Islamic world, for which he is celebrated.

Dard (1721–85)

Charges we've heaped against ourselves.
The task for which we came is done.

Can this be life or just some storm?
Life anyway has caused this wreck.

What use these roses, morning breeze?
We're here a moment, soon to leave.

All sights we've taken in, my friends.
Stay on, but now we must be gone.

Don't take it hard—we'll know in time.
The spell You cast will answer all.

You see me here with love-torn heart.
My friend, how many are there healed?

Wet-eyed we joined the party (like
the candle) and wet-skirted left.

They look for Him somewhere beyond:
those Shaikhs have left their house and gone.

wet-eyed, wet-skirted: a candle begins by melting at the top and ends by melting at the bottom. Similarly, when we are born, we weep. At death we leave life stained with sin—'wet-skirted'.
those Shaikhs: those who have not grasped the real truth, but seek God only in terms of formal religion.

Outside ourselves *we* could not tread:
each way we turned, He closed our path.

We came alone into the world,
but find Him with us now we leave.

All so unreal! Mere sparks, we've seen
the business through at last and gone.

Cup-bearer! In this mill of leaving,
while you've strength, pass round the cup.

Dard, can you explain these crowds—
where they've all come from, where they've gone?

Mir (1722–1810)

My plans all overturned, a failure every
medicine I've tried. You see how heart-ache's
laid me low?

Undeniable the very life she breathes.
My luck that in her first communication
lay my death.

Considering my state, the moments when
I lacked respect were few. I went along
with her in every way, bent over backwards . . .

If only she would lift her veil right now!
What use her doing it for all when I
have shut my eyes for good?

Nothing for it in the black and white of our world
but to weep the whole night long, or, somehow,
pass the time till dark.

Her wish, at length to take the morning air . . .
The rose won by her face, the cypress made
her body's slave.

cnp: the container of mystical knowledge.

Quicksilver those wrists. I held them once
and let them go . . . What a fool to listen
to her promises, how green!

No good my pleas to her at any time.
However hard I tried she shrugged me off
—so proud—with added interest.

Not easy for a shy gazelle to put
aside its fear. Whoever tamed you had
a magic touch. He worked a miracle.

Why question Mir's religion now? Caste-mark
on his forehead, seat taken in the temple . . .
He said goodbye to Islam long ago.

Insha (*1756–1818*)

We're dressed and ready, comrades waiting for the word.
Some gone on ahead, while we just sit and wait.

Spring breeze, don't tease me with your scent. Let go.
Dog-tired I am and all you want to do is play.

Their thoughts, cup-bearer, fly beyond the furthest star
while revellers in the tavern reach their wildest hour.

Like the traveller's footprint on the road of longing
I find I'm stuck and can't get free. What can I do?

My follies, night and day, have got me in this fix.
I look to any shade beneath a wall for shelter.

Patience, what is that? Fame and honour? Well,
I've wept and worried for the lot. I'm now resigned.

My heart, don't let your courage swell. Don't kiss her now
Intoxication has not fired her yet. She's cold.

This shyness, madam, that you bring today is new.
At least a hundred times before we've sat like this!

Since when, Insha, has heaven's revolution granted
peace? For these few friends who sit with us our thanks.

Ghalib (1797–1869)

Desires in thousands fill my mind,
each one I ache to try. A number
satisfied, but still too few.

My executioner scared? She'll have
my blood on her hands? All my life
it's drained away, like all these tears.

Our confidants, to whom we turned
for comfort in our suffering, now
bear the worse scars from her knife!

That tale we hear of Adam leaving
Paradise has nothing—such dishonour—
on *my* exit from her street!

What standing then, my torturer,
if your artful tresses, coiled for height,
become so loosened they collapse!

You want to have a message reach her?
Just put the writing in *my* hands.
At dawn I'm out, my pen well primed . . .

It's turned out, in these present times,
that I'm the one to soak up wine.
Old Jamshed's cup has come again!

Death in love's the same as life.
The sight of her, the infidel
who's killing us, itself revives.

Now, Ghalib, where's the tavern door . . .
our Mister Temperance? This much I know—
yesterday I passed him going
in as I came out!

*

artful tresses: tall stature and long hair are ideal qualities of the beloved. Her hair when built up adds to her height. The secret would be revealed if it hung loose.
Jamshed: the Persian king who is said to have invented wine and was renowned for his cup in which he could read the future. Ghalib was well known for his partiality to wine.

My foolish heart, what's wrong with you?
No medicine will cure this ache.

So keen for her, yet she is cold.
God, what a business it is!

I have a tongue in my head too.
If only she'd ask me what *I* need!

If You alone exist, O God,
then why all this commotion now?

What are these beauties with their sweet,
bewitching looks, alluring sighs?

Those perfumed coils and tresses, that glance
from under blackened lids? Explain.

All we hope—that she be faithful.
Faith? She's never known the word!

Beyond all blessings I can give
I sacrifice my life for you.

Agreed, your Ghalib's worthless. But why
do you complain? You had him free!

Momin (1800–52)

That understanding we both came to—
you may perhaps recall. Yes, that—
our promise to be faithful to the last.
You may perhaps recall . . .

Those blessings granted me before,
the favour that you showed to me,
in every detail they're remembered.
You may perhaps recall . . .

Once there was this love between us,
once a bond that held us tight.

Once the two of us were lovers.
You may perhaps recall . . .

Listen then. The promise you made
was years ago. Yet now there's not
a single word it ever came true.
You may perhaps recall . . .

A quarrel the night we came together,
not one thing to which you'd agree.
No, no! The petulant way you spoke.
You may perhaps recall . . .

The one you counted as your lover,
the one you said you'd trust for ever.
I'm still the same poor Momin. Yes,
you may perhaps recall . . .

Zafar (1775–1862)

This famous poem, ascribed to the luckless king of Delhi who was exiled after the 1857 Mutiny, may well not be his.

No light in any eye is me,
I beat in no one's heart.
No use to man or child,
a pinch of dust is all I am.

Ruin's apparent here in my looks.
My love has taken leave of me.
I reap a spring whose garden
knew its death last fall.

Pointless your going to my grave
with either prayer or flower.
Who'd ever light a candle there?
That shrine of helplessness is me.

I sing no new life into souls.
Who'd want to hear my song? I am
the cry of endless separation.
Bitter anguish fills my call.

Zafar is no one's lover now,
a challenger to none for sure.
Destruction has become my lot.
The land I am is blitzed.

Iqbal (1877–1938)

That song, my shaken nightingale, is still unformed.
Better keep it in your breast a while . . .

Reason is mature when circumspect; if love
is circumspect it isn't yet mature.

Love jumped—no fears—right into Nimrod's fire;
while reason, from the roof, gaped at the scene.

The Messenger's word is all love needs to come alive;
while reason still can't take it in . . .

Love's way is freedom, overthrowing fate.
But you're the latter's priest and temple-bound.

The cup-bearer, angry at my temperance, cries out:
'You're still, deep down, a seeker after ends!'

Life's quantity and quality? Its scale is unrelenting
effort. Your gauge, still, a count of dawns and dusks.

Spring cloud, how much longer this lean grant of dew?
They're still dry-cupped, my mountain tulips.

My wine is Arab. Those who pass it round are not.
Wine-bibs, they still shrink from my jug.

This breeze across the garden carries news of Iqbal.
His new bird trapped and struggling in the net . . .

Nimrod's fire: referring to the legend of Abraham being cast into the fire by the tyrant Nimrod (after Qur'an 21 : 68–9).
a seeker after ends: in matters of real desire, one may not consider the outcome.
my wine is Arab: I am a true Muslim.

Tamil

Tamil, the second classical language of India, belongs to the Dravidian family. It has a literary tradition going back 2,000 years and has over 40 million speakers, chiefly in South India, Sri Lanka and Malaysia.

The present selection begins with poems from the Eight Anthologies of *sangam* ('academy') literature, the earliest recorded Tamil poetry. In these, the 'interior' (*akam*) poems are dramatic monologues in which five landscapes (hill, seashore, forest, arable land, desert) and their contents (birds, beasts, trees, tribes, characteristic arts and occupations) correspond to the phases of love (first union, anxious waiting, infidelity, elopement, patient waiting and reunion); the 'exterior' (*puram*) poems are meditations, panegyrics, heroic and sometimes grim elegies. Both kinds of anthology often contain work by the same poets, many of whose names are derived from their poems: for example, Cempulappeyanirar means 'the poet of the red earth and pouring rain', after the poem of his given here.

The poem by Nammaṛvar is from the medieval *bhakti* (devotional/mystical) tradition which spread throughout the Hindu world (cf. the Sanskrit poet Jayadeva and the Bengali Vaishnava poets, qq.v.), while the extract from Kampan offers a taste of the great epic poet who was heir to both the classical 'inscapes' and the religious feeling of *bhakti*.

Among modern poets, Bharati was a path-finder and liberator for Tamil, and Piccamurti ends the selection with a satirical poem about India's national bird, the peacock.

from the 'Eight Anthologies' (c. 1st–3rd cents.)

'interior' poems

WHAT HER FRIEND SAID

The great city fell asleep
but we did not sleep.
Clearly we heard, all night,
from the hillock next to our house
the tender branches of the flower-clustered tree
with leaves like peacock feet
let fall
their blue-sapphire flowers.

Kollan Aṛici

WHAT HE SAID

What could my mother be
to yours? What kin is my father
to yours anyway? And how
did you and I meet ever?
But in love our hearts are as red
earth and pouring rain:
mingled
beyond parting.

Cempulappeyanirar

WHAT HE SAID

My love is a two-faced thief.
In the dead of night
she comes like the fragrance
of the Red-Speared Chieftain's forest hills,
to be one with me.

And then, she sheds the petals
of night's several flowers,
and does her hair again
with new perfumes and oils,
to be one with her family at dawn

with a stranger's different face.

Kapilar

WHAT SHE SAID

Only the thief was there, no one else.
And if he should lie, what can I do?

There was only
a thin-legged heron standing
on legs yellow as millet stems
and looking

for lampreys
in the running water
when he took me.

Kapilar

WHAT SHE SAID

Before I laughed with him
nightly,

the slow waves beating
on his wide shores
and the palmyra
bringing forth heron-like flowers
near the waters,

my eyes were like the lotus
my arms had the grace of the bamboo
my forehead was mistaken for the moon.

But now

Maturai Eṛuttalan Centamputan

WHAT SHE SAID

Only the dim-witted say it's evening
when the sun goes down
and the sky reddens,
when misery deepens,
and the *mullai* begins to bloom
in the dusk.

But even when the tufted cock
calls in the long city
and the long night
breaks into dawn,
it is evening:

even noon
is evening,

to the companionless.

Milaipperun Kantan

WHAT HE SAID

O did I not think of you?
and thinking of you,
did I not think and think again of you?
and even as I thought of you
was I not baffled
by the world's demands
that held me to my work?

O love, did I not think of you,
and think of you till I wished
I were here to sate my passion
till this flood of desire
that once wet the branch of the tall tree
would thin
till I could bend and scoop a drink of water
with my hands?

Auvaiyar

'exterior' poems

RELATIONS

Like a hunted deer
on the wide white
salt land,
a flayed hide
turned inside out,
one may run,
escape.
But living
among relations
binds the feet.

Oreruṛavanar

ELEGY ON A YOUNG WARRIOR

O heart sorrowing
for this lad
                    once scared
of a stick
lifted in mock-anger
when he refused
a drink of milk,
                    now
not content with killing
war-elephants
with spotted trunks,
                    this son
of the strong man who fell yesterday

seems unaware of the arrow
in his wound,
his head of hair is plumed
like a horse's,
                    he's fallen
on his shield,
his beard still soft.

Ponmutiyar

Nammaṛvar (?9th cent.)

POSSESSION

Poets,
  beware, your life is in danger:

the lord of gardens is a thief,
  a cheat,
master of illusions;

he came to me,
  a wizard with words,
    sneaked into my body,
          my breath,

with bystanders looking on,
    seeing nothing,

he consumed me
  life and limb

and filled me
  making me over
into himself.

Kampan (11th/12th cent.)

A RIVER

Turning forest into slope,
field into wilderness,
seashore into fertile land,
changing boundaries, exchanging
landscapes,
          the reckless waters
roar on like the pasts
that hurry close on the heels
of lives.

Caressing the lovers' hair,
the lovers' bodies, the lovers' limbs
concubines take away whole hills
of wealth yet keep little
in their spendthrift hands
as they move on:
          so the waters
flow from the peaks to the valleys
beginning high and reaching low.

Born of Himalayan stone
and mingling with the seas,
it spreads, carelessly various,
one and many at once,
like that Original Thing
even the measureless Vedas
cannot measure with words.

Through pollen-dripping groves
clumps of champak
lotus pools

waterplaces with new sands
flowering fields cross-fenced
with creepers

like a life filling and emptying
a variety of bodies

the river flows on.

Subramanya Bharati (1882–1921)

A NEW HYMN TO THE SUN

Sun,
what did you do
with the dark?
chase her away?
do her in
and devour her?

Or did you embrace
and hide her away
in your arms of light?

Is the dark your enemy,
something you eat?
or love maybe:
did she get so dark
not knowing where you were
all night?

And when you arrived,
did she lose herself
in you, your light?

Maybe you're brother
and sister,
and your mother
asked you both
to take turns
watching over the world.

Don't you die,
are you immortals?
I praise you both,

and especially you,
O Sun.

N. Piccamurti (1900–76)

NATIONAL BIRD

Having spelt it out in blood
they were determined
to rouse the nation,
put an end
to the oppression and bungling.
Going to the forest
once for game
a hyena ran into them,
rolled its eyes and laughed;
a black bear rose before them
like a storm;
a viper, a whip-snake and a python,
their mouths close to the ground,
fed themselves without stirring;
a lion's tumultuous roar
shattered to bits the four corners of the world.
Returning, they staggered along,
hands trembling, legs faltering;
saw a peacock, and were thrilled.
Thinking, 'It's pointless begging, one must trespass;
it's no good asking, one must grant',
a few plucked the tail
with its thousand eyes
and returned overjoyed,
shooing off, with feathers,
poverty, disease, sorcery, witchcraft,
exclaiming, 'Begone, go away.'
Others pulled its tongue out
thinking it to be specific.
And still others, 'The peacock neck is ours',
broke it and hurried off.

The rest tore its body to shreds,
claiming, 'It's ours, too',
roasted and ate it.
As they turned homewards,
hunger assuaged,
the inarticulate land
groaned aloud.

Mongol

Mongol literature centred round the figure of Jenghiz Khan from the 13th-century *Secret History of the Mongols* until conversion to Buddhism in the 16th century brought influences from China and Tibet. These were in turn supplanted in the 20th century by Socialist Realism, when Outer Mongolia became the Mongolian People's Republic. The best poetry remains in the oral epic tradition, of which two examples are given here. The first was collected in northern Mongolia in the late 19th century, the second from a modern poet-singer of Huhehot, Inner Mongolia.

ERINDZEN MERGEN

Erindzen Mergen, best of men
born to rule the western world
had a palace of white bricks
built against the First Mountain
raised beside the Milky Sea
with fifteen hundred windows
    a snow-bright smoke-hole
    with bronze-bright gate-posts
    a cast-iron gate
    weighing seventy pounds
a cast-iron parapet
    weighing eighty pounds:
the many-hued gem-tipped arch
had a tiger and a lion
    engraved and chiselled
    on its right fillet
an antelope and ibex
    engraved and chiselled
    on its left fillet
and a hawk and an eagle
    engraved and chiselled
    on its underside.
He had a rust-red sword, fit
for ten thousand heads of men.

    Harnessed and ridden
in winter was his horse, its

neck a hundred fathoms long
its rump a day's journey broad
    four hoofs flashing fire—
a fox-hued, noble Arab.
    For riding nearby
    on great errands he
    had a golden steed:
    for riding to hunt
    on small errands he
    had a golden steed:
    for the mountains of
    Altai and Khangai
    on their thirteen crests
he had a many-hued troop.
    The Tüyn valley was
filled with ten thousand red bulls
    The Tüis valley was
filled with ten thousand grey sheep:
a steward, Alia Shara
    grazed horses, ten times
    a hundred thousand.

Born to rule the northern world
    Bajin Dor Khan asked:
'Erindzen Mergen, best of men
what kind of a man is he?
If you have looked, come and tell!'
Two excellent seers were called
and having seen they came: 'Oh
Erindzen Mergen, best of men
is a formidable man:
there's no killing him,' they said.
    And Bajin Dor Khan
led his three thousand soldiers
led his thirty-two heroes
    prepared himself, took
    his tough golden bow
    formed and fashioned from
    seventy yak-horns—
    such a golden bow
    made smooth and fashioned
    from ninety yak-horns:
    prepared himself, took

his sword of fine gold
with mother-of-pearl pommel
with Torvo-sandalwood grip.

On Erindzen Mergen, best of men
three years he made war: to kill
Erindzen Mergen, best of men
he had not the strength.
Erindzen Mergen, best of men
galloped then and strove
with Bajin Dor Khan
and destroyed Bajin Dor Khan
took Bajin Dor Khan's people:
wives and children too
sooty pots too, took
care too of the goat-woman
who brought her only daughter.
An eighty-day feast was made
a sixty-day jubilee
and he lived in peace
happily ever after.

Pajai (1902–)

BIRTH OF THE HERO

In the beginning
when the first world
had just taken shape
when the fire-red sun
was but a star
when the First Mountain
was but a hill
when the First Sandal-tree
was but a bush
when the Ganges
was but a swamp
when Kasyapa Buddha
was but a wandering monk
before the beginning
in the world of Asia

in great and mighty days
Geser the Bold was born.

If the cold wind does not rise
the leaves do not whisper:
if there had been no need
Geser the Bold
would not have been born.
When the laws led men astray
when the wicked foe raised his head
Geser the Bold was born:
when the terror of this golden world
the scourge of the people
the Ogre, the dangerous foe
brings suffering
when terror and suffering loom
Geser the Bold, the lively
delivers the land.

Kirghiz

The world's longest poem is probably the Kirghiz folk epic *Manas*, which runs to half a million lines. It includes the 13,200-line 'little epic' *Er-Töshtük*, versions of which exist in two other Turkic languages—Kazakh and Tümen-Tatar. Two short extracts from it are given here: the first concerns the meeting of Er-Töshtük with the monstrous crone the Jelmoghuz; the second concerns the hero's meeting with a giant in the underworld.

from MANAS

Töshtük, son of Eleman
        saw the Crone. Her hair
was white as a swan's feathers
her body bore seven heads
she sat astride a mortar
her face was monstrously strange
and her poisons were deadly:
no good could be expected
        from this miscreant.
        She was so wrinkled
        she had no face left:
no man had come back alive
from meeting and fighting her.
        Töshtük, ever since
        he had been Töshtük
        and ridden a horse
had never seen such a fright—
on her back a blue felt coat
in her hand a hide-scraper.
        Seeing this old witch
the brave son of Eleman
felt his heart fill with anguish:
she seemed the great soul-stealer
the terrible deceiver
the true destroyer of lives.

*

When Töshtük set foot

in the Underworld
the earth shook. He walked
in the Crone's footsteps. At first
they were wolf-tracks: he followed.
Then they grew like tiger-tracks.
He rode on, saw a Giant
lying on the ground
with one ear for a mattress
the other for a blanket
his lower lip in the earth
and stinking of rottenness
his upper lip raised so high
that it hung with icicles:
his hand reached out to Khokand
and his leg to Bukhara.

'Your hand reaches to Khokand
and your leg to Bukhara
your lower lip is rotten
your upper lip is frozen:
what kind of a man are you?
I am just a traveller
going about my business:
get out of my way!'

The Giant lay there, answered:
'I would gladly step aside
for you, young hero!
My name is Moon-Ear.
But I learn that Er-Töshtük
has come from the world above:
I would like to challenge him.'

When Er-Töshtük heard these words
he dismounted, and Moon-Ear
who was lying on the ground
clambered to his feet.
They attacked, grappled
with each other. Er-Töshtük
seized the Giant by the ears
dashed him against forty hills.
Then, having cut off his head
he went on his way.

Kamassian

Kamassian is one of the Samoyed languages which with the Finno-Ugrian make up the Uralic family. The last community to use the language was discovered in 1914 at the confluence of the Yenisei and Angara rivers in central Siberia. Its entire known literature consists of the celebrated folk poem given here.

LAMENT

Where I wandered
  my black hills
are left lying:
the ways I trod
  with green grass
are overgrown.

My black hills
are left lying
  my white peaks
are left idle
  our strength
is left lying:
  of my clan
I am left lying idle
  from my kin
I am left astray.

Where I fished
  my lakes
are left idle—
I see them no more:
my tent-poles, lying
  are rotten
my tent-sides, sewn
are dried out, gone.

Vogul

Vogul or Mansi is a Finno-Ugrian language whose 7,000-odd speakers hunt and fish in the Ob basin of western Siberia. Its oral literature, hitherto unchallenged by Soviet efforts to promote written work, has attracted a good deal of attention. Of the two epic-style poems given here, the first has shamanistic features which point to origins of considerable antiquity, while the second has been traced to an 18th-century chieftain. The third poem, a lyric of uncertain date, praises a village called Khōslōkh; the translation omits the name. Not much is known of Vogul prosody: the source text of the first two poems has little evidence of formal organisation beyond an elevated style, whereas that of the third suggests a rhythmic pulse which the translation attempts to match.

SONG MADE BY TUR MY GRANDFATHER

On the upper reaches of White Loon River I lived:
a lifelong singer, I had made some fifty songs.
One day short as this iron arrow's flight
I tried to hold a song to please the heart
inside this ten-ribbed chest, but I could not.
To the banks of White Loon River I made my way
for water, with my hollow mouth humming:
a boy running down there caught my song
and when I came away it was already
all over the village with its hundred houses—
he had somehow taken my song!
I sat
but having sat I could not, so I went
across to call on my uncle, chief of the town.
'My lad,' he said, 'are you starving, or what?'
'I have made some fifty songs and now
I have composed a song to please the heart
and a boy running down there has taken it
all round the village with its hundred houses:
give me your splendid whip for mounting a horse!'
'Though you should chase it with the splendid whip
for mounting a horse, you will not catch it up.'
As a three-pronged arrow craftsman-carved in horn

flies above the smooth star-glittering ice
my song had slipped away down the spreading river.
Earth and heaven shook with the sound of my song
when it was sung: a man with lively hands
was strumming it upon his five-stringed wood.

Now I have come into a grievous bed:
like yellow silk I spill my precious soul.
My father's many sons are making me
a plankless coffin: in black mother earth
they bury me. After my holy week
they come up to the grave to hold a wake:
upon my plankless coffin's one-tongued top
I tap. An evil-minded woman chatters:
'It's the good father he has left behind
he's groping for.' A kindly woman says:
'It's no good kinsman he has left behind
he's groping for—it is his five-stringed wood.
Why didn't you put it in with him?
That's why he taps his plankless coffin's top.'
So they put in my five-stringed wood with me
and from my father's many sons I take
this in my mouth: it is a splendid gift.

SONG OF CONVERSION

In all lands of the many-landed earth
I hear them speak of the four-cornered cross:
in all lands of the many-landed earth
I hear all bend to the four-cornered cross.
Inside the one-roomed house my father built
I sit. A loud thundering din bursts out,
bursts with a mighty boom somewhere. I go
out into the square of my spacious town
and with my twin blackcurrants I look up
towards my lofty sky-god: not a wisp
of cloud, even as small as a roach-scale
do I see anywhere. And then I look
down by the winding river's bend: a ship

in my mouth: the instrument symbolises the song. Now that his authorship is recognised, the singer can rest in peace.

all splendid with a prow like a hen's beak
dips there. Strong iron-bellied guns they are firing
many iron-bellied cannon they are firing
and our black mother earth shakes under them.
I take my arrow-quiver of black iron
into my two ten-fingered hands: I place
myself at the head of my army, march
and turn the splendid ship with the hen's beak
away.

A two-roomed house I build, here take
my rest. A loud thundering din bursts out,
bursts with a mighty boom somewhere. I go
out again in shirtsleeves of Russian linen
look by the winding river's bend, and see
many iron-bellied cannon they are firing.
I lose my presence of mind: two slit-arsed Cossacks
seize me as if I were a garganey
new-fledged this summer, not yet fit to fly.
Then I look up: the bishop, whoremonger
himself is brought, and I am put in fetters
my father never knew, and I am thrown
into a dreadful place where the dogs lie.
For how long I know not they carry me:
the lowest of my father's seven chests
I take with me, and suddenly I am brought
into Tobolsk bright as the morning star.
Into some lousy house there I am thrown
such as my father never saw: a full
week at the full moon I am food for lice.
All the corners of the four-cornered chest
my father filled, I empty: then a lord
powerful with silk buttons comes to me
and like a beast with ready tongue he warbles
so sweetly to me. All the compartments
of the four-cornered chest my father filled
are empty. Now with buttons like my lord's
powerful with silk buttons, I am buttoned
under the neck, with buttons round as loaves
I button up myself, on me is hung
a gold four-cornered cross. My father's dish
he used to fill with foal-fat for the god
is laid aside until the thousandth day.

SONG ABOUT MY VILLAGE

Bleak headland of the village
bleak headland where the young women walk
bleak headland where the young men walk.

My dear sand, white as cranes' feet
something to sing about
something to be glad about.

Dear bleak headland of my village
bordered on one side
by the sharp-pointed forest bordering,
bordered on the other side
by the pearl river flowing—
    flowing round it indeed
    bordering it indeed.

All my dear church-pointed pines
all my dear churchlike pines
stand there, so many,
appear there, so many.

The dear path where the young women walk
the dear path where the young men walk
is overgrown with no twigs
is overgrown with no grass.

Abkhaz

The various heroic tales, in verse and prose, which make up the legends of the Nart family may justifiably be regarded as the national epic of the North Caucasus. The stories, whose ultimate origins are disputed, are most widely attested in the folk traditions of the speakers of Ossetic, an Iranian language; Balkar-Karachay, a Turkic language; Chechen and Ingush, of the Nakh subgroup of the North-East Caucasian language group; and Circassian (i.e. Adyghe and Kabardian) and Abkhaz, of the North-West Caucasian group. None of these languages existed in written form, to any great extent, until the Soviet period. Abkhaz, with some 90,000 speakers in the Soviet Union (plus a sizeable though indeterminate number in Turkey), is characterised by a large number of consonantal phonemes—one dialect has 67. In the poem given here, with which Abkhaz literature makes its English début, stress has been marked on names; Zartézhw is pronounced approximately *zar-toozh.*

MOTHER OF HEROES

No sun, she sheds warmth
no moon, she sheds light—
Princess Satanéi.
Pad-pad go her heels
as she passes by.
She walks Kubán's banks
mother of a hundred sons—
Princess Satanéi.

A thousand flax-stalks she plucks
and winds them round her.
A huge bare beech she beholds:
one kick, and over it goes.
She tears it out of the ground
she turns it this way and that
she trims its branches:
so she fashions a spindle
and lays it across her knee.
Then a huge rock she beholds:
one poke, and a hole
she has bored in it.

So her spindle has a weight.
What a whirring as she spins!
What a clatter as she weaves!
What a thud as she bleaches!
    In one day she spins
    she weaves, she bleaches
the clothes of her hundred sons.
    No, not in one day
for this is her constant task
    standing in Kubán.

Once the whirr of her spinning
and the thud of her bleaching
rang as she walked Kubán's bank
    when, weary, she stopped.
    She took off her clothes:
naked as when she was born
    on the bank she stood.
The cold air cooled her body
    white as a new cheese
    and bright as amber
shining like a living sun:
    to cool her soft skin
she slipped into the water.

She surfaced and looked around:
in the shade on the far bank
she beheld the Narts' cattle
huddled and stamping. 'Well, well,
my sons' cattle,' she murmured
    and was very glad.
Looking closer she noticed
something among the cattle:
a tree?—no, too small for that
a rock?—no, for that too big.
The beasts rubbed their horns on it
scratched off swarming flies with it.
'Ah, Zartézhw the Narts' herdsman—
it must be!' she decided
    and she gave a shout
which awoke the Narts' herdsman.
His brows, blowing in the breeze
shot up to his scalp, amazed:

with eyes open wide
he beheld something standing
shining brighter than the sun
lighting up both banks.

'Heavens! What is this, at noon
brighter than the sun
and blinding me so?' he said.
He got up, walked through the herd
rubbing his eyes with his hands.
He stopped, looked across once more:
Princess Satanéi
lovely in the cold Kubán!
The poor herdsman went wild, his
blood boiled almost audibly:
he felt that he was on fire
so sore his soul, hurt his heart.
Now, though wide awake
he was speechless, motionless.
At first he stood there confused
trying to keep calm
but he, such a lady's man
could not master himself now.

The Princess stood on the bank
shining. He called out: 'Halloo!
Was that you shouting, Princess?
Was it to me you shouted?
If it was you, poor Princess
may I cross and speak to you?
Why hide? Let us have it out!'
The Princess had not plagued him:
many nights and many days
she had dreamed of, longed for him.
Hearing him on the far bank
she answered: 'Yes, it was I
who dared to hail you
but cannot say why from here.
Come across and I will tell.'
Hearing this, Zartézhw's heart
wavered where he stood.

'What shall I do? Here's a flood:

if I go in I shall drown
if I go in I shall die.
For you, what would I not do?—
but my soul is dear to me.'
'Damn you for a bitch's son!
I lower myself to you:
I might have known your answer.'
The Princess glowed hot and bright
turned her back on him, swam off.

The herdsman looked where she went.
His wrath stirred, his anger swelled:
'Did I dream, or was it she?
If no dream, I am ashamed!'
Into wild Kubán he dived—
almost tore himself in two.
No good: Kubán spewed him back.
    His soul grew wilder:
he seized his staff, dared again
but luckless Kubán swept on
spewed him back once more, beaten.
But waters could not damp him:
fearless, he trusted his strength.
Staff in hand he dived again
but again the river won.

The Princess, dressed and ready
on her bank stood spinning yarn
glancing at him now and then.
    Poor fellow! she thought:
would the water bear him off?

What should the proud herdsman do
stranded on Kubán's far bank?
It was all like a nightmare
    and he called to her:
'Ah, too wide! What shall I do?
Ah, too wide! What shall I do?
One thing I will say—listen!
Tie up your delicious hair
    tidy your fine skirt
    reveal your fair neck
    and show me your face!'

'So that is it, eh?' she said.
She turned to him, struck a pose—
struck a pose, and what a pose!
    No sun, she shed warmth
    no moon, she shed light—
standing there on the far bank!

    With his heart raging
    with his blood boiling
speechless a moment he stood.
Then, gathering all his strength:
'So, across, across!' he cried.
A cloud-dark arrow he hurled:
    like lightning it flashed
like thunder it shook the ground
like mist it enveloped all.

Princess Satanéi, till now
fearless, darted to and fro
by a rock threw herself down.
The arrow flew, struck the rock
stamped a man's features on it
in the twinkling of an eye:
    the mist had lifted
    silence had fallen.

Princess Satanéi emerged
saw where the arrow landed:
look, a man's face, clearly drawn!
Knowing this for a wonder
she would cut it out, take it.
The herdsman had seen all, said:
'If you would learn what this means
you must ask Áinar the smith.'
'O mother, what shall I do?
Where shall I go? I thought I
could do all a woman can.
O poor Zartézhw, your wonder—
how am I to release it?'
'O bright Princess Satanéi
take it to Áinar the smith.
His right hand holds the hammer
    his left hand the tongs

his right foot works the bellows:
he lacks no strength nor wisdom.
He will raise the face for you.'

Off went Princess Satanéi
came back with Áinar the smith
    showed him the man's face:
    he knelt by the rock
    hammered at the thing
prepared to chisel it out.
Three days and three nights he worked:
Princess Satanéi stood by.
On the third day he freed it
and gave it to the Princess.
    And he said to her:
'Clasp this under your right arm
and nine months hence a warrior
will be born. At that moment
your neighbour's mare will give birth
to a steed none will mount and live:
no steed will be so mighty.
    Now you must do this:
before the Narts' new brother
    comes into the world
let no one go near that steed.
When the Narts' brother is born
he will know what he must do.'

Princess Satanéi agreed.
With the face under her arm
she went, kept it there nine months
in the warmth of her fair skin
showed it, spoke of it to none
    waited for the day.

Georgian

The Georgian language, though spoken by fewer than three million, has a richness and a poetry—both popular and literary—that nations ten times larger might envy. The literary language dates back to the 5th century; secular literature emerged from religious and historical texts to a golden age in the reign of Queen Tamar in the 13th century. After centuries of Mongol and Persian domination, Georgian poetry recovered in the 18th century to follow more European modes. At the beginning of the 20th century Vazha Pshavela infused folk themes into poetry of colossal grandeur, and in their different ways Galaktion Tabidze and the poets of the 'Blue Horns' group developed European Symbolism into a genuinely original lyricism; one of this group, Galaktion's cousin Titsian Tabidze, has been powerfully translated by Pasternak. Folk poetry, at its greatest in the grim heroics of the Khevsuri mountain clans, is still very much alive.

The language has the consonantal richness and grammatical complexity typical of Caucasian languages: it has perhaps the greatest variety of possible syllables in any known language, a wealth of synonyms and a syntactical sophistication that one associates more readily with the world's major languages.

THE YOUTH AND THE LEOPARD

These were the words of the beardless youth:
'I crossed the rocky mountain ridges,
I went on a hunt, I set off on
the paths that cross the bare, sharp rocks.
High on the crags I came across
a herd or two of mountain goats.
I fired my gun at a great-horned goat,
the horns crashed down to the river's bank.
I had stumbled on a leopard's lair,
the time was the middle of the night.
The leopard flew out in my path,
he filled my god-given eyes with rage.'

Leopard and youth closed in to fight,
they made the earth beneath them quake,
they sent the boulders tumbling down,
they smashed the forest branches off.

The youth was running short of time,
the hilt of his sword was red with blood,
he puts up his shield but cannot fend
the quick-limbed leopard of the rocks.
Its claws lash out and rip apart
the hem of his armoured coat of mail.
Now the youth laid both his hands
to clutch the crosspiece of his sword.
Slowly his sabre cut into the beast,
the time had come for it to fall.
He hurled the leopard from the rock
and turned the sandy river-banks red.
High on the rocks the youth himself
lay on his side and breathed his last.

Who will tell this to his mother?
Fortune-tellers, soothsayers sit at her door.
'After all, our hunter's arrows
were not used up to no avail.'
His mother was walking to and fro,
weeping had filled her eyes with tears.
'A leopard fell upon my son,
a raging, savage leopard. Now
they have blacked out each other's daylight,
my son with the sword, the beast with his limbs.
The leopard could not have been a coward,
my son did not face a gentle beast.
Each has slaughtered his enemy;
shame on them, for neither lives.'

As she wept, she bound the wounds
the leopard's claws had left on her son.
'Child, you are asleep, not dead,
it's hard work that has worn you out.
How could the wild beast rip apart
the shirt of chain-mail that you wore?
You must have been a match for him,
your arms flagged as you swung your sword.
The leopard would not give you time,
nor did you let him have a chance.
The shield you were clutching in your hand
could now no longer cover you;
nor could the leopard use his limbs,

the sword had shattered his bone in two.
This much, no more, I shall weep for you,
your death is not a cause for tears.
Farewell, the sign of the cross be with you;
for this is the gateway to the grave.
At least I have brought up one real son,
a warrior who fought a savage leopard.'

As she slept, the ghosts appeared
now of the leopard, now of her son.
Now the leopard seemed to rip
the iron bodice off her son;
now it seemed her son was winning,
flinging the leopard head over heels.
And, strange to tell, after such dreams
she would awake with sobs and tears.
At times she would think, 'Who ever heard
of any son whom no mother reared?
Perhaps the leopard's mother too
is, like me, crying day and night.
I shall leave and go to her
and give her comfort in her grief,
so that she tells me all her tales
and I shall tell her of my son,
for she is sorrowing for her son,
killed without pity by the sword.'

Shota Rustaveli (c. 1200)

from THE KNIGHT IN THE PANTHER SKIN

This exotic romance, the greatest work of Georgian literature, tells the adventures of Avtandil, an Arabian paladin who is hopelessly in love with his king's daughter, and Tariel, an Indian knight who wears a panther skin, as they search for the latter's beloved who has been kidnapped by evil spirits. Love triumphs in the end.

from the Prologue

Poetry is above all else a branch of wisdom,
godly in source and sense, sustenance for the listener;
still more does it please the virtuous man who hears it.
Verse is good at saying long things shortly.

Just as a long race and great gallop prove a horse,
or the field, true aim and skilful swing a polo-player,
so speaking and drawing out long poems proves the poet;
how can his speech falter or the poem begin to wane?

Now see a poet and the verse he writes;
how can Georgian words fail or the poem turn base?
He'll not run out of Georgian or impoverish his words,
but strike the polo-stick with skill and do heroic deeds.

A man is not a poet who writes just a thing or two;
let him not think he is the equal of good poets.
Should he write a few vile lines that miss the mark
and then say, 'Mine is best', he is a stubborn mule.

Secondly, the lesser verse of men who are part poets,
unable to perfect their words and make them pierce the heart:
I'd compare them to youthful hunters' arrows,
useless for killing big beasts, fit only to slaughter small game.

A third kind of poem is for feasts and singing,
for lovemaking, for rejoicing, for drinking with friends;
these give us pleasure, if only spoken clearly,
but he is no poet who cannot say things at length.

Tariel's tale of killing the lion and panther

'I shall tell you in detail of all that has happened to me
and then let your true wise heart be the judge.
I was waiting for you but found the waiting hard,
I could stand the cave no more, I felt like a ride in the fields.

'I reached the ridge over there after crossing the reeds;
a lion and a panther had met and were rushing towards each other.
They seemed like lovers, I was happy to see them,
but what they did to each other was to stun and dismay me.

'They first played gently, then they clung on stubbornly,
they struck out with their limbs, not shrinking from death.
The panther lost heart—for women will flee—
the lion hung on and no one could have calmed him.

'The lion appalled me; I called out, "You are mad;
why hurt your beloved? Shame on your manhood!"
With drawn sword I went for him, let the blade pierce him,
I struck at his head, killed him, freed him from care.

'I flung down the sword, made up my mind, grabbed hold of the panther,
I tried to kiss it, for the sake of her who makes me burn.
It growled at me, struck me with blood-shedding claws,
I could endure no more; maddened, I killed it.

'Try as I might, I could not have calmed down the panther;
I raged, swung and hurled it down, and let it lie.
I recalled the time I had embraced my beloved,
I all but died; do not wonder that my tears pour down.

'Now, brother, I have told you the grief that troubles me.
I am not meant to be alive, let such an outcome not amaze you.
I have parted with life, yet death is hard to come by.'
And so the youth ended, sighed and began to weep.

Avtandil too was weeping and shedding tears with him:
he told him, 'Resign yourself, don't die, don't tear your heart.
Though grief has laid you low, God will show mercy.
Did He not bring you together, though man might part you?

'Troubles dog the lover and make his existence sorrowful,
but delight is given at last to him who overcomes first grief.
Love is needed to bring us close to death,
to drive the learned mad and make the unlearned wise.'

Vazha Pshavela (1860–1915)

from THE SNAKE EATER

The folk hero Mindia eats snake-flesh to escape from demonic captivity. Instead of death, he is given the power to understand animals and plants. But marriage drives him to cut down trees for firewood and kill goats to feed his children. He loses his magic powers, leads his village to perdition in war and kills himself.

But when spring is in the air,
the land wakes up; freedom and joy
waft everywhere, young buds appear,

the green grass hugs the flowers close,
then Mindia, all eyes and ears,
roams the mountains and the fields.
Every creature, plant he meets,
he greets. Nature calls out 'Hail',
decked out in flags. The flowers throw
their proud and painted heads up high.
As one they roar 'Long live Mindia!'
The trees begin to rustle their leaves,
the grass and herbs sway in the breeze,
each herb sets up a murmur, a din,
'I am the cure for this disease.'
The next calls 'I am that ill's cure.'
Mindia plucks them, takes them off
before the morning dew has gone.

It is as though the flowers think
nothing of their seething life,
so long as they may heal disease.
They yearn to be of use to man,
to flesh and bone beset by ills.
Thus act the flowers, but the trees
weep and Mindia alone
understands their moans and cries.

Their weeping made his life upset:
he took his axe up to a tree,
said 'This is the one that I must fell',
swung the axe and in mid-swing
heard the tree beseech him: 'No,
don't kill me, Mindia, I beg,
don't blot out my life, don't stun
a helpless and defenceless tree.'

His arms went limp, he blankly gazed
up at the sky and turned towards
another tree: it moaned still more.
Empty-handed, he made for home,
he could not cut up wood to burn
and, not to have a cold, chill hearth,
he gathers hay or withered stubble
or straw or dung. He now makes do
with any fallen twigs he finds,

nevertheless gives thanks to God,
when the day begins and when it ends.

He urges others: 'Men, don't do
a sinful thing: don't fell trees;
make do with stubble or dry twigs.'
No one listens: his advice
seems to them a madman's speech.
'God made trees to meet our needs.'
And to this day, who thinks twice
to spare the aspen or the beech?

When he starts to reap the corn,
his mind is utterly deranged,
his shirt hangs open as he cuts
one stem here, another there.
He tramples down the field of corn,
crushes the stalks and lays them waste;
while his arms have strength to swing
he whirls around, a human awl;
at last, tired out, he folds up, falls
and prostrate sprawls down on the earth.
Should you ask him why he behaves
like this, the answer comes:
'You cannot grasp what you have said,
that's why you think my actions mad.
If only you knew, how they themselves
plead with me to mow them down.
You should see ten thousand stems
offer themselves of their own accord,
set up a clamour on seeing me
approach like a god, sickle in hand:
"I'm the one to cut down, Mindia;
I beg you, do not pass me by."
"No, me!" another calls out, "for
I am more frightened by the sky.
When I see a patch of mist
my body crumples, limp with fear.
Woe, should the hail slash at my throat!"
Still louder, yet another flower
cries out: "Do not abandon me;
I pray God give you strength and joy."
They drive me mad with furious sounds,

I am bewildered with compassion.
Two hands, two eyes are not enough
to take them all; and I myself
am on the brink of breaking down.
Hailstones make the corn afraid,
as men fear being left to starve,
and yet the sickle cuts a swathe
far more deadly than the hail!
The ripe and golden ears of grain
save themselves for men to use;
they do not wish to rot and waste
for crows and kites to peck at them.
That is why they urge us on,
in one loud roar, to reap them down.
They yearn to be our food and bread,
to sate the hungry so that we
can pray for rest for the deceased
and call upon the heavenly powers.'

Galaktion Tabidze (1893–1958)

THE WIND BLOWS

Oh the wind, how it blows, how it blows.
The wind blows the leaves off afar,
arches trees, trees in ranks, trees in hosts.
Tell me where, where you are, where you are.

How it rains, how it snows, how it snows.
You're not to be found any more.
Your image pursues me, it haunts
everywhere, every day, every hour.

From the sky drizzle far misty thoughts.
Oh the wind, how it blows, how it blows.

Titsian Tabidze (1895–?1938)

POEM-LANDSLIDE

I don't write poems . . . it's me they write,
my life and the poem's unfold alike.
I call a poem a torrent, a landslide
that sweeps you off and buries you alive.

April was the month that I was born in,
apple-trees opened their blossom to the skies.
Whiteness rains on me, and in a torrent
the rain, as tears, is gushing from my eyes.

That's how I know that when I come to die
the poem I speak, however, will remain,
strike a poet's heart and thus buy
intercession—I can't complain.

'A boy grew up,' they'll say, I think,
'by a stream in Orpiri, in poverty.
Poems were his food and drink,
he wouldn't move except for poetry.

'And he was tortured to the day he died
by Georgian sun and Georgian earth.
Happiness was a thing he was denied,
happiness he surrendered to his verse.'

I don't write poems . . . it's me they write,
my life and the poem's unfold alike.
I call a poem a torrent, a landslide
that sweeps you off and buries you alive.

Armenian

The Armenians, the oldest Christian nation in the world, have been to Islam more or less what the Jews have been to Christendom—a conscience, an intellectual force, a nation identifying itself in largely religious terms, for which it has suffered dispersion and genocide.

The earliest Armenian poem is a fragment concerning the birth of the legendary Vahagn (*vah-agn*, bringer of fire) quoted in a chronicle written in the 5th century, when the Armenian alphabet was devised; a good deal of folk poetry survives, including epic. The mystic St Gregory of Narek is an important figure of the Middle Ages: the poem given here from his *Book of Lamentations* is part of the liturgy for the vigils of the major feasts. The fall of the monarchy in the 11th century began a long fallow period notable mainly for minstrels like Nahabed Kouchag, who at least brought poetry into the secular sphere. A Renaissance in 19th-century Venice, Istanbul and Tbilisi, the Georgian capital, led eventually to the development of the two literary dialects of today—the Western, used by diaspora writers and open to French influence, and the more conservative Eastern (now Soviet). Vahan Tekeyan, Siamanto and Daniel Varouzhan are Western poets; the latter two were among the two million Armenians murdered by the Turks in 1915. Of Eastern poets, the best known is Yeghishe Charents, with his blend of patriotic and revolutionary elements as in the famous 'radio poem' given here, with its image of the poet as a broadcasting station.

Few nations of comparable size—there have never been more than four million Armenians—have a culture of such liveliness and sophistication.

BIRTH OF THE FIRE-GOD (*pre-Christian*)

Heaven and earth laboured
the crimson sea too laboured
            and in the sea
the red reed laboured.
From the reed's tip
            smoke rose
from the reed's tip
            flame rose
            and in the flame
a youth was running:
he had hair of fire
            a beard of flame
and his eyes were suns.

St Gregory of Narek (*c*. 945–*c*. 1003)

SPEAKING WITH GOD FROM THE DEPTHS OF THE HEART

Sweetly accept, O mighty Lord God,
    the supplications of one who has brought you bitterness
Approach with compassion one who is shamefaced
Disperse, O all-giving, the shame-begotten woes
Lift off, O merciful, the unbearable burdens
Cut off, O resourceful, the habits that deal death
Crush, O ever victorious, the pleasures of the deceiver
Drive off, O high one, the murk that leads astray
Seal off, O life-giver, the inroads of the tempter
Scatter, O all-seeing, the captor's evil devices
Smash, O inscrutable, the fighter's assaults.

Inscribe with the sign of the cross the skylight of my roof
Shelter with your arm the ceiling of my temple
Mark with your blood the threshold of my room
Sign the path of your supplicant
Strengthen with your right hand the pallet of my repose
Cleanse of snares the cover of my bed
Support with your will my tortured soul
Keep pure my body's breath which you have bestowed
Place around me the swarm of your heavenly host
Line them up against the order of devils
Give the repose of bliss to my sleep at dead of night
    through the intercession of the holy Mother of God and all the elect
Keep intact the windows of the sight, the faculties of the mind,
    fearlessly holding off upheavals, distractions, nightmares, fancies:
Through remembrance of hope in you I shall be kept from harm.

And waking from the heaviness of sleep
    to most sober watchfulness
    to soul-renewing cheerfulness
Standing before you
I will send heavenward
This voice of supplication fragrant with faith
To you, most blessed King of unutterable glory
Joining in song with those gathered in heaven who praise you

For you are glorified by all creatures
for ever and ever. Amen.

Nahabed Kouchag (c. 1500–92)

I've never made confession to a priest:
seeing one, I have turned away in haste.
Seeing a pretty girl, towards her I've pressed,
knelt in her service, to her breast confessed.

*

I'm young, you're young:
the time is ripe.
Your waist
is like a drawn
bow in my hand:
it bends.

Your nipples hang
full as the grape.
Your breast
is like the dawn:
I open and
night ends.

Vahan Tekeyan (1877–1944)

MY ONLY ONE

My only one, watching me in despair
From the reflecting well,
Like you, with you, I watch you too down there
Wretched and sorrowful.

Which of us has the greater pity when
Dumbly we watch each other?
All this time we have mourned your once bright twin
Beside you, your dead brother.

One night I dreamt, soon after he was hurt,
That panting in the dark

Dragging an enormous furniture cart
I saw a black shape lurk,

To whom with anxious, fearful voice I cried:
'Comrade, my sight is dim—
And yours?' Though we were walking side by side
There was no sound from him.

I did not know the wretch by now had gone
Where mortal creatures go.
He never spoke. You saw him later on:
He never saw you, though.

When from the yawning well you look at me
And I look at him dead,
He seems to me, floating there ceaselessly,
Like a drowned martyr's head.

My only one . . . For you my faint heart fears,
Seeing you—thanks to you:
Now I implore you as I weep your tears,
Do not forsake me too.

Siamanto (1878–1915)

THE DANCE

And choking back the tears in her blue eyes,
In a field of ashes where Armenian life was dying still,
The German witness spoke of our horror.

Unspeakable the tale I tell—
What I with humanly relentless eyes
From my safe window overlooking hell,
Gnashing my teeth and terrible with rage,
Saw with these eyes, relentlessly human.
In the ash-heap that was the Garden City
The bodies were piled up to the treetops
And from the waters, the springs, the streams, the road
The angry babble of your blood
Still speaks into my ear of its revenge.

Do not be shocked by the unspeakable,
But let man know man's crime against mankind,
Two days under the sun, going to the grave,
Man's evil to mankind
Let all the world's hearts know.
That morning dark with death was a Sunday,
The first to break in vain on broken bodies,
When in my room from evening to daybreak,
Bent over a stabbed girl's agony
With my tears I was watering her death.
Suddenly, clad in black, a bestial mob
Brought twenty young wives, fiercely whipping them,
And lewdly singing in the vineyard stood.

Leaving my half-dead patient on her pallet
I went out on my hellish balcony:
The black mob filled the vineyard, thick as trees.
One brute roared at the young wives: 'You will dance,
Dance when we beat the drum!'
And the Armenian women longed for death
As on their flesh the whips came cracking down.
The twenty, hand in hand, began to dance . . .
The tears flowed from their eyes like wounds:
O how I envied her who lay behind me,
Hearing her curse creation with a quiet
Gargle as the poor sweet Armenian girl
Released her dove, her lily to the stars . . .

I shook my fists uselessly at the crowd.
'You will dance!' howled the savage mob;
'Dance till you die, beautiful infidels,
Dance with bare breasts, and smile at us, and no complaints!
For you no weariness, for you no shame:
You are slaves—dance with limbs, with heads uncovered,
Dance till you die, and give us all a thrill!
Our eyes are thirsty for your curves, your deaths.'

The twenty sank exhausted to the ground.
'Get up!' The naked swords flickered like snakes.
Then someone fetched a pitcher of kerosene.
Human justice, I spit in your face.
Without delay the twenty were anointed.

'Dance!' roared the mob; 'this is sweeter than all the perfumes of Arabia!'
They touched the naked women with a torch.
And there was dancing. The charred bodies rolled.

In shock I slammed my shutters like a storm,
Turned to the one gone, asked: 'These eyes of mine—
How shall I dig them out, how shall I, how?'

Daniel Varouzhan (1884–1915)

ORIENTAL BATH

Lazily the green-domed bath's inner door
Opens, the pulley-weight thudding against
Its sweating ebony, and creaks exhausted
Behind the houris who walk slowly in.
They are all naked, lovely, their arms folded
Over their gorgeous breasts which are heaped up
With swelling tears, their nipples darkly fair;
Their mother-of-pearl sandals clop on the floor;
Their hearts' delighted gasps, their tinkling voices
Inside the bath become a booming peal;
Like stars in the dim swirling mist their eyes
Glimmer, the steam wraps its damp swathes about
Their bodies which are melting into sweat.
The houris bathe: on the hot navel-stone
Some lie and seem to swoon into a dream;
Through the dome's tracery the sun's white beams
Are sifted down like a rich rain of pearls,
The steam becomes a silver sea in which
The swans of Oriental Pleasure swim.
Their towels, stuck like seaweed to their thighs,
Are tossed aside; their bodies turn to statues
And plait by plait they loose their hair like seas
From which stray gems occasionally fall.
O tresses, tresses!—now the whole bath-house
Seems afloat, and the marble navel-stone
Turns brown from the rich surging of their waves;

houris: nymphs of the Muslim paradise (Qur'an 56: 34).
navel-stone: the central platform above the furnace.

And then they comb with golden combs—long, long,
Out to the end of endless tresses go
Their fingers, ceremoniously slow,
Swimming among the sparks of diamond rings;
They swoon sometimes, and sometimes suddenly
They shudder when a cold dew from the dome
Drops on the secret hollow of their necks.
Now look!—the taps, a hundred marble taps
They open one by one with babbling gush.
The ash-grey steam swirls upward, cloud on cloud,
The empty basins come alive, the water
Flows everywhere and sings melodiously.
The houris bathe: gathered around the basins
Canova's Graces seem to clasp each other,
Entwining teats, entwining supple arms,
Entwining glistening legs and navels—phials
Of perfume sweet with grains of melted musk.
Their thighs spread on the marble as they sit
And drink the joy of water lapping them;
Listen!—the golden bowls ring on the stones
(While hardwood bowls, like hearts, too often crack)
Serving their nakedness no tongue can tell.
They stir the clay, the cool thyme-scented clay,
The lump of nectar—our forefathers' food—
And slap it into turbans on their hair
And smear it into foam upon their breasts.
By the cool poultice and the slimy mortar
The houris are refreshed: they rub their bellies
Smooth as pebbles velvet has anointed.
The waters boil, wash the adorable Furies,
The soaps lather once more to purify
The Purities, stickily radiant:
The water, trickling round the navel-stone
And out to fill the very sewer with fragrance,
Is grey with clay and bitter, scouring lime
And as it flows it sometimes sweeps away
Brown tufts of matted hair and armpit curls
And down from these live statues, luminous
Cypresses which begin to feel exhausted,
Filling and draining their last bowls. Once more
The basins overflow, the bath echoes,

Canova's Graces: Antonio Canova (1757–1822), Italian neoclassical sculptor.

The boiling water runs, the houris bathe:
Then, their skins glowing like a flame-bright rose,
Their pupils faint, their bowls upon their heads,
Each clutching in one arm her swelling breasts,
They hurry out in single file gasping,
Poppy-red apparitions in the steam . . .
O richly rolling curls upon your breasts,
O drenched curls heavy with a weight that drips
On your bare feet as mother-of-pearl dew!
How shall I tell your anointing, your adorning
When you are dry and when like idols dressed?
O let me kiss the fingers which you plunge
Into the henna-box like a bleeding heart,
And kiss your frankincense-anointed hair
Which in the moonlight will perfume the pillow,
Your mascara'd eyebrows, misty eyelashes,
Breasts which with necklaces of glittering gold
Become the bright torch of the nuptial bed,
And kiss your navels where enfolded lurk
Arabia's opium, Africa's musk!
Now you are going home, laden with gems . . .
O let the flagstones freshen with your steps,
Let the cold bite your lips, redden your cheeks,
Let your damp robes, your fluttering hems exhale
And spill the thymy fragrance of your bath,
Flooding the crossroads, squares, as you walk by;
And let the bread left over from your lunch,
Stowed in the bowls and covered with the towels,
Shed the sweet smell of its exotic spices,
For then the Oriental City's streets
Will know that in your footprints May is blooming,
That over the cool pavements Spring will pass.

Yeghishe Charents (*1897–1937*)

INTO THE FUTURE (1920)

My infinite soul is filled now
with a babble of noise and song,
my heart is filled with electricity
flowing bright and strong.

My soul is a radio station now
facing men and the whole world
and it is high, high, the station of my soul,
like Ararat it is high and steadfast,
mighty, terrible.

In these glowing, windswept, babbling times
it falls to me to sing the song
of a million hearts both far and near today,
to fling the present joy, the great upswing
of my comrades in their countless millions
toward the times to come
it falls to me today.

That is why my song is victorious
that is why my voice today
is stubborn, steadfast as eternity.

That is why
colossal as the great
Eiffel Tower
on the threshold of past and future ages
mighty, tall
I am standing at my full height
and I am singing.
And my soul now, a radio station,
is sending its song red as fire
far and wide
to every heart that lives,
everywhere.

My soul is singing, ringing full of fire.
I know, before my song today
facing my soul's red sparks
every soul is a radio station
wherever it may be,
every soul that lives, that has being,
that is carrying in its arms
the same great mystery, the vast mystery
of these glowing times,
the bright mystery of these glowing times,
every soul
that with its iron arms today

is singing, lashing,
and seeking new rest and a lullaby
in the rebellion of a million arms.

Do you know that now
here in my ravaged land of Nayiri
and far and wide
in red Moscow
in yellow Tibet
in San Francisco, in vast London
and in Singapore
in every place, everywhere
the world is pregnant with a new song . . .

Hey! Far and near
in pits
in factories
in wide steppes and in forests
in every place, everywhere
my countless brothers lulled by the song
of iron, bronze, soil and mine:
who today has our fiery will
our red might and our
universal
glowing good fortune?

Who has them today?

It is we who are new, in our countless thousands.

Like a vast iron discus
our brave brothers'
universal will
we have already hurled
into the winds of the coming world
into the Future.

Nayiri: Assyrian name (13th cent. BC) of the Lake Van region, where the first Armenian nation state, Urartu, was formed in the 9th cent. BC.

Persian

Sir William Jones introduced English poets and writers to the beauties of Persian poetry before Edward Fitzgerald's justly famous *Ruba'iyat of Omar Khayyam* made Persian themes more widely known. The four-line stanza, called the *ruba'i*, is only one element in a literature that includes the epic form; *qasidas* which are monorhymed odes of sometimes quite extensive length; strophic poems; the rhyming hemistich form called the *masnavi*, used both for the epic and in voluminous didactic poems; and the *ghazal*, lyric monorhymed verses comparable with the sonnet.

This poetry emerged in the 8th and 9th centuries. Some of its forms and metres, which have followed strong but flexible conventions, were derived from Arab poets. From the beginning, however, imagery and subjects appeared with a sophistication owed to ancient origins in old Iranian minstrelsy and Central Asian hymns. Also, references to gardens and fruits were more Persian than a feature of desert Arab ballads. The latter, on the other hand, implanted in Persian poetry their originally nomadic theme of lovers separated and consequent erotic longing.

Persian poetry belonged to the Iranian lands between the River Oxus and the Persian Gulf. In this area, once it had achieved written form a thousand years ago, poetry did much to establish and spread a standard form of the Persian language. It has remained one of the most cherished and universally shared possessions of the Iranian people, to whose conversation it gives frequently used proverbial allusions and often-quoted verses.

Written at first for the entertainment, praise and sometimes subtle admonition of princes and powerful patrons of the poets, Persian poetry developed to express man's spiritual needs as well as cries to the great for leniency and generosity. The selection below is scanty for what is a large store of poems, but it traces this movement away from realistic naturalism into abstract topics, and shows the tenacity and adaptability of a well-founded tradition.

The expression of spiritual needs became more urgent and profound after the 11th century, when Persia's frequent invasion by nomadic tribes from Central Asia brought turmoil and suffering that drove men to look inward for renewal of religious faith and peace of mind. Sufism found in Persian poetry one of its chief vehicles of expression, so that Persian poetry is forever linked to the types of Muhammadan mysticism, and the quest of the soul for return to God, covered by the name Sufism, a name derived from the wool, *suf*, from which the Dervish, the pious ascetic, had his cloak made.

The translations offered aim to display as clearly as possible what the originals say. Persian poets were expected to reveal all the beauties and versatility of which their language was capable. To do this took an ingenuity, within distinct prescribed forms, which defies imitation, and to substitute alien verse-forms in translation could obscure the nature of the original. Hence in this selection obtrusively versified translations are avoided; an unadorned literalism seems to give a more honest version.

Rudaki (?–940/1)

All the teeth ever I had are worn down and fallen out.
They were not rotten teeth, they shone like a lamp,
a row of silvery-white pearls set in coral;
they were as the morning star and as drops of rain.
There are none left now, all of them wore out and fell out.
Was it ill-luck, ill-luck, a malign conjunction?
It was no fault of stars, nor yet length of years.
I will tell you what it was: it was God's decree.

The world is always like a round, rolling eye,
round and rolling since it existed: a cure for pain
and then again a pain that supplants the cure.
In a certain time it makes new things old,
in a certain time makes new what was worn threadbare.
Many a broken desert has been gay garden,
many gay gardens grow where there used to be desert.

What can you know, my blackhaired beauty,
what I was like in the old days?
You tickle your lover with your curls
but never knew the time when he had curls.
The days are past when his face was good to look on,
the days are past when his hair was jet black.
Likewise, comeliness of guests and friends was dear,
but one dear guest will never return.
Many a beauty may you have marvelled at
but I was always marvelling at her beauty.
The days are past when she was glad and gay
and overflowing with mirth and I was afraid of losing her.
He paid, your lover, well and in counted coin
in any town where was a girl with round hard breasts,
and plenty of good girls had a fancy for him
and came by night but by day dare not
for dread of the husband and the jail.

Bright wine and the sight of a gracious face,
dear it might cost, but always cheap to me.

My purse was my heart, my heart bursting with words,
and the title-page of my book was Love and Poetry.
Happy was I, not understanding grief,
any more than a meadow.
Silk-soft has poetry made many a heart
stone before and heavy as an anvil.

Eyes turned always towards little nimble curls,
ears turned always towards men wise in words,
neither household, wife, child nor a patron—
at ease of these trials and at rest!
Oh! my dear, you look at Rudaki
but never saw him in the days when he was like that.

Never saw him when he used to go about
singing his songs as though he had a thousand.
The days are past when bold men sought his company,
the days are past when he managed affairs of princes,
the days are past when all wrote down his verses,
the days are past when he was the Poet of Khorassan.

Wherever there was a gentleman of renown
in his house had I silver and a mount.
From whomsoever some had greatness and gifts,
greatness and gifts had I from the house of Saman.
The Prince of Khorassan gave me forty thousand dirhems,
Prince Makan more by a fifth,
and eight thousand in all from his nobles
severally. That was the fine time!
When the Prince heard a fair phrase he gave, and his men,
each man of his nobles, as much as the Prince saw fit.
Times have changed. I have changed. Bring me my stick.
Now for the beggar's staff and wallet.

*

Your cruel heart is never satisfied,
You shed no tears at my predicament.
How strange that I should love you more than life,
Though you are harsher than a thousand foes!

*

You have stolen colour and fragrance from the rose,
Red for your cheeks and perfume for your tresses.
The stream becomes rose-coloured when you bathe,
The lane musk-scented when you comb your hair.

Firdawsi (?934–1020/1 or 1025/6)

from THE BOOK OF KINGS

Sohrab enters Iran to replace its weak king with his own father Rustam, whom he has never met; but, thanks to the intrigue of a neighbouring ruler who has designs on the throne himself, Rustam is the Iranian champion and no match for his son.

At dawn the sun blazed up,
The warriors lifted their heads from sleep.

Sohrab accoutred himself for battle,
His head turned on war, his heart warm from revelry.

With a roar he came out into the arena,
The bull-headed club grasped in his hand.

Of Rustam he asked, his lips parted in laughter—
You'd have said they'd been boon companions all night—

'How was the night, how do you feel on rising
And why have you set your heart on strife?

Throw away quiver and vengeful sword;
Splay those impious claws on the ground.

Let us dismount together
And gladden our fierce faces with wine,

And let us make a pact before God,
Repenting of our seeking for combat;

Then while others fight,
You may bear me company and be an ornament to our feast.

My heart prompts me with love for you
And waters my cheeks with tears of shame.

As surely you come of heroes' stock,
Tell me of your ancestry—

Now you have come to contend with me,
You've no need to conceal your name.

Are you not Zal's son, the great Sam's grandson,
The famous Rustam, Zabul's elect?'

Rustam answered: 'O seeker for fame,
Never did we hold such discourse as this:

Last night our talk was of wrestling;
I'm not deceived, stop trying these ruses.

Though you be young, I am no child:
Now my loins are girded for battle.

Let us try our strength, the outcome will be
What the world's Guardian decrees and orders.

I've had too many ups and downs
To be a man for deceitful words and guile.'

Sohrab said, 'O aged one,
Though my counsel does not take root,

My wish was that in due season
Your life should leave your body in your bed;

While your heirs erected your tomb,
The spirit would take wing and your body be left in the grave.

But since your life is now at my disposal,
By God I'll destroy you.'

They dismounted from their chargers;
Corseleted, helmeted, they moved alert to spring,

The chargers left pawing the stones,
The two stepped forward full of foreboding.

They grappled like lions,
Blood and sweat poured from their bodies.

From first light till the shadows lengthened
Each pitted his strength against the other.

Sohrab struck out like a furious elephant,
Sprang from his place like a roaring lion.

He snatched at Rustam's belt and pulled
With such force it seemed he rent the ground.

He grunted with rage and spleen
As he threw Rustam the Lion down.

He gripped him like an elephant in must,
Lifted him off the ground and brought him down again.

He sat athwart Rustam's chest,
His clutching hands, face and mouth full of dust,

With the action of a lion that swipes
With its forefoot and trips up a wild ass.

He drew a bright blade
To cut the head from the body.

Rustam saw and shouted,
'What you don't know should now be told.'

He said to Sohrab, 'Hardy lion-snatcher,
Lasso-thrower, grasper of scimitar and club,

Different from this is our rule,
Other than this our lore's usage:

He who engages in a wrestling bout
And lays a noble's head in the dust,

The first time he has him on the ground,
Does not cut off his head even in rage.

If a second time he gets him down,
Achieves a lion's name in throwing him,

Then it is lawful to behead him;
It is on this that our custom rests.'

By this trick he sought to escape
From being killed in the dragon's grip.

The bold youth gave heed
To the old man's speech, though he should not have,

First out of rashness, secondly, from Fate,
And thirdly, from the brave candour of youth.

He set him free and went his way,
Into a desert where gazelles fled before him.

Farrokhi (?–1037/8)

from QASIDA OF THE AMIR'S BRANDING-GROUND

The grass like soft blue silk veils the face of the meadow:
The hills swathe their heads with embroidered silks from China.

The ground breathes scents innumerable, as from the musk-deer's gland:
Countless leaves, like parrots' feathers, are decking the willows.

Last night, at midnight, the breeze brought in the scent of the spring:
Hurrah for the northern breeze and the spring's fragrance!

You'd say the wind had powdered musk in its sleeve:
You'd say the garden had an armful of pretty playthings.

The narcissus is wearing its necklace of white pearls,
The flame-of-the-forest its earrings of Badakhshi rubies.

The rose-tree bears on its branches cupfuls of red wine:
The sycamores stretch down their human five-fingered hands.

Gay-skirted garden, branches which play the chameleon,
Pearl-coloured streams, and pearls from the clouds like rain.

Badakhshi: Badakhshan, a province bounded by the River Panj (a tributary of the upper Oxus), north of Afghanistan, and famous for its ruby mines, which are mentioned by Marco Polo, who speaks of the 'Balasa rubies' in 'Balashan'.

You are right, supposing that bright robes of honour are here—
The garden full of handsome forms at the prince's branding-ground.

So glad with all delight is this royal branding-ground
That the age stands wondering at it for its revelry.

You see green over green, like a sky above the sky:
You see tent after tent, like castles of silver.

In each pavilion a lover lies with his drunken friend:
On each patch of greensward one joys in the sight of his love.

The lawns resound with the harps of neat-fingered minstrels,
And rowdy the tents with the drink that the pages serve.

Kissing and dalliance of lovers, coquetry and soft denials,
The minstrels' strings and the singing, the drinkers asleep or fuddled!

At the pavilion's gate of the monarch, the Blest with Victory,
A fire has been made for the branding, as bright as the sun.

The fire goes up like spears with pennants of gold brocade,
Hot as the temper of youth, gold like gold for the testing.

The branding-irons like branches of coral, ruby-red:
Each one in the heart of the fire like ripe seeds in a huge pomegranate.

Rank upon rank of slave-boys who have known no sleep all night:
File upon file of ponies, awaiting the brand.

On his river-fording charger, the great-hearted monarch
Stands in the midst, like Isfandiyar, his noose in his hand

(Curled, like the curling locks of heart-snaring youths,
Strong as the bonds of friendship tried through the years)

The just prince Abu Muzaffar, a king of many confederates,
Joyful with zest for joy, fulfilled with desire of fulfilment.

Isfandiyar: a hero of ancient Iranian legend.

Each one over whom he flings his wide-spreading noose,
Imprinted on buttocks and face and thigh, receives his name.

Thus on the one hand he brands; on the other he pours forth gifts—
To the poets whom he holds with a bridle, and the guests he retains
with a headstall.

'Unsuri (?–1039/40)

Three things have modelled themselves on three of yours—
Rose on cheek, grape on lip, beauty on face.
Three things each year are taken from three of mine—
Grief from heart, tears from cheek, fancy from eye.

Minuchihri (?–c. 1040/1)

AUTUMN WINE

Up and bring me my beaver fur—autumn draws on:
The wind blows chill from Khwarazm.

Look, the scatter of leaves from the vine—
You'd say they were spattered like dyers' shirts.

Surprised, the farmer gnaws his finger—
No flower petal left nor pomegranate in field or garden.

His train torn away from the spring peacock—
His feathers plucked and thrown into a corner,

He is left wounded and lonely, in the midst of the garden;
None will sit laughing and chatting in his company now.

Those bright feathers of his will not be refastened—
Not till October's gone, not till March return.

Don't you notice at night how the marigold grieves—
Its cheeks grown pale and its forehead wrinkled?

Khwarazm or Khorezm: the region on the lower reaches of the River Oxus, south of the Aral Sea and east of the Caspian. The area would be associated, in the mind of the poet and his audience, with furs imported into northern Persia, as well as with the northerly winds that made wearing furs desirable.

Its heart is black, its cheeks like the yellow rose,
As if it had drunk the musk-flavoured wine the night before.

Its smell overpowers the scent of jasmine and musk;
Its cheeks are sallow like a sickly lover's.

Look at the lemon, marvel at its nature—
A hard long tit hanging downwards,

Yellow and white, but more white than yellow,
Yellow without and white within;

Silver within, gold dinar without,
The silver within stuffed with royal pearls.

The orange like two silver pans of a balance,
Their undersides gilded with red gold;

They're heaped with camphor, sweet rose-water and jewels;
A cunning little magic goldsmith

Has welded the two rims together again
And pricked all the surface with a needle.

And the pomegranate shaped like a simple cup
Where the ruby has poured in all its colour;

It has put a parcel of red gems into the cup,
With a flimsy yellow caul thrown over them;

At the summit a musk-pod has opened,
With golden filings stuffed within.

And the apple—a white sugar-ball turned on a lathe,
Three hundred times dipped in tincture of safflower.

Its cheeks are freckled with specks of coral,
Its backside swathed in an emerald-green breech-clout;

In its womb two or three tiny chambers,
A piccaninny asleep in each, like a pitch-ball.

At first light when the farmer comes outside,
He neither pauses nor drags his feet:

He makes for the vineyard and opens its gate to see
What the daughter of the vine is up to and what's to be done.

Not a single virgin girl shows him her face,
All are either pregnant or with morning sickness.

The farmer came up and looked at them closely;
He drew a sharp knife and slit their throats;

Then he squeezed them into his basket,
Pressing hard to cram them all in.

He set them on his back and carried them home,
Emptied them out and placed them in store.

After that he put them in the press,
And trampled them again and again—

Till their veins burst and their bones came adrift,
Their backs, heads and sides all squashed together;

They're not let out of prison night or day,
Till all at once the blood comes clear from the flesh;

Then he pulls out the veins and the skeletons,
To throw them away as trash,

But he takes up the precious blood, every drop,
And pours it back into that dungeon.

Three months go by without sign or word:
He knows none will be taken for this blood.

On the day appointed, glad and smiling, he rises briskly,
To go out and unseal the prison door.

When he looks down at the captives in his dungeon,
A hundred candles and lamps dance on his lips and teeth.

He sees many roses and jasmine flowers—
More than any garden or flowerbed can show.

Abu Sa'id ibn Abi'l-Khair (967–1048)

Love flowed like blood through every vein of mine,
Drove out all else and filled me with the Friend.
My Friend embraces every limb of me,
Only my name remains, the rest is He.

Mu'izzi (1048–1124)

O King, the morning drink's a splendid thing,
All who seek pleasure love the morning drink.
At every hour wine is a source of mirth,
At dawn it is elixir itself.

Omar Khayyam (1048–1131)

QUATRAINS

He began my creation with constraint,
By giving me life he added only confusion;
We depart reluctantly still not knowing
The aim of birth, existence, departure.

*

If the heart could grasp the meaning of life,
In death it would know the mystery of God;
Today when you are in possession of yourself, you know nothing,
Tomorrow when you leave yourself behind, what will you know?

*

The cycle which includes our coming and going
Has no discernible beginning nor end;
Nobody has got this matter straight,
Where we come from, and where we go to.

*

quatrains: '*ruba'iyat*' in Persian.

Today is the time of my youth,
I drink wine because it is my solace;
Do not blame me, although bitter it is pleasant,
It is bitter because it is my life.

*

If my coming here were my will, I would not have come;
Also, if my departure were my will, how should I go?
Nothing could be better in this ruined lodging
Than not to have come, not to be, not to go.

*

The firmament secretly whispered in my heart,
'Do you know what sentence fate laid on me?
If my revolving were in my control,
I would release myself from this circling.'

*

Alas, the book of youth is finished,
The fresh spring of life has become winter;
That state which they call youth,
It is not perceptible when it began and when it closed.

*

When we were children we went to the Master for a time,
For a time we were beguiled with our own mastery;
Hear the end of the matter, what befell us:
We came like water and we went like wind.

*

The parts of a cup which are joined together
The drunkard does not hold it lawful to break:
So many delicate heads, legs, hands,
Through whose love were they joined, by whose hatred smashed?

*

I saw an old man in the wine-shop.
I said, 'Have you any news of those who have gone?'
He replied, 'Take some wine, because like us many
Have gone, none has come back.'

*

I was in the potter's shop last night
And saw two thousand jugs, some speaking, some dumb;
Each was anxiously asking,
'Where is the potter, and the buyer and seller of pots?'

Rumi (?–1273)

from THE GREAT COLLECTION

A vast collection of lyrics composed under the name of Shams of Tabriz, the shadowy figure reputed to have brought Rumi from the study and teaching of scholastic theology into the way of Sufi mysticism. Allusions to magic and to the special properties of precious and semi-precious gems worn in rings are common in these poems.

Go comrades, fetch in my friend;
Bring one moment the fugitive idol;

With sweet ditties and golden pretexts
Bring home the fair moon of delightful aspect,

And if he protests and promises 'Another time I'll come',
All the promises are false—he'll be cheating you.

He has breath of miraculous fervency by magic and by enchantment
To tie knots in water and bind the wind.

When my love enters full of grace and joy,
Sit down and behold the wonders of God.

Where's the beauty of all beauties when his beauty shines forth?
His sun-bright cheeks put other lamps out.

Go light-foot heart to Yemen, to my darling,
Bear greetings and service to the unpriced agate.

*

When you lowered my body down into its pit
I was estranged and cut off from the intimates of the Presence.

Suddenly down in the pit a moon became my companion
Who threw into my brain the madness of a thousand desires.

All men seek release from prison and durance; not I—
Where could I go, outside where turn, he being here?

Without prison walls I could not be alone with him;
Honey is not clarified without the heart's labour.

One glance at one's own kind—his image is shattered:
Eying them is distraction; seeing him, desire's fulfilment.

If Joseph is the comrade, none cares how he's come by;
Hug the depth of the pit, it is our Joseph's special domain.

Whoever's incurred such a sentence as this, runs open-eyed
And expectant to prison, to seize such sweetness as this.

I heard the stars: 'If anyone gets
Track of that moon's brightness, let us know.'

When you attain this jewel such grace is yours
That you go like Moses and cross the seven seas.

Because of lovers' jealousy news of him doesn't reach the moon and stars:
When moon-like he shines forth, the heavens melt away.

I'm ashamed to describe his face, for God's sake shut my mouth:
When will the water-seller's bottle hold the waters of the sea and of the ocean as well?

from THE MASNAVI

An encyclopedia of human experience set out in exemplary tales to teach the virtue of following the spiritual path. It is pre-eminently this work that has earned for its author the titles *Maulavi*, 'the Divine', and *Maulana*, 'our Master'.

One came and knocked at the door of the friend,
Who said, 'Who are you, comrade?'

He replied, 'It is I.' He answered, 'Go away, it is not the time:
At such a banquet as this, no place for the unprepared.'

What but the fire of separation and absence can make
The unprepared ready and deliver him from false feeling?

That wretch went away a year in journeying;
In separation from the friend he was scorched with flame;

He was made ready in the fire, then he returned,
Again he walked round the house of the companion.

He knocked at the door with every diffidence and politeness
Lest any discourteous word should escape his lips.

The friend called to him, 'Who is at the door?'
He answered, 'It is yourself at the door, O ravisher of hearts.'

The reply came, 'Now since you are myself, myself come in:
There is no room in the house for two I's.'

Amir Khusrow Dehlavi (1253–1325)

Last night I dreamt you brought me wine
and poured and poured until my dreams were full,
each one watered till the tendrils grew.

And then I heard you pouring more again for two
and thought I saw my tears reflecting you . . .
I wasn't sure, until I woke to find
my body bathed in wine and wrapped in vines
or was it you?

I never knew who turned my night to day
before the dawn had time for dew.

Hafiz (c. 1325/6–90)

Boy, set the bowl on fire with light of the wine:
Minstrel, sing the world's business is ours for the asking.

You who do not know the delights of our endless drinking,
We've seen the Friend's cheek reflected in the cup.

What price the charms of erect forms
When our straight pine shows itself off?

On the Day of Reckoning I fear the religious elder's lawful bread
Won't compete with our forbidden liquor.

He whose heart love has vivified never dies—
Our persistence is recorded in the chronicle of the Universe.

Should you breeze pass over the beloveds' garden,
Take care to give our message to the darlings—

Say, 'Why purpose to blot out our name from memory?
The time will come when you recall our name no more.'

Hafiz, scatter the seeds of weeping from your eyes—
Perhaps the bird of consummation is heading for our snare.

*

Come, hope's palace is no more than a jerry-built house:
Bring wine, for life's foundations are rooted in wind.

But that man's zeal enslaves me, who under the sky's blue wheel,
Is tied to nothing coloured by dependence on the world.

How can I tell you what good news the Angel of the Unseen
Brought me last night, flat out on the wine-shop's floor?—

He said, 'O high-towering falcon, perching on the tree of Heaven;
No place for you, this corner of affliction's town!

They are whistling you home from the battlements of the Empyrean:
How did you come to be in this place of snares?'

I give you a piece of advice—mark it and practise it;
This saying was taught me by my Master on the Way:

Don't look to hold this tottering world to her bond:
She is the withered hag of a thousand bridegrooms.

*

Now that the cup of clear wine is in the hollow of the rose's hand,
The nightingale has a thousand tongues in its praise.

Ask for a book of poems and take the path to the fields:
This is no time for school and debating an exegete's commentaries.

The schoolman was drunk yesterday and gave this sentence:
'Though forbidden, wine is better than the wealth of endowments.'

Cut yourself off from people and take the Phoenix for pattern—
The fame of recluses spans the world's horizons.

It is not for you to choose between the dregs and the pure:
Whatever our wine-server has served is choiceness itself.

Humours of rivals and the conceits of colleagues
Are the tale of likening mat-weavers to the worker in gold thread.

Be quiet, Hafiz, guard these subtleties like pure gold—
The town's counterfeiter is the keeper of the treasury.

*

Tresses dishevelled, sweat broken out, lips laughing, drunk,
Shirt in shreds, a song on her lips, wine-cup in hand,

Eyes looking for trouble, petulant,
At midnight last night she came to my pillow and sat.

She bent her head down to my ear and grievingly said,
'O my crazy lover, are you asleep?

'A man of esoteric knowledge they give such nocturnal wine as this,
Would be love's blasphemer if he were not wine's devotee.'

Go hermit—don't carp at drinkers of the dregs:
We were given no other boon but this on the Day of the Covenant:

What He poured into our cup we drank,
Whether it was liquor of paradise or the wine of drunkenness.

The wine-bowl's laughter and the beauty's curling tresses—
They've broken many a repentance like that of Hafiz.

*

Day of the Covenant: a reference to God's question to mankind after the Creation, *alastu birabbikum*, 'Am I not your Lord?' Mankind replied 'Yes', thus sealing a compact with God alone, to bear witness for Him forever, and against itself should it ever deny God. See Qur'an 7: 173.

When God formed the shape of your heart-opening eyebrows,
He tied my affair's undoing to your glances.

From my and the bird of the meadow's heart he took ease away
The moment he wrought your eye's and tunic's brocade.

Many a knot in my labour and the rose-bud's heart
The rose-breeze undid when it set its heart on desiring you.

The Wheel's turning made me content with your bonds,
But to what avail since it tied the outcome to your will?

Don't wrinkle my poor heart like a musk-bladder:
It closed a deal with your knot-loosing tress tip.

O time of union, you were the life of another;
My heart knew no hope but was set on fidelity to you.

Through your cruelty I said, 'I'll leave the town';
Laughing she replied, 'Go, Hafiz, who's stopping you?'

*

I saw last night how angels knocked at the wine-shop's door—
Those who kneaded Adam's clay and threw it in the mould.

Dwellers in the precinct behind the veil and chastity of the Kingdom
Dispensed intoxicating wine to me, dweller in the dust.

Heaven could not bear the burden of the contracted fealty:
The lot they drew came in the name of bedlamite me.

Dispense forgiveness of the seventy-two sects' bickering;
Losing sight of reality they went the way of delusion.

Thanks be for this, that peace has come between Him and me;
The blessed are filling the grateful cup while they dance.

The fire isn't that whose flame the candle laughs with:
It's the one the harvest of moths was caught in.

Nobody like Hafiz has unveiled the cheek of thought,
Not since speech's tresses were first combed with the pen.

Abu Talib Kalim (?–1651/2)

. . . Half my life spent attaching my heart
to this and that;
the rest, detaching it again.

Hatif of Isfahan (?–1783/4)

THE MESSAGE

One of the five strophes of Hatif's most famous poem, which, with its two-line refrain, is considered among the greatest Persian expressions of Sufism. The poem has powerful resonances for the Persian reader: despite its late date, it is written in the Classical style and uses a pre-Islamic word for the 'Revealing Angel'.

Last night, my heart tossed and torn with love,
I went to the wine-seller's street.
I found a choice and cheerful crowd there,
The old wine-seller the host of the party.
Servants were at their stations
And topers seated shoulder to shoulder,
The host on his dais,
The tipplers ranged round him.
Some were drunk, some had passed out,
Their hearts made pure.
The heart was talkative but the lips silent:
Eternal Grace had opened
Eyes to the Truth, ears to the Secret.
The only speech, one to another's 'Here's to you!'
And the other's 'Drink up'.
Their ears for the harp, their eyes on the bowl,
Theirs was all that could be wished for in this world or the other.
I respectfully went in and said,
'You whose heart harbours the Revealing Angel,
I'm a sick lover in dire need;
Look at my wound and devise a cure.'
The Elder laughing quipped back,
'Ah, the slave of the Lord of Reason,
What is in common between you and me?
The daughter of the vine veils herself in shame from you.'
I said, 'But my life is consumed away, give me one drop

To quench my raging fire
That was burning me up all last night;
Not tonight, please, another like the last.'
Laughing he told me to take the cup.
I seized it and he said, 'Good, that's enough.'
I swallowed a draught and got
Free of reason's torment and the burden of the senses.
When I came to myself I saw just one,
The rest only outlines and patterns.
Suddenly the Revealing Angel in the court of Heaven
Whispered this saying in my ear:
'There is the One and no other but He;
He is the One—there is no God but He.'

Iraj (1874–1924)

A VEILED GIRL

Pet onion!
        in your layers of veil and gown;
all beauty in one mirror, or
a turnip in a sack?
No matter where I look:
                up or down,
you're not my pet or sweet
or even a human bean—
wrapped in that black and purple skin
you are an aubergine.

Ancient Egyptian

The following three sections concentrate on the Ancient Near East's two great literary traditions, those of Egypt and Mesopotamia, flavoured with a third, that of Ugarit. Egypt and Mesopotamia were the two creative matrices of civilisation in the Ancient Near East, and were the source of the great bulk of its literature. The surviving material, vast as it is, is probably only a fraction of the total. The two traditions differ considerably; for instance, there was no epic in Egypt, whereas it was a very considerable genre in Mesopotamia. Both traditions contributed greatly to the development of Greek and Hebrew thought and style, and hence to the entire Western tradition.

Pyramid texts

Carved on the inside walls of the smaller and later Pyramids, these consist of 759 spells or Utterances, most of them brief and disturbing, some long and incantatory. They are spoken to safeguard the journey of the dead king to the West (the other world) and the peaceful succession of his son.

THE KING PRAYS TO THE SKY-GODDESS

(*Utterance 350, for King Teti, c. 2250 BC*)

O great strider
Who sows greenstone, malachite, turquoise—stars!
As you are green so may Teti be green,
Green as a living reed!

THE KING HUNTS AND EATS THE GODS

(*from Utterances 273–4, for King Unas, c. 2300 BC but probably much older*)

Sky rains, stars darken,
The vaults quiver, earth's bones tremble,
The planets stand still
At seeing Unas rise as power,
A god who lives on his fathers,
Who feeds on his mothers!

Unas is master of cunning
Whose mother knows not his name;
Unas's glory is in heaven,
His power is in lightland;
Like Atum, his father, his begetter,
Though his son, he is stronger than he! . . .

Unas is the bull of heaven
Who rages in his heart,
Who lives on the being of every god,
Who eats their entrails
When they come, their bodies full of magic
From the Isle of Flame. . . .

Unas is he who eats men, feeds on gods,
Master of messengers who sends instructions:
It is Horn-grasper in Kehau who lassoes them for Unas,
It is Serpent Raised-Head who guards, who holds them for him,
It is He-upon-the-willows who binds them for him.
It is Khons, slayer of lords, who cuts their throats for Unas,
Who tears their entrails out for him,
He the envoy who is sent to punish.
It is Shesmu who carves them up for Unas,
Cooks meals of them for him in his dinner-pots.

Unas eats their magic, swallows their spirits:
The big ones are for his morning meal,
The middle ones for his evening meal,
The little ones for his night meal,
And the oldest males and females for his fuel.
The Great Ones in the Northern sky light him fire
For the kettles' contents with the old ones' thighs,
For the sky-dwellers serve Unas,
And the pots are scraped for him with their women's legs. . . .

Unas has risen again in heaven,
He is crowned as lord of lightland.

Atum: the Creator.
Isle of Flame: part of the celestial topography.
Shesmu: god of the oil and the wine-press.

He has smashed bones and marrow,
He has seized the hearts of gods,
He has eaten the Red, swallowed the Green.
Unas feeds on the lungs of the wise,
Likes to live on hearts and their magic;
Unas abhors licking the coils of the Red
But delights to have their magic in his belly. . . .

Wisdom Literature of the Old and Middle Kingdoms

Most ancient peoples had a tradition of gnomic poetry. Some of the Egyptian writings are sources for the Biblical Proverbs, and are telling even today.

from THE INSTRUCTION ADDRESSED TO KAGEMNI (*c. 2200* BC)

The tent is open to the silent,
The seat of the quiet is spacious.

*

A little something stands for much.

from THE INSTRUCTION OF PTAHHOTEP (*c. 2200* BC)

The limits of art are not reached,
No artist's skills are perfect;
Good speech is more hidden than greenstone.

*

Follow your heart as long as you live,
Do no more than is required,
Do not shorten the time of 'follow the heart'.

*

Speaking is harder than all other work.

*

Red, Green: symbols of Lower Egypt.

If you take to wife a *shepenet*
Who is joyful and known by her town,
If she is fickle and likes the moment,
Do not reject her, let her eat,
The joyful brings happiness.

*

Hearing well is speaking well.

*

Hearing is better than all else,
It creates good will.

from THE INSTRUCTION ADDRESSED TO KING MERIKARE (*c. 2100 BC*)

Even one day gives to eternity.

*

No river lets itself be hidden,
It is good to work for the future.

*

Caution prolongs life.

*

For god knows every name.

from THE COMPLAINTS OF KHAKHEPERRE-SONB (*c. 1900 BC*)

Hearts are greedy.

shepenet: guesses at the meaning of this have ranged from 'fat woman' to 'dancer'.

from THE DISPUTE BETWEEN A MAN AND HIS *BA* (*c. 1800 BC*)

A man longs for death. In disgust, his *ba* or soul threatens to leave him. The man says:

Death is before me today
Like a well-trodden way,
Like a man's coming home from warfare.

Death is before me today
Like the clearing of the sky,
As when a man discovers what he ignored.

Death is before me today
Like a man's longing to see his home
When he has spent many years in captivity.

Religious poetry

Religion in Egypt was polytheistic, but with a tendency to associate and equate the gods with each other, as happened in later Greek literature.

from THE INSTRUCTION ADDRESSED TO KING MERIKARE (*c. 2100 BC*)

Well-tended is mankind—god's cattle,
He made sky and earth for their sake,
He subdued the water monster,
He made breath for their noses to live.
They are his images, who came from his body,
He shines in the sky for their sake;
He made for them plants and cattle,
Fowls and fish to feed them.
He slew his foes, reduced his children,
When they thought of making rebellion.
He makes delight for their sake,
He sails by to see them.
He has built his shrine around them,
When they weep he hears.

from THE GREAT HYMN TO THE ATEN
(*c. 1350 BC*)

Akhenaten, the father of Tutankhamun, attempted to replace the established religion of Egypt with a militant monotheism, and proclaimed the unreality of all gods except for the Aten, the sun-disc. At times the hymns inspired by this short-lived revolution resemble the Psalms, especially Psalm 104.

Earth brightens when you dawn in lightland,
When you shine as Aten of daytime;
As you dispel the dark,
As you cast your rays,
The Two Lands are in festivity.
Awake they stand on their feet,
You have roused them;
Bodies cleansed, clothed,
Their arms adore your appearance.
The entire land sets out to work,
All beasts browse on their herbs;
Trees, herbs are sprouting,
Birds fly from their nests,
Their wings greeting your *ka*.
All flocks frisk on their feet,
All that fly up and alight,
They live when you dawn for them.
Ships fare north, fare south as well,
Roads lie open when you rise;
The fish in the river dart before you,
Your rays are in the midst of the sea.

Who makes seed grow in women,
Who creates people from sperm;
Who feeds the sun in his mother's womb,
Who soothes him to still his tears.
Nurse in the womb,
Giver of breath,
To nourish all that he made. . . .

You made the earth as you wished, you alone,
All peoples, herds and flocks;
All upon earth that walk on legs,

ka: vital force, personality.

All on high that fly on wings,
The lands of Khor and Kush,
The land of Egypt.
You set every man in his place,
You supply their needs;
Everyone has his food,
His lifetime is counted.
Their tongues differ in speech,
Their characters likewise;
Their skins are distinct,
For you distinguished the peoples. . . .

He makes waves on the mountains like the sea,
To drench their fields and their towns.
How excellent are your ways, O Lord of eternity!
A Hapy from heaven for foreign peoples,
And all lands' creatures that walk on legs,
For Egypt the Hapy that comes from *dat*.

Your rays nurse all fields,
When you shine they live, they grow for you;
You make the seasons to foster all that you made,
Winter to cool them, heat that they taste you.
You made the far sky to shine therein,
To behold all that you made;
You alone, shining in your form of living Aten,
Risen, radiant, distant, near.
You made millions of forms from yourself alone,
Towns, villages, fields, the river's course;
All eyes observe you upon them,
For you are the Aten of daytime on high.

You are in my heart,
There is no other who knows you,
Only your son . . .
Akhenaten, great in his lifetime;
And the great Queen whom he loves, the Lady of the
Two Lands,
Nefer-nefru-Aten Nefertiti, living forever.

Khor and Kush: Syria and Nubia.
Hapy: the Nile.
dat: the Underworld.

from A HARPER'S SONG (*c. 1310 BC*)

Harper's songs were often sceptical meditations on death inscribed in tombs. In this one, 'life is but a dream' first finds expression in Western literature.

As to the time of deeds on earth,
It is the occurrence of a dream;
One says: 'Welcome safe and sound'
To him who reaches the West.

from THE BOOK OF THE DEAD (*1500–700 BC*): JUDGEMENT

The Book of the Dead is a magnificent collection of spells to guide their possessor through death and judgement, and to secure for him eternal life.

Hail to you, great God, Lord of the Two Truths!
I have come to you, my Lord,
I was brought to see your beauty.
I know you, I know the names of the forty-two gods,
Who are with you in the Hall of the Two Truths,
Who live by warding off evildoers,
Who drink of their blood,
On that day of judging characters before Wennofer.
Lo, your name is 'He-of-Two-Daughters',
And 'He-of-Maat's-Two-Eyes'.
Lo, I come before you,
Bringing Maat to you,
Having repelled evil for you.

I have not done crimes against people,
I have not mistreated cattle,
I have not sinned in the Place of Truth . . . (*& so on*)

I am pure, I am pure, I am pure, I am pure!
I am pure as is pure that great heron in Hnes.
I am truly the nose of the Lord of Breath,
Who sustains all the people . . .

Maat: order, truth, justice.

O Wide-of-stride who comes from On: I have not done evil.
O Flame-grasper who comes from Kheraha: I have not robbed.
O Long-nosed who comes from Khmun: I have not coveted.
O Shadow-eater who comes from the cave: I have not stolen.
O Savage-faced who comes from Rostau: I have not killed people.
O Lion-twins who come from heaven: I have not trimmed the measure.
O Flint-eyed who comes from Khem: I have not cheated.
O Fiery One who comes backward: I have not stolen a god's property.
O Bone-smasher who comes from Hnes: I have not told lies.
O Flame-thrower who comes from Memphis: I have not seized food.
O Cave-dweller who comes from the west: I have not sulked.
O White-toothed who comes from Lakeland: I have not trespassed . . .
(*& so on for the forty-two gods*)

I am one pure of mouth, pure of hands,
One to whom 'welcome' is said by those who see him;
For I have heard the words spoken by the Donkey and the Cat,
In the house of the Open-mouthed;
I was a witness before him when he cried out,
I saw the splitting of the *ished*-tree in Rostau.
I am one who is acquainted with the gods,
One who knows what concerns them.
I have come here to bear witness to *maat* . . .

Wisdom literature of the New Kingdom (1550–1080 BC)

from THE INSTRUCTION OF ANY

This text is unique in didactic literature, in that it contains its own subversion: Any's son rebels against his father's moralising, insisting that he has a right to be different.

Pray by yourself with a loving heart,
Whose every word is hidden.

*

A deep water whose course is unknown,
Such is a woman away from her husband.

*

A quarrelsome man does not rest on the morrow.

*

Fill your eyes with all the flowers
That your eye can see.
One has need of all of them.

*

A woman is asked about her husband.
A man is asked about his rank.

from THE INSTRUCTION OF AMENEMOPE

Another thing is good in the heart of the god:
To pause before speaking.

*

If a man's tongue is the boat's rudder,
The Lord of All is yet its pilot.

*

The heart of man is a gift of god,
Beware of neglecting it.

from THE IMMORTALITY OF WRITERS

Man decays, his corpse is dust,
All his kin have perished;
But a book makes him remembered,
Through the mouth of its reciter.
Better is a book than a well-built house,
Than tomb-chapels in the West;
Better than a solid mansion,
Than a stela in the temple!

Is there one here like Hardedef? . . .
Is there another like Ptahhotep? . . .
Death made their names forgotten
But books made them remembered!

Hardedef: composer of a wisdom book of the Old Kingdom (c. 2400 BC).

Love songs (c. 1400–1200 BC)

Egypt was not only a funereal country, as these love songs show. The translations are a creative reworking in a contemporary idiom, in contrast to the simple, direct versions elsewhere in this section.

Aim him straight at the house of your reticent lady,
  storm, full cargo and sail, her true love's nest.
(Oh throw the temple gates of her wide,
  his mistress readies for the sacrifice!)

Fill her with singing, with hurrying dances,
  wines, strong ale . . . (her Western places!) . . .
Waylay propriety. Then pay reward:
  finish her off in the night!

Thus will you hear her hushed saying,
  'Have me . . . close in your arms.
Even when dawn breaks in on tomorrow,
  let us be this way still.'

*

How clever my love with a lasso—
          she'll never need a kept bull!
She lets fly the rope at me
          (from her dark hair),
Draws me in with her comehither eyes,
          wrestles me down between her bent thighs,
Brands me hers with her burning seal.
          (Cowgirl, the fire from those thighs!)

*

          I strip you of your tangled garlands,
Once you are back again, O drunken man
          sprawled deep in sleep (and gone) in bed.
I stroke your feet
          while children . . .
                    (*Here the papyrus begins to tatter*)
. . . cry out wild with longing . . .

*

Astray or captured, all bear witness
        to the consummate skill of this lady,
Shrewd at her craft and perfected by heaven.
        Her hand has the feel of new-blown lotus,
Her breast the delicate scent of ripe berries,
        her arms twine like vinestems, and tangle,
And her face is a snare of fine-grained redwood.
        And I? who am I in this recital?—
The proverbial goose
        (and my love it is lures me)
Tricked by her tasty bait
        to this trap of my own ingenious imagining.

*

When the fig feels called to speak its mind,
        moving leaves begin to whisper:
If ever she decided to ask it,
        I would quietly die for my mistress.
        (Was ever lady so noble as Me?)
If ever her quickened slaves were not there
        it is I who would play humble servant.

I was brought from a wet, hostile land,
        uprooted as plunder for my beloved.
She had them set me in the orchard;
        she saved me.

But the dear never lets me spend my day drinking
        nor fills my insides with sweet ditchwater.
How in the world can a girl enjoy life
        with such terrible thirst and not drinking?
By my deathless soul (if it survives)
        sweetheart, fetch me some water!

*

My heart remembers how I once loved you,
        as I sit with my hair half done,
And I'm out running, looking for you,
        searching for you with my hair down!

If ever I get back, I'll weave
        an intricate hairdo down to my toes.
Love, there's so much time now to finish . . .

Ugaritic

On the Syrian coast, Ugarit was the source of a fine epic literature, until its destruction c. 1195 BC. It tells us much of Canaanite mythology, and thus of Biblical polemic. *The Tale of Aqhat*, an exciting saga of murder and revenge, revolves around the struggle for Aqhat's bow, which begins in the excerpt given here. The bow was made for Aqhat's father, Daniel, by the craftsman-god Kothar-and-Khasis. The other main character, Anat, is the most fascinating of Ugaritic goddesses, passionate, violent, intensely jealous.

from THE TALE OF AQHAT (*recorded c. 1830 BC*)

The gods are feasting, drinking;
They dine off milk-fed lambs,
Succulent flesh, cut with salt knives.
Draughts of wine they drink in flagons,
The blood of grapes in cups of gold.
They fill their cups, fashioned in silver,
Drink flagon after flagon.
The stewards, ever busy,
Bring bubbling new wine into Baal's house,
Into El's house: the old is finished.
Jar pours on jar.
   Drawing the shaft back, taut and steady,
Aqhat aligns the marvellous bow,
Devised by Kothar-and-Khasis,
Skilled in speaking, cunning in carving.
   She lifted up her eyes and gazed;
Anat stared at the bow of Aqhat.
Fair was its form, lovely to look at,
Its glittering arrows raced the lightning,
Lightning that teases cowering waters.

salt knives: the salting and spicing of carving-knives is still widely practised in the Near East.
Baal: god of rain and fertility, whose death and resurrection may well have been reenacted each year.
El: somewhat senescent head of the pantheon (literally 'god'), whose permission was required for every deed.

Anat wished to align the bow,
To aim the arrows, taut and steady,
The skilled work of Kothar-and-Khasis.
Horns carved like serpents twist and stare.
The beaker falls from Anat's hand,
The flagon from her fingers falls,
In the dust wine trickles.
She lifted up her voice and cried:
'Listen, noble Aqhat, listen!
Silver is yours, if you should wish it,
Gold, if you prefer! Only give me . . .
Give me your bow, grant me your quiver!'
  And noble Aqhat answered:
'The finest ash of Lebanon,
The finest tendons of wild bulls,
The finest horns of swift gazelles,
Filaments from the thighs of bulls,
And the fine reeds from the wide marshes,
Give these to Kothar-and-Khasis,
And let him frame a bow for you,
A quiver for the Widow,
Sister-in-law of Nations.'
  The fair Anat replied:
'Wish, Aqhat, wish; life will I send you—
Ask, hero, ask; deathless I make you.
There you will number years with Baal,
Count seasons with the sons of God;
As Baal, when he returns to life,
When all is ready,
Expectant,
The Master-player gives him to drink,
He plays and sings, shapes spells about him,
A sweet voice plays, I tell you truly—
I offer noble Aqhat life for ever!'
  Then noble Aqhat speaks:
'Do not deceive me, O fair maiden,
Your lies are hateful to a hero.
Death is man's fate,
What will he take?
What will he take?
Death is man's way,
A white glaze on my head,
Ash sprinkled on my crown,

The death of all, my death,
With the dead I will die.
I will say yet more: I will ask you—
A warrior's bow: do women hunt with it?'
  Anat's mouth is full of laughter,
While her heart is wry, and schemes:
'Consider well, my noble Aqhat,
Consider well, retract your answer!
On paths of pride lest I should meet you,
In stubborn ways lest I should find you,
Under my feet lest I should trample you,
Loveliest, most virile of men!'
  Her feet whirr as she leaves the earth,
She travels to the Source of Rivers,
Surge of abysmal waters,
Passes into the royal compound,
Retreat of El, Father of Years.
She fell prostrate before his feet,
Worshipped, and paid him homage.
Bitterly she reviled Aqhat,
Daniel's darling, man of healing.
She lifted up her voice, and cried:
  '. . . Aquat . . .
    . . . him . . .'

(*Tablet broken*)

Mesopotamian (Sumerian, Akkadian)

Mesopotamian literature presents us with a continuous tradition, even though it was written in two very different languages, Sumerian and Akkadian. Sumerian is older, and became a purely literary language c. 2000 BC, rather like Latin in the Middle Ages.

from THE EPIC OF GILGAMESH
(*Akkadian, early 2nd millennium BC*)

One of the world's great epic poems, *Gilgamesh* tells of the lives of Gilgamesh, King of Uruk, and his friend Enkidu. After the death of Enkidu, Gilgamesh wanders over the world in quest of eternal life, until he reaches the Land of the Far Away, where live Utnapishtim and his wife, who alone have been granted immortality by the gods. Utnapishtim, the Mesopotamian Noah, declares that Gilgamesh's quest is hopeless, and tells him the story of the Flood. The poem continues:

Utnapishtim said, 'As for you, Gilgamesh, who will assemble the gods for your sake, so that you may find that life for which you are searching? But if you wish, come and put it to the test: only prevail against sleep for six days and seven nights.' But while Gilgamesh sat there resting on his haunches, a mist of sleep like soft wool teased from the fleece drifted over him, and Utnapishtim said to his wife, 'Look at him now, the strong man who would have everlasting life, even now the mists of sleep are drifting over him.' His wife replied, 'Touch the man to wake him, so that he may return to his own land in peace, going back through the gate by which he came.' Utnapishtim said to his wife, 'All men are deceivers, even you he will attempt to deceive; therefore bake loaves of bread, each day one loaf, and put it beside his head; and make a mark on the wall to number the days he has slept.'

So she baked loaves of bread, each day one loaf, and put it beside his head, and she marked on the wall the days that he slept; and there came a day when the first loaf was hard, the second loaf was like leather, the third was soggy, the crust of the fourth had mould, the fifth was mildewed, the sixth was fresh, and the seventh was still on the embers. Then Utnapishtim touched him and he woke. Gilgamesh said to Utnapishtim the Faraway, 'I hardly slept when you touched and roused me.' But Utnapishtim said, 'Count these loaves and learn how many days you slept, for your first is hard, your second like leather, your third is soggy, the crust of your fourth has mould, your fifth is mildewed, your sixth is fresh and your seventh was still over the glowing embers when I touched and woke you.' Gilgamesh said, 'What shall I do, O Utnapishtim, where shall I go? Already the thief in the night has hold of my limbs, death inhabits my room; wherever my foot rests, there I find death.'

Then Utnapishtim spoke to Urshanabi the ferryman: 'Woe to you, Urshanabi, now and for ever more you have become hateful to this harbourage; it is not for you, nor for you are the crossings of this sea. Go now, banished from the shore. But this man before whom you walked, bringing him here, whose body is covered with foulness and the grace of whose limbs has been spoiled by wild skins, take him to the washing-place. There he shall wash his long hair clean as snow in the water, he shall throw off his skins and let the sea carry them away, and the beauty of his body shall be shown, the fillet on his forehead shall be renewed, and he shall be given clothes to cover his nakedness. Till he reaches his own city and his journey is accomplished, these clothes will show no sign of age, they will wear like a new garment.' So Urshanabi took Gilgamesh and led him to the washing-place, he washed his long hair as clean as snow in the water, he threw off his skins, which the sea carried away, and showed the beauty of his body. He renewed the fillet on his forehead, and to cover his nakedness gave him clothes which would show no sign of age, but would wear like a new garment till he reached his own city, and his journey was accomplished.

Then Gilgamesh and Urshanabi launched the boat on to the water and boarded it, and they made ready to sail away; but the wife of Utnapishtim the Faraway said to him, 'Gilgamesh came here wearied out, he is worn out; what will you give him to carry him back to his own country?' So Utnapishtim spoke, and Gilgamesh took a pole and brought the boat in to the bank. 'Gilgamesh, you came here a man wearied out, you have worn yourself out; what shall I give you to carry you back to your own country? Gilgamesh, I shall reveal a secret thing, it is a mystery of the gods that I am telling you. There is a plant that grows under the water, it has a prickle like a thorn, like a rose; it will wound your hands, but if you succeed in taking it, then your hands will hold that which restores his lost youth to a man.'

When Gilgamesh heard this he opened the sluices so that a sweet-water current might carry him out to the deepest channel; he tied heavy stones to his feet and they dragged him down to the water-bed. There he saw the plant growing; although it pricked him he took it in his hands; then he cut the heavy stones from his feet, and the sea carried him and threw him on the shore. Gilgamesh said to Urshanabi the ferryman, 'Come here, and see this marvellous plant. By its virtue a man may win back all his former strength. I will take it to Uruk of the strong walls; there I will give it to the old men to eat. Its name shall be "The Old Men Are Young Again"; and at last I shall eat it myself and have back all my lost youth.' So Gilgamesh returned by the gate through which he had come, Gilgamesh and Urshanabi went together. They travelled their twenty leagues and then they broke their fast; after thirty leagues they stopped for the night.

Gilgamesh saw a well of cool water and he went down and bathed; but deep in the pool there was lying a serpent, and the serpent sensed the sweetness of the flower. It rose out of the water and snatched it away, and immediately it sloughed its skin and returned to the well. Then Gilgamesh sat down and wept, the tears ran down his face, and he took the hand of Urshanabi; 'O Urshanabi, was it for this that I toiled with my hands, is it for this I have wrung out my heart's blood? For myself I have gained nothing; not I, but the beast of the earth has joy of it now. Already the stream has carried it twenty leagues back to the channels where I found it. I found a sign and now I have lost it. Let us leave the boat on the bank and go.'

After twenty leagues they broke their fast, after thirty leagues they stopped for the night; in three days they had walked as much as a journey of a month and fifteen days. When the journey was accomplished they arrived at Uruk, the strong-walled city. . . .

from THE BABYLONIAN CREATION EPIC
(Akkadian, mid-2nd millennium BC)

When there was no heaven,
no earth, no height, no depth, no name,
when Apsu was alone,
the sweet water, the first begetter; and Tiamat
the bitter water, and that
return to the womb, her Mummu,
when there were no gods—

When sweet and bitter
mingled together, no reed was plaited, no rushes
muddied the water,

the gods were nameless, natureless, futureless, then
from Apsu and Tiamat
in the waters gods were created, in the waters
silt precipitated,

Lahmu and Lahamu
were named; they were not yet old,
not yet grown tall
when Anshar and Kishar overtook them both,
the lines of sky and earth
stretched where horizons meet to separate
cloud from silt. . . .

from INANNA'S JOURNEY TO HELL
(*Sumerian, 3rd millennium BC*)

Inanna, versatile goddess of the date-cluster, of fertility and love, visits her sister Ereshkigal, queen of the Underworld. As the price of her return, she surrenders her own husband, the shepherd Dumuzi, later known as Tammuz.

Little devils are chattering to great ones,
'Come on, we'll go to Inanna,
we'll sit in her lap so holy-O.'

The devils went in to Uruk,
they seized Inanna, the holy one.

'Come away down, Inanna,
down to the great Dark City,
there where your wilful heart took you,
down into hell, down
to the home of Ereshkigal,
come away down, Inanna.
But, Inanna, you are not to put on
your beautiful dress,
the *Ma*-dress, *Pala*-dress,
dress of your sovereignty,
come away, come away down, Inanna.
Take off your crown, Inanna,
of the holy salutation,
come away, come away down.
Do not make up your face,

not now, Inanna,
but come away down to the underworld,
come away down to hell.'

They held on fast to holy Inanna
and stricken with terror she gave Dumuzi
into the power of the devils.
They said,
'This boy, put fetters on his feet,
truss him up, pinion his neck in stocks.'

They flew at his face with hooks and bits
and bodkins, they slashed his body with a heavy axe,
they made him stand and made him squat;
they pinioned that boy by the arms
and covered his face with a mask
of agony; he held up his hands
to the sun in heaven:
'Utu, Utu, I am your friend,
I married your sister,
I am someone you know.
She went down to the pit and all
for that she has given me over,
me in her place in hell to sojourn.
Utu, just judge that you are,
do not let them take me away!
Transform my body, take away my hands,
save me from out of the power of my devils
and never let them find me.
I will glide through the upland meadows
like a *sag-kal* snake and escape
with my soul to her home, to my sister
Geshtinanna.'
Utu received his tears, changed his body,
took away his hands, and Dumuzi glided
through the uplands like a *sag-kal* snake;
his soul plunged with the falcon's stoop
that follows a sparrow, he carried it straight
to the home of Geshtinanna.

Utu: the sun-god, brother of Inanna.

But despite all his ruses, Dumuzi is not saved. There are many laments for Dumuzi. Here are two.

Who is your sister? I am she.
Who is your mother? I am she.
Day dawns the same for you and me.
This is the same day we shall see.

*

There can be no answer
 to her desolate calling,
it is echoed in the wilderness,
 for I cannot answer.
Though the grass will shoot
 from the land
I am not grass, I cannot come
 to her calling.
The waters rise for her,
I am not water to come
 for her wailing,
I am not shoots of grass
 in a dead land.

from THE MESSAGE OF LUDINGIRA TO HIS MOTHER (*Sumerian*)

A certain Ludingira sends a message to his mother, inquiring after her health. He gives the messenger a number of 'signs' by which to recognise her. Here are two.

My mother is brilliant in the heavens, a doe in the mountains,
A morning star abroad at noon,
Precious carnelian, a topaz from Marhashi,
A prize for the king's daughter, full of charm,
A *nir*-stone seal, an ornament like the sun,
A bracelet of tin, a ring of *antasura*,
A shining piece of gold and silver . . .

*

My mother is rain from heaven, water for the finest seed,
A harvest of plenty, which grows a second crop,
A garden of delight, full of joy,
A watered pine, adorned with pine cones,

A spring flower, a first fruit,
An irrigation ditch carrying luxuriant waters to the garden plots,
A sweet date from Dilmun, a date chosen from the best.

from A LATE BABYLONIAN RELIGIOUS TEXT (*Akkadian*)

The long fragmentary poem from which this is taken completely eludes explication; it is weird and brilliant and unlike anything written in ancient times.

Into your genitals in which you trust I will make a dog enter and tie shut the door;
I will make a dog enter and will tie shut the door; I will make a *hahhuru*-bird enter and it will nest.
Whenever I leave or enter
I will give orders to my *hahhuru*-birds,
'Please, my dear *hahhuru*-bird,
Do not approach the mushrooms.'
Ditto. The smell of the armpits.

You are the mother, Ishtar of Babylon,
The beautiful one, the queen of the Babylonians.
You are the mother, a palm of carnelian,
The beautiful one, who is beautiful to a superlative degree,
Whose figure is red to a superlative degree,
is beautiful to a superlative degree.

from A LAMENT (*Sumerian, c. 1900 BC*)

A wailing oh, a wailing oh, could he only hold back the lament!
Lord of my city, Great Mountain Enlil, a wailing oh!
Lord of my city, Great Mountain Enlil, a wailing oh!
Over the shack, this young man is shedding tears,
A dirge over the storehouse, this girl is mourning.
This young man is shaking in tears,
This girl is shaking in tears,
This girl is crying.

PROVERBS (*Sumerian*)

Beer is like a jumper; the teeth are its staircase.

*

In my heart I am a human being, but in my eyes I am not yet a man.

*

You are played by the day, you are played in the evening,
Oh tearful lyre, must you constantly stand by?

*

Fate is a furious storm blowing through the land,
Fate is a dog who makes one walk behind him.

*

The fox having urinated into the sea,
'The whole of the sea is my urine,' he said.

Turkish

According to Chinese sources Turkish literature began in the 2nd century BC but the extant records are those of Orhon cuneiforms, generally dated 8th century AD. As the Turks moved westward different branches of the language came into existence. The most important is Çagatay, which evolved its own literature quite separate from Ottoman. There is also Oğuz, the forerunner of modern Turkish: the most notable work it produced is *The Book of Dede Korkut*, whose prose narrative is punctuated with superb verses. Ottoman literature began about the early 13th century, soon founding in poets like Yunus Emre and Eşrefoğlu a mystical tradition of considerable value in Islamic culture. Persian forms began to exercise an influence on Ottoman poets, who gradually adopted and used them, creating a new Turkish language now known as Osmanli. Persian-inspired poetry began in the mid-16th century, reaching its peak perhaps in the work of Nedim, the most prominent and the most Turkish poet of Lâle Devri (the Age of Tulips). Westernisation started in the late 19th century, and the work of Ahmed Haşim and his contemporaries combines Persian metres with themes prompted by the French Symbolists. The emergence of modern Turkey produced a poetry more aware of its local, popular roots: poets turned to the syllabic metres of folk poetry, and the old Osmanli literary style gave way to the more direct language characteristic of most Western poetry today. The incomparable Nazım Hikmet and his generation demonstrate the great advance Turkish poetry has made this century; the bulk of what follows bears witness to a vigorous modern presence embracing both Eastern and Western concerns.

from THE BOOK OF DEDE KORKUT
(compiled c. 13th cent.)

The young Oğuz prince Uruz accompanies his father Kazan on a hunting expedition near the Georgian border: the Georgians attack and capture Uruz. Kazan, not knowing this, returns home, where the boy's distraught mother questions him in the lines which follow. The tale ends happily: after a counter-attack in which his mother takes part, Uruz is freed.

My lord Kazan,
Luck of my head, throne of my house,
Son-in-law of the Khan my father,
Loved of the lady my mother,
He to whom my parents gave me,

Whom I see when I open my eyes,
Whom I gave my heart and loved,
My prince, my warrior, Kazan!
You rose up from your place and stood,
With your son you leaped on to your black-maned Kazilik horse,
You went out to hunt over the great mountains with their lovely folds,
You caught and laid low the long-necked deer,
You loaded them on to your horses and turned homeward.
Two you went and one you come; where is my child?
Where is my son whom I got in the dark night?
My one prince is not to be seen, and my heart is on fire.
Kazan, have you let the boy fall from the overhanging rocks?
Have you let the mountain-lion eat him?
Or have you let him meet the infidel of dark religion?
Have you let them tie his white hands and arms?
Have you let him walk before them?
Have you let him look fearfully around, his tongue and mouth dry?
Have you let the bitter tears flow from his dark eyes?
Have you let him cry for his lady mother, the prince his father?

My son, my son, O my son,
My portion, my son!
Summit of my black mountain yonder, my son!
Light of my dark eyes, my son!
The poison winds are not blowing, Kazan, yet my ears are ringing.
I have not eaten garlic, Kazan, yet I burn within.
The yellow snake has not stung me, yet my white body rises and swells.
In my breast, which seems dried up, my milk is leaping.
I cannot see my only son, and my heart is aflame.
Tell me, Kazan, about my only son.
If you will not, I shall curse you, Kazan, as I burn with fire. . . .

I meant to rise up from my place and stand,
To mount my black-maned Kazilik horse,
To go among the teeming Oghuz,
To find a chestnut-eyed daughter-in-law,
To set up white tents on the black earth,
To walk my son to his bridal bower,
To bring him to his heart's desire.
You did not let me attain my wish,
May my dark head's curse seize you, Kazan.

My one prince is not to be seen, and my heart is on fire.
Tell me what you have done,
Or I shall curse you, Kazan, as I burn with fire.

Yunus Emre (?1238–?1320)

Knowledge is to understand
To understand who you are.
If you know not who you are
What's the use of learning?

The aim in learning is
To understand God's Truth.
Because without knowledge
It is wasted hard labour.

Do not say: I know it all,
I am obedient to my God.
If you know not who God is
That is sheer idle talk.

Twenty-eight syllables
You read from end to end.
You name the first 'alpha'
What can it possibly mean?

Yunus Emre says also
Let me receive what I need.
The best possible thing
Is to find perfect peace.

Eşrefoğlu (?–1469)

O my God do not part me from thee
Do not part me from thy sight

To love you is my faith and belief
Do not part my belief from my faith

I've withered, become like the Autumn
Do not part the leaves from the branch

My Master is a rose, I his leaf
Do not part the leaf from the rose

I, a nightingale in my love's garden
Do not part his beak from his song

All the fish breathe in water they say
Do not part the fish from the lake

Eşrefoğlu is thy humble slave
Do not part the Sultan from his servant

Nedim (?1681–1730)

SONG

Come, let's grant joy to this heart of ours that founders in distress:
Let's go to the pleasure gardens, come, my sauntering cypress . . .
Look, at the quay, a six-oared boat is waiting in readiness—
Let's go to the pleasure gardens, come, my sauntering cypress.

Let's laugh and play, let's enjoy the world to the hilt while we may,
Drink nectar at the fountain which was unveiled the other day,
And watch the gargoyle sputter the elixir of life away—
Let's go to the pleasure gardens, come, my sauntering cypress.

First, for a while, let's take a stroll around the pond at leisure,
And gaze in marvel at that palace of heavenly pleasure;
Now and then, let's sing songs or recite poems for good measure—
Let's go to the pleasure gardens, come, my sauntering cypress.

Get your mother's leave, say it's for holy prayers this Friday:
Out of time's tormenting clutches let us both steal a day,
And slinking through the secret roads and alleys down to the quay,
Let's go to the pleasure gardens, come, my sauntering cypress.

Just you and I, and a singer with exquisite airs—and yet
Another: with your kind permission, Nedim, the mad poet;
Let's forget our boon companions today, my joyful coquette—
Let's go to the pleasure gardens, come, my sauntering cypress.

Ahmet Haşim (1884–1933)

PROMISED LAND

Let it play with your hair, this gentle breeze
Blowing from the seven seas.
If only you knew
How lovely you are the way you gaze at the edge of the night
Steeped in the grief of exile and longing, in sorrow.

Neither you
Nor I
Nor the dusk that gathers in your beauty
Nor the blue sea,
That safe harbour for the distress that assaults the brain—
We spurn the generation which knows nothing of the soul's pain.

Mankind today
Brands you merely a fresh slender woman
And me just an old fool.
That wretched appetite, that filthy sight
Can find no meaning in you or me
Nor a tender grief in the night
Nor the sullen tremor of secrecy and disdain
On the calm sea.

You and I
And the sea
And the night that seems to gather silently,
Without trembling, the fragrance of your soul,
Far away
Torn asunder from the land where blue shadows hold sway,
We are forever doomed to this exile here.

That land?
Stretches along the chaste regions of imagination, and
A blue nightfall
Reposes there for all;
At its outer edges, the sea
Pours the calm of sleep on each soul . . .

There, women are lovely, tender, nocturnal, pure.
Over their eyes your sadness hovers,
They are all sisters or lovers:

The tearful kisses on their lips can cure,
And the indigo quiet of their inquiring eyes
Can soothe the heart's suffering.
Their souls are violets
Distilled from the night of despair,
In a ceaseless search for silence and repose.
The dim glare from the moon's sorrows
Finds haven in their immaculate hands.

Ah, they are so frail—
The mute anguish they share,
The night deep in thought, the ailing sea . . .
They all resemble each other there.

That land
Is on which imaginary continent, and
Dimmed by what distant river?
Is it a land of illusions—or real,
A utopia bound to remain unknown forever?

I do not know . . . All I know is
You and I and the blue sea
And the dusk that vibrates in me
The strings of inspiration and agony,
Far away
Torn asunder from the land where blue shadows hold sway
We are forever doomed to this exile here.

Nazım Hikmet (1902–63)

A SAD STATE OF FREEDOM

You waste the attention of your eyes,
the glittering labour of your hands,
and knead the dough enough for dozens of loaves
    of which you'll taste not a morsel;
you are free to slave for others—
you are free to make the rich richer.

The moment you're born
    they plant around you
mills that grind lies

lies to last you a lifetime.
You keep thinking in your great freedom
    a finger on your temple
        free to have a free conscience.

Your head bent as if half-cut from the nape,
your arms long, hanging,
you saunter about in your great freedom:
    you're free
        with the freedom of being unemployed.

You love your country
as the nearest, most precious thing to you.
But one day, for example,
    they may endorse it over to America,
and you, too, with your great freedom—
you have the freedom to become an air-base.

You may proclaim that one must live
not as a tool, a number or a link
but as a human being—
then at once they handcuff your wrists.
You are free to be arrested, imprisoned
    and even hanged.

There's neither an iron, wooden
    nor a tulle curtain
        in your life;
there's no need to choose freedom:
you are free.
But this kind of freedom
    is a sad affair under the stars.

DON QUIXOTE

The knight of immortal youth
at the age of fifty found his mind in his heart
and on a July morning went out to capture
the right, the beautiful, the just.

Facing him a world of silly and arrogant giants,
he on his sad but brave Rocinante.

I know what it means to be longing for something,
but if your heart weighs only a pound and sixteen ounces,
there's no sense, my Don, in fighting these senseless
windmills.

But you are right, of course, Dulcinea is your woman,
the most beautiful in the world;
I'm sure you'll shout this fact
at the face of street-traders;
but they'll pull you down from your horse
and beat you up.
But you, the unbeatable knight of our cause,
will continue to glow behind the heavy iron visor
and Dulcinea will become even more beautiful.

Cahit Sıtkı Tarancı (1910–56)

ROBINSON CRUSOE

Robinson, my clever Robinson
you don't know how I envy you.
If you could only show me your island,
there I would find peace of mind.

I'll be the ship, you be the captain.
We can unfurl the sail one morning.
The sea becomes our shadow in the sun.
The journey. And suddenly we're at our island.

I wish you could be my interpreter,
introduce me to the fish,
to wild birds and flowers,
say to them about me: 'He's one of us.'

I know how to climb trees.
I can tell a fruit that's ripe.
I can also manage breaking stones,
making fires, cooking food.

Robinson, understanding Robinson,
if your island hasn't sunk yet
take me there
before the seaways close.

Fazıl Hüsnü Dağlarca (1914–)

ECHO

When a poet
Dies
God
Feels it first

HEADACHE

We call it headache—
The wingbeats
Of a dead bird
Pounding on our forehead

HALİM THE THIRD

Majestic and sacred, I am Halim the Third,
Ruler of Rulers.
Here in my white hands
The morning of my people begins.

Every moment I breathe
Carries my warmth to unknown virgins;
In my continuance I unveiled
The taste of time.

The world as dimensions
Hangs upon my dispensation.
In the peace of my body
Castles find their peace.

I freed poetry, science, victory
In the wake of great eagles.
On seas and on lands,
Let generations rejoice.

The dark and blue skies
Are meant for my head,
To my endless blood
My love is an endless parallel.

Noble, strong, handsome and absolute
As far as the mind can conjecture
I am Halim the Third.
Mountains everywhere, who are *you*?

Orhan Veli Kanık (1914–50)

FOR THIS COUNTRY

What haven't we done for our country?
Some of us died
Some of us gave public speeches.

TWEEZERS

Neither the atom bomb,
Nor the London conference;
Tweezers in one hand,
A mirror in the other;
Does she care about the world?

Oktay Rifat (1914–)

ONCE UPON A TIME

From behind each tree you appeared
in such great numbers that I felt alone,
and amid the gust of your mad movements
my ladder against the fortress whirled away.

I met you at the corner of each street,
you were so absent that I cried, lost myself.
Within clouds reminiscent of ancient seas
floated rocks gnawed down with your blood.

What a pity! You vanished in great numbers
as if coexistent with a time that never was.
I bent and picked up the sky from the ground,
the sky you had carelessly dropped, dropped.

STARS

Near the book a notebook
near the notebook a glass
near the glass a child
in the child's hand a cat.
And far away stars stars.

Melih Cevdet Anday (1915–)

OUR TABLE

On the way back from the funeral cocks were crowing
Upon the April soil of an empty afternoon.

The sky, like a small morning-glory,
Suddenly faced us. We went into a tavern.

Our table gave little crackling sounds,
The tree remembering it had been alive.

İlhan Berk (1916–)

THE GATE OF AHMET THE FIRST

Massive processions of fires and slaughters and deaths and massacres
Out of such a night you summon me
You say enough of this wreck and ravage and enmity let them end
at the gate of Ahmet the First never to rear their heads again
Let us no longer know assassination
Take one step and an expanse opens before us so wide as to never
diminish
Fires offer no solution hostilities set nothing right
Look how far I am from you yet nothing is different
Our awakening one morning ruins nothing improves nothing
Only love plucks me away only love carries me to places I never knew
We trudged long and here we came to a stop.

the Gate of Ahmet the First: one of the entrances to the Sultans' Palace in Istanbul, named after a 17th-century sultan whose peace treaty with Austria put an end to Ottoman expansion westward; the Ottoman Court called itself the Sublime Gate (Topkapı).

Cahit Külebi (1917–)

IN THE WAR

Fathers went home feeling guilty every evening
In the war
The mothers' milk dried up
The children wept
The men joined the army
The women were skin and bone
The girls grew pale in the war

As for those who fought
Only their memory remains

Behçet Necatigil (1917–)

HARBOUR

Ships whose masts are torn in violent storms
Come for refuge—we think we have found them.

They do not see us—only the distance.
We mend, repair. They go, we stay.

Then at night—let it be the last, last.
Send no others! we beg of the sea.

And our loneliness grows
More monstrous still.

Attilâ İlhan (1925–)

ISTANBUL GATE OF FELICITY

from 'Suite in the Ottoman Mode'

world war years with the beauty of a frightened woman

when the *good cheer* kept vigil at the kuzgunjuk landing
turned like the pessimistic cadets of kuleli toward sultan reshad

and no one was there for the last autumnal ferry
no helva vendors from beykoz or phonographs with odeon horns
pouring out songs in an ancient mode only the captain's cymbals
alla turca made in yildiz and lifted from the bazaars

istanbul straits with the sulkiness of a wounded vulture

when monocled german officers argued at kramer's beerhouse
moltke versus bismarck in their fissured tongue
downing three bitter dark green doubles of pilsen beer
torpedonet heroes rich in numbers as the imperial band
return to the galician front under the cold russian rain
swept night and day by long range battery fire
red crescent tents blossoming like wet flowers
enormous flowers of extremely bloodstained white
back to the galician front the operetta remedy

in *ikdam* false news of victory on the syrian front

at the ministry of war the commander in chief enver pasha
with colonel suleyman of military secret intelligence
knows nothing of how time passes until morning worship
in the unfiltered glass-shattering darkness of a cellar
before an execution the nervous motions of prayer
of cowardly shadows in bekiraga prison
the sticky sweat crawling on yakub jemil's temples
the torn *union and progress* membership card on the floor
the rattle of a mauser being loaded the order to shoot
the lilacs fade like lightning in the water jug there is no cure

those world war years with the beauty of a frightened woman

Can Yücel (1926–)

ALEA IACTA EST

Attila crossed the Danube
Hannibal crossed the Alps
Caesar crossed the Rubicon

And I crossed
My self
Burning all the flowers behind me

Cemal Süreya (1931–)

SONG ABOUT EXECUTIONERS

Since the Bourgeois Revolution
One hundred and fifty years ago
Monsieur Guillotine, a Parisian lawyer
Reads of suicides in the morning paper
With tears in his eyes

Señor Bullet in Spain
Your glance could wander off
Towed by some cloud
Unless of course you were blindfolded
Like Lorca

And what's to be said about
Mr Electric Chair
Credit investments apart
A better symbol
Than William James

The gushing blood is a salute
To Cain, to Ezra Pound
In parentheses to Raskolnikov
The head misunderstanding continues
To order the feet about
But Herr Axe's job is done

Citizen condemned to die
When the chair is pulled from under you
If you can husband your breath
You will live a short span longer
For death as proffered by Rope Effendi
Is one of polite delay

Arabic

Arab poetry is one of the great literatures of the world, and yet it is little known in the West. While the love songs of the Moors in Spain were the inspiration of medieval troubadours and Arab themes have permeated European verse, until recently Arab poetry has been available only to an enthusiastic few. Why this should be the case is a puzzle. It is possible that in the past the supremacy of Latin blinkered the Western reader. Later Edward Fitzgerald's *The Ruba'iyat of Omar Khayyam* established a model for the translation of Islamic poetry and formed a taste, which subsequent translators of Arab poetry have found it difficult to overcome. Certainly the reason for Western neglect is not that Arab poetry is alien to us. Indeed, the English-speaking reader is far more at home with Arab poetry than with Arab music, architecture and design.

The language is rooted in everyday speech. Further, a tradition which combines lyric intensity with an outlook which is empirical and humanistic has obvious parallels with important strands in Western tradition.

The Arab poet's attitude to nature is one of reverence which in some cases amounts to mysticism. It has its origin in a basic fact of existence: plants in the Arab world imply water and water signifies life. There are other factors. Before Muhammad pagan Arabs believed that spirits resided in certain trees and rocks. After Muhammad poets continued to animate the world. Particular places in the landscape were linked with old camp sites and past events which in the poet's mind and the tribe's memory made them pregnant with association. The opening section of the best known form, namely the *qasida*, is dedicated to the remembrance of these locations. The personification of nature is underlined by some love poets who, being forbidden to voice their emotions directly to the girls they loved, communicated their feelings by addressing flowers and animals in the same terms and with the same passion that they would normally reserve for the mistresses they worshipped. The poems they wrote strove to match in beauty the objects they described.

Another strong element in Arab poetry is its modern tone. Moreover, the techniques the classical poets employed, especially the jump-cut which without warning suddenly shifts the poem from one experience to another, from direct to indirect speech and from one emotion to another, anticipate tactics pioneered in the West by Rimbaud, Pound and Eliot. However, the history of Arab poetry is not the history of one or two kinds of poetry. It is the history of a tradition which includes the oral epic, the love poem, the courtly lyric, the panegyric, the boast, the wine song, the moral satire, the mystical address and the philosophical meditation, each created by individual poets with their own distinct styles.

All the major periods of Arab poetry are represented in the pages which follow.

Find al-Zimmani (?–530)

We forgave the Banu Duhl and we said,
'They are brothers'. We hoped they would be friends.
They became aggressive. We had to fight.
The evil we suffered we quickly repaid.
We were a pride of lions hunting at dawn.
We hit them and hacked them. Blood spurted from guts
Like a jet of wine from a leather bottle.
Fools regard good manners and sympathy
As marks of weakness. When decency fails
The safety of the tribe depends on force.

Munakhal al-Yashkuri (?–597)

It was raining. I walked into her room.
She was young, lovely and dressed in white silk.
When I touched her she waddled back, a sand grouse
Tottering to a stream. We kissed and she breathed
Like a fawn. She pressed against me and said
'Yashkuri, there's no fire in your body.'
'Stop teasing. I'm tired out. You've stolen my strength.'

Urwa ibn al-Ward (?–615)

When a man fails to provide for himself
He moans about money and blames his friends.
His family long to be rinsed of their blot.
To get what you want you must take your chances,
You must roll up your sleeves and stick to the job.
Walk now in God's country and earn your keep
So people don't nag and you can live in peace.

*

I must go and make money. I have learnt
To fear poverty: people despise the poor.
A bankrupt in their house is an insult.
If you are honest, well bred and much liked
The dew will dry, your wife scold, your child scorn.
Men view the rich with awe, they hold their breath.
A rich man has a god who forgives.

Abu Mihjan (?–652)

I know what the Merciful said of drink;
But give me a glass, man, and pour it neat
So I can load my sins. I drink it straight
To attain a noble fall. I relished fire
And, despite the world, satisfied my needs.

*

When I die bury me by a vine tree
Whose roots will dampen my bones. Don't bury me
In the desert where I can't touch a drop.

Majnun Laila (?–682)

When Laila was a small tomboy her friends
Could see no bumps on her blouse. I loved her.
As children we were shepherds of the flock:
I wish the lambs, and ourselves, had never moved.

*

My soul clung to her soul
Before thought and later
Our love was centred in drops.

Our love cried in the cradle,
It fused our lives and grew.
When we die, it won't die,

It will survive to light
The darkness of our grave.

*

I saw a gazelle nibbling in a garden:
I thought it was Laila in the sunlight.
Gazelle, eat in peace, I come as a friend.
Take your time, I'll be your castle. When I flash
My sword it glowers. When I lunge, it slices.

Shaken I saw a wolf attack the gazelle
And sink its fangs and claws in her belly.
I hit the wolf with an arrow which shot

The life out of its throat. My anger cooled,
And my pulse settled. A gentleman will avenge.

*

How can a pain in the chest be softened?
The darts of death are closer than your hands.
Too much loss; too much want; absence. I tremble,
You can't come to me, I can't come to you.
Our love is a small bird tied by a child,
The bird sips the lake of death and the boy
Goes on with his game. He doesn't have the sense
To feel the bird's pain: and the wings can't fly.
I know a thousand roads, a thousand places,
But without a heart there is nowhere to go.

Jamil (?–701)

Let us live till we grow old.
But should we die let my grave

Lie beside yours. When they've raked
Your mound I'll try to join you.

Forbidden to meet under the sun
Our souls dance in the moonlight.

If I don't express this love
The pain will never cease to hurt.

Waddah al-Yaman (?–709)

She said: Don't come to my door, my father's old-fashioned.
I said: Secretly I'll snatch you, my sword's tough and sharp.
She said: A castle blocks your path; I said: I'll ram it.
She said: The sea divides us; I said: I shall swim.
She said: I'm watched by seven brothers; I said: I'm unbeaten.
She said: God is above; I said: My Lord's merciful
And forgives. She said: I've run out of arguments,
So my love, when dreams are told instead of stories,
Fall on me like dew, let the night be ours alone.

Umar ibn Abi Rabi'a (644–711)

I'm obsessed with a girl who suspects me.
Once, when she strummed her lute, and sang, and sang,
I told her: 'I wish I could be the back
Of your lute so when your arms cradled me tight
I'd lie in your lap.' She wept, turned her head,
'Why do you make such remarks? If you thought
I'd be cold and distant, you wouldn't have spoken.'
'Come off it, my dreams don't worry your little mind.'

*

They told her I married.
She hides her anger and says
To her sister, 'He can wed
Ten girls for all I care.'
The women point, her nerves crack.
'I feel odd, my heart's left
My breast, and my bones melt.
This news scorches my whipped soul.'

Arji (?–738)

My people forgot me: they lost a captain
They could use in war to protect the front.
I was left to face disease and old age,
Now the daggers of death are thrust at my throat.
I was made to look small, and seem a man
Without a name; I who am kin of Amr.
Every day I'm dragged manacled from my cell.
How much can I take? How much injustice
Can I endure? Caliph, if you hear me
You will know the depth of my gratitude.
I shower gifts on the man who breaks my chains,
But my taunting jailer I will tear apart.

Abu al-Shamaqmaq (?–796)

If I sailed a ship, the spray would dry
And the waves would harden.

If I watched a ruby glitter in my hand,
It would turn to glass.

If I drank the sweet Euphrates' water,
I would swallow salt.

I appeal to God and my patron,
My hawks fly like hens.

*

When I sat in that empty house the cold
Turned me to flint, a dog freezing a vixen.

Only date stones and rubbish left by rats
Stocked the larder. The flies swarmed to a dustbin.

Life scuttled out of the cracks and ran for food,
But the cat stayed. He was sick and begged God

To let him catch a mouse. Not a whisker.
His head, bent with boredom, looked out of joint.

When I spotted him with his nose in his paws,
Slinking and morose, I said, 'Cheer up,

You're king of the cats.' My words were kindly.
'I've lost my sense of fun. I can't endure

This drab hovel stripped like a desert. My head
Lolls with hunger, I crawl like a shadow.'

'Go if you must. Take care and best of luck.
When you find a butcher, make yourself useful.

Should you hear I've got some money and milk,
Come back, and settle down. You'll get bored with
butchers.'

The cat said, 'God bless dear friend', then crept out
Like a little crook who has bribed his release.

Abbas ibn al-Ahnaf (750–809)

Love has trees in my heart, and they
Are watered by pent-up rivers.

The black-eyed girl who's so demure,
And speaks coyly like a high flute,
Nudged sleep from my head. My liver
Turned to fire and I cried with pain.

I loved those tears which swamped my eyes,
Twin pupils drowned beneath a liquid sky.

*

When I visit you and the moon
Isn't around to show me the way,
Comets of longing set my heart
So much ablaze, the earth is lit
By the holocaust under my ribs.

*

Abbas I wish you were the shirt
On my body, or I your shirt.
Or I wish we were in a glass
You as wine, I as rainwater.
Or I wish we were two love birds
Who lived alone in the desert,
No people.

*

Zalum said, and she was never unfair,
The man who compared me to the moon
Was mistaken: the moon has no damson eyes,
Nor idle charm that makes for boredom.

Abu Nuwas (762–813)

When she left me, stopped writing notes,
My desire hurt. The thought of her
So upset me I nearly died.
I got Satan into a corner
And, blubbing like a child, told him,

'She's hooked me: tears and lack of sleep
Cause my eyes to look like ulcers.
Unless you make that girl love me,
And you can, I won't write poetry,
I won't listen to songs, and I won't
Pickle my bones with drink. Day and night
I'll fast, pray and read the Qur'an.
I'll follow the path He commands.'
Shamefaced she was back in a flash.

Ibn al-Rumi (835–896)

When a baby is born the world shows him
Its walls and ditches. Why else should the child weep?
Once lonely and confined, now loved and free,
He yet seems to fear the hidden threats of life.
It is strange how the soul senses the earth's mysteries.

*

I have a country I'd never sell
Nor let anyone own. It has
Become the body of my soul.
If it was taken I would die.
People love the landscape of their youth.
When they think of home they recall
Their childhood and long to return.

Buhturi (821–897)

Cheerful Spring, laughing and swaying, has come.
His beauty almost talks. Last night Nayruz
Tiptoed through the dark and stirred sleeping buds.
A touch of dew frees petals to utter words
They could not say before. Spring dresses the trees
In a country smock embroidered with flowers.
He blesses our eyes with colours we thought forbidden.
The garden breeze is so gentle you imagine
It carries the breath of contented lovers.

Abdullah ibn al-Mu'tazz (861–908)

The cavalry of dew is mounted on flowers
Stirred by the whip of the wind.

The field gallops as it stands.

*

Watch now the beauty of the crescent moon as it ascends,
Ripping the darkness with its light; look, a scythe of silver
Mowing a black prairie that's clustered with white narcissi.

*

I don't want to drink in ruins under a sky
The belly of a wild ass.

Nor under a roof that sieves rain with broken walls
Which let in great mounds of soil.

I want to drink in the morning when heaven appears
Wearing a kaftan of voile;

And the Eastern breeze goes for a stroll through a garden
Full of blossom lapped with dew;

And the bright sun is like a newly minted dinar.

Mutanabbi (915–965)

Our forebears stayed in the world for a spell
Each spending his days in search of comfort.
Although a few may have found happiness
They all choked with dismay when they went.
Throughout life man scratches the sore time inflicts,
His sunniest days are edged with black despair.
When time grows a stick, man sharpens a spear.
It's not worth fighting for the things you want.
The noble choose death to shame, but there's little point.
Hero or coward death is bound to come.
You're a fool not to face it. Our spirits
Fear the future, but rest when all is ended.

Abu al-Ala al-Ma'arri (973–1058)

Needles have stitched a death shroud with our life thread;
It caps our temples. The searching intellect

Sees light as newly created and darkness
As the dimension from which it was born.

Don't pray for a kingdom in case you try
To seize power with force. Kings are sad creatures.

Each sunset warns quiet men who look ahead
That light will end; and each day postman Death

Knocks on our door. Although he does not speak,
He hands us a standing invitation.

Be like those skeleton horses which scent battle
And fear to eat. They wait chewing their bridles.

*

The comet, has it nerves or is it dead;
Has it a mind, or is it burning rock?

Some people believe in a world after death,
While others say we're only vegetables.

I advise you to avoid ugliness
And do what's good, for I've learnt the soul

Near death repents, repents its gouty skin
Which began so fresh, and may do again.

*

Sin and crime, Raven, sin and crime,
They're all guilty; no creature's pure.

Take the food you need from the plains
And try to live in the treetops,

I'll not blame you. If your wings snuffed
Out the night light, I'd defend you.

Man frightens the lion in its den
And never gives the jackal any peace.

Thieves who tempt their neighbours to crime
Might as well hustle grapes to vineyards.

Man corrupts the life around him
And rats on friends who seek his help.

If you farmed man's estate, and made
It rich, stones would be your salary.

Hafsa bint Hamdun (10th cent.)

I've a lover who checks his feelings,
    But when I leave he's full of pride.
'Who's pleased you more?' he boasts. 'Have you,'
    I ask, 'slept with a better woman?'

Wallada (?–1091)

Good God, I was born to live a noble life
And the way I walk shows my elegance.

I present my cheek to my admirer
And I give my lips to whoever wants me.

*

If you were loyal to our union
You wouldn't have fallen for my servant.
You left a ripened branch for a twig.
I am the moon, but God help me
You were struck by a tiddly star.

Nazhun (11th cent.)

The nights are great, but Sunday's fantastic.
When the chaperone slept you would have seen
Only this remarkable couple. You might have watched
The sun wrapped tight in the arms of the moon,
A shivering deer in the claws of a lion.

Mariam bint Abu Ya'qub (11th cent.)

What does one expect from a woman
Of seventy-seven made of cobwebs?
She crawls like a baby to her stick,
And stumbles, a convict in shackles.

Hafsa bint al-Haj (?–1189)

The garden didn't smile when we walked in its lanes
But displayed green envy and yellow bile.
The river didn't ripple with pleasure when we stood
On its bank; and the dove cooed with dislike.
You mustn't think the world is lovely and kind
Just because you are good. Look how the sky
Switched on the stars to spy on our embrace.

*

Shall I join you or will you come to me?
My heart is always glad to meet your needs.

My mouth is a spring and my hair a shade.
I'm sure you'll be thirsty when you break at noon.

*

I send my poems to call you,
As they sing they'll please your ear.

A garden waiting to be seen
Floats its perfume on the air.

*

Ask the lightning that shocks the sky
On a calm night if my lovers
Remember me. My God, it makes
My heart shudder and my eyes rain.

Yusuf al-Khal (1917–)

PRAYERS IN A TEMPLE

1

The stone speaks. The stone becomes bread, becomes wine, becomes. The stone is the sky, lucky is the one who has wings.

Ah, how much I love you tonight.

For the first time I've embraced you like this. I strip naked inside you—I am. For the first time I am the stone—the sky.

Your eyes . . . Your body is a child swimming in the water. I love the child and the water, the water and the child.

In the wilderness nothing is friendly except the stone, in spite of its roughness one lies on it and is comfortable.

Let this moment be for us. The stone is the sky and we are its wings.

2

When I wake, the river wakes with me, flows and fills the plain. I will set the sail of the day. I am alone. The friend I was expecting has not yet arrived.

When I wake, the light is sitting in front of me. Why don't you wake up, silly wound, take up your bed and walk away.

The walls are crumbling. The eyes of the air are fluttering. The foot is stamping on the pavement. No murmur in the light. Screaming is the secret word.

When I wake, my love wakes with me.

3

My legs are made of reeds, I will look for a crutch.

I've found it: a blond silk thread.

I will walk to the end of the earth. In the plains. On the mountains. At night. During the day. I will walk like a dream reached on waking.

My love is with me. My body is with me. My God is with me. Get up, fate, and let me have your place.

4

From a distance my oak tree shades me and takes care of me. Stretches its arms to me. It has a nest with two sparrows.

And here I am singing. In the courtyard there is an apple tree whose fruit gives juice for my throat.

I love my oak tree very much. Because of it I am here. Because of it I sing.

During the day I dream of the shade, and at night I embrace it and fall asleep.

I will lift the sun with my wings. I nail it, and it does not move. My oak tree's shade is my only comfort.

5

Tonight I've climbed the ivory towers. My stairs were your blue hair.

Ah, and on your altar I offered sacrifices: a pair of turtle-doves and a ewe I fattened for the sacrifice. And here I am descending to the foot of the mountain with my only child. The wounds of joy are screaming, and my days are as silent as the hand.

At dawn I will take my sheep to pasture, and in the evening I will sing for them the song of homecoming.

And now let me scream.

My body is receding, leaving me like a stranger—a rider I've never seen before.

6

Your eyes are streams of appeal. How delicious is your soft mouth. Your tongue makes the body, and your breathing gives the breath of life.

What a goddess you are! Your paradise is no temptation to sin. All its fruits are for me. I am its first man.

Embrace me, happiness. On your body I sailed my boat whose oars are lusts that never die.

Let the winds bring what they want. I am an experienced sailor, my boat is the cedar of love.

Embrace me, my little goddess. Fold your horizons around me. Love me more than love. My past is a deep fathomless wound.

7

Do not fold your dress like this. Let him enter. Let him ascend. Your breasts are peaks. Their slopes are tempting, opening to the dreams of the body.

In your garden I will plant a scion of roses.

And if I'm still alive in the autumn, I will uproot the boxthorn bushes and replace them with light and wind.

Today let us rejoice.

For some time my tongue has not tasted honey. My nails no longer wound.

Stand naked before me and I will show you the keys of life.

Ah, let him enter!

The light of life is faint. Its presence always draws on procreation.

8

Your bedroom window is suspended on a cloud. Why do you open it and disappear?

Who will prepare the table today, unroll before me the carpet of joy, embrace my loneliness in the shade, and save my face from shame?

My existence is a wave of secrecy which your strange body deciphers.

No slaves on my ships, nor slave girls, pines, fine purple clothes and jewellery of glass and stone.

Only one word and little action on my ships.

And now the city is surrendering to assault. Its walls are falling.

I am like Thammuz. My blood is a drink for the thirsty and my body is a feast for lovers.

We are all hungry for the body and thirsty for the essence of the soul.

Nizar Qabbani (1923–)

A PERSONAL LETTER TO THE MONTH OF JUNE

Month of June, explode in our antique skulls
Sweep away thousands of synonyms
Sweep away maxims and ancient wisdom
Rip up our old dirty linen
Slash the skin of our ugly faces,
Change, turn extremist and rebel against conventions,
Shoot the past

June: a reference to the Six-Day War of June 1967.

Be the gun and the crime;
After the hanging of God on the gate of the city
Prayers lost their value
Belief and unbelief lost their value.

Abdul Wahab al-Bayati (*1926–*)

THE SINGER AND THE MOON

1

I saw him playing with hearts and rubies

2

I saw him dying

3

His shirt stained with strawberries
A dagger in his heart
Cobwebs
All around his broken flute
And the green moon in his eyes
Sets across the terraces of the night and of the houses
As he lies on the pavement dying in silence

Buland al-Haidari (*1926–*)

CONVERSATION AT THE BEND IN THE ROAD

Haven't you slept . . . sad guard,
When do you sleep?
You, who have not known sleep in the light of our lamp
for a thousand years,
You, who have been crucified between his outstretched
palms for years,
Don't you ever sleep?
—For the twentieth time . . . I want to sleep
I fall asleep but can never sleep
For the fiftieth time
I fell asleep and couldn't sleep

For sleep to the sad guard
Remains like the edge of a knife
I'm afraid of sleeping
I'm afraid of waking to dreams.

Let them burn Rome . . . let them burn Berlin
Let them steal the Wall of China
You have to sleep . . .
It's time this sad guard
Had a rest for a moment . . . he sleeps
—I sleep . . . and Berlin burns every second
And every hour a wall is stolen from China
Between one blink and another a dragon is born
I'm afraid of sleeping
For sleep to the sad guard
Remains like the edge of a knife.

Mouin Besseiso (1926–)

TO RIMBAUD

When Rimbaud became a slave-trader
And threw his net
Over Ethiopia
To catch black lions
Black swans
He abandoned poetry . . .
How honest was that little boy . . .
But many poets
Became slave-traders,
Usurers,
And did not abandon poetry;
Representatives of publicity agencies
Dealers in faked paintings
And did not abandon poetry.
In the sultan's palace their poems were turned into
Doors and windows
Tables and carpets
And they did not abandon poetry . . .
They praised,
Received medals and titles,
Gold, silver and stone cups

And they did not abandon poetry . . .
The gendarme's stamp,
The gendarme's footmark on their poems
And they did not abandon poetry . . .
How honest was Rimbaud . . .
How honest was that little boy . . .

Adonis (1930–)

THE MARTYR

(a dream)

When I saw the night in his burning eyelids
There was no tree in his face, or stars.

I raged round his head
Like the wind, and fell to pieces
Like a shattered flute.

A MIRROR FOR THE TWENTIETH CENTURY

A coffin bearing the face of a boy
A book
Written on the belly of a crow
A wild beast that comes with a flower

A rock
That breathes with the lungs of a lunatic:

This is it
This is the Twentieth Century.

Muhammad al-Maghut (1934–)

THE POSTMAN'S FEAR

Prisoners everywhere
Send me all you have
Fears screams and boredom

Fishermen of all beaches
Send me all you have
Empty nets and seasickness

Peasants of every land
Send me all you have
Flowers rags
Mutilated breasts
Ripped up bellies
And torn out nails
To my address . . . any café
Any street in the world
I'm preparing a *huge file*
About human suffering
To present to God
Once it's signed by the lips of the hungry
And the eyelids of those still waiting
You wretched everywhere
What I fear most is
God could be *illiterate*

Shauqi Abu Shaqra (*1935–*)

THE FAN AND THE OBSERVATORY DOME

The world, as fine as a razor-blade, cuts my chin. The police chase me like fish.

I play, making a paper star. The Magi follow its light. An Ethiopian servant holds my fan.

I fly on a straw towards the windows and put out the honeymoon lantern.

I climb the rays of the teeth. Incense rises from me. I carve an angel which could be eaten on the road like a raisin.

I sit like a ball outside the playground eating snow. I travel on a reed. I carry coloured eggs, fledgelings and oil.

Wearing shorts, like a notebook, I jump from the observatory dome to the planets. I open my shirt and breathe air.

I have made a lion from a stone. The gnats and the secrets of the small world will fall on it.

Unsi al-Haj (1937–)

GIRL BUTTERFLY GIRL

A girl dreamt she was a butterfly
She got up
And didn't know whether she was
A girl dreaming she was a butterfly
Or
A butterfly dreaming it was a girl

After hundreds of years
The air at night
My children,
Was a boy and girl frolicking like a butterfly
Who dreamt it was a boy and a girl
Or
A boy and a girl dreaming they were a butterfly

The wind grew strong
A butterfly
My children,
Fell to pieces outside

Samih al-Qasim (*1939–*)

THE CLOCK ON THE WALL

My city collapsed
The clock was still on the wall
Our neighbourhood collapsed
The clock was still on the wall
The street collapsed
The clock was still on the wall
The square collapsed
The clock was still on the wall
The house collapsed
The clock was still on the wall
The wall collapsed
The clock
Ticked on

Hebrew

Hebrew poetry has a continuous history of over 3,000 years, and it is obviously impossible, in a small selection, to give more than a few highlights. The three great peaks of Hebrew poetry are here mainly represented—the Bible (the titles given are editorial), the Golden Age of Spain (1000–1300) and the Zionist Renaissance. But there was no period in which Hebrew poetry was not cultivated, and in every age there was poetry of interest and value. A larger selection would include that of the Apocrypha and of the Dead Sea Scrolls; the extraordinary type called *piyyut* (a word derived from the Greek, like our English word 'poetry'), which was written in the early Middle Ages, and is almost untranslatable because of its complex allusiveness; the poetry of the epigones of the Golden Age, and the precursors of the modern age.

In a survey of the entire range of Hebrew poetry, one's impression is of continuity and unity. The Biblical experience informs the whole, despite the wide variety of language, forms and mood. Even a modern poet like Bialik, expressing an alienation and unease foreign to the Bible, is imbued with the language of the Bible and its Talmudic commentaries, so that the Biblical élan is present in counterpoint and tension with moods of uncertainty and irony. In the Bible, poetry—as opposed to the plain prose of the narrative sections—is inspired utterance; there is no 'speaking in the language of current discourse', but a well-defined poetic diction, which by its headlong rhythms and esoteric expression signifies the presence of ecstasy, abnormal perception, even magic. This ability to move into another psychical dimension arose from a consciousness of salvation and election, and of living in the broad stream of *Heilsgeschichte*. In Spain, the poetic diction becomes conscious and refined; it is based on Arabic models and backed up by systematised theory. Yet the Biblical impetus is still there, and in Judah ha-Levi and Solomon ibn Gabirol we have new Hebrew prophets whose 'fountain of the tongue' has been loosed. And in the modern movement the utterance, while closer to ordinary language, has again become vatic and almost rule-free, but with the pathos of search, rather than the carelessness of authority. The burden of the long centuries lies on the modern Hebrew poet, even in his effort to throw it off. He must come to terms, somehow, with Jewish destiny, and the overwhelming presence of the Bible. He must make sense of his history, even the senseless horror of the Holocaust. The revival of the Jewish people as a nation must be put into its perspective, for the very fact that the poet writes in the new, living Hebrew, rather than in any of the languages which have deeply impressed the Jewish mind (Greek, Arabic, Spanish, German, English), shows that there is a continuity of culture from the very earliest times to the present—a continuity which is not fossilisation or stagnation, but a living, developing tradition.

Biblical poetry is religious (with some exceptions, for example the love songs of *The Song of Songs*, which were only later turned by exegetes into religious allegories). In Spain a Hebrew secular poetry arose, side by side with religious poetry. Modern Hebrew poetry is mainly secular, social and personal, but with constant religious overtones, whether of commitment or protest. Judaism is a religion which is never far removed from the secular, because of its insistence on the value of this world as a field of human responsibility. *Isaiah* can be a source of knowledge about female adornments, and the *Psalms* about musical instruments. The interplay between the religious and the secular is one of the perennial features of Hebrew poetry.

English literature, in the past, has received a powerful impetus from languages have many similarities in movement, syntax and consonantal pattern. The Authorised Version is the greatest translation of all, not for reasons of accuracy (it is full of errors) and not, as some have alleged, because it transcends the original, but because it captures so well the rhythm and vigour of the Hebrew. Nevertheless there is always room for new translations of the Hebrew Bible, and some modern versions have excellent qualities, and draw the modern mind closer to the source. In the translation of modern Hebrew verse some fine work has been done. For medieval Hebrew poetry, especially the religious poetry, one has to rely in the main on rather dated Victorian translations, and there is a wide-open field here for a translator of courage and confidence.

English literature, in the past, has received a powerful impetus from Hebrew poetry in translation. Post-Biblical Hebrew poetry, however, is little known to the average reader of English. It is to be hoped that the new interest in Judaism by Christians will extend to the realm of literature, and that Hebrew poetry since the first century AD will receive the attention it deserves.

THE BLESSING OF BALAAM (*10th cent. BC*)*

And when Balaam saw that it pleased the Lord to bless Israel, he went not, as at other times, to seek for enchantments, but he set his face toward the wilderness. And Balaam lifted up his eyes, and he saw Israel abiding in his tents according to their tribes; and the spirit of God came upon him. And he took up his parable, and said,

Balaam the son of Beor hath said,
  and the man whose eyes are open hath said:
he hath said, which heard the words of God,
  which saw the vision of the Almighty,
  falling into a trance, but having his eyes open:
How goodly are thy tents, O Jacob,
  thy tabernacles, O Israel!
As the valleys are they spread forth,
  as gardens by the river's side,

* See Contents List for sources of Biblical passages.

as the trees of lign aloes which the Lord hath planted,
and as cedar trees beside the waters.
He shall pour the water out of his buckets,
and his seed shall be in many waters,
and his king shall be higher than Agag,
and his kingdom shall be exalted.
God brought him forth out of Egypt;
he hath as it were the strength of an unicorn:
he shall eat up the nations his enemies,
and shall break their bones,
and pierce them through with his arrows.
He couched, he lay down as a lion,
and as a great lion: who shall stir him up?
Blessed is he that blesseth thee,
and cursed is he that curseth thee.

THE LAMENT OF DAVID FOR SAUL AND JONATHAN (*8th cent. BC*)

The beauty of Israel is slain upon thy high places:
how are the mighty fallen!
Tell it not in Gath,
publish it not in the streets of Askelon;
lest the daughters of the Philistines rejoice,
lest the daughters of the uncircumcised triumph.
Ye mountains of Gilboa,
let there be no dew, neither let there be rain,
upon you, nor fields of offerings:
for there the shield of the mighty is vilely cast away,
the shield of Saul, as though he had not been anointed with oil.
From the blood of the slain,
from the fat of the mighty,
the bow of Jonathan turned not back,
and the sword of Saul returned not empty.
Saul and Jonathan were lovely and pleasant in their lives,
and in their death they were not divided:
they were swifter than eagles,
they were stronger than lions.
Ye daughters of Israel, weep over Saul,
who clothed you in scarlet, with other delights,
who put ornaments of gold upon your apparel.
How are the mighty fallen in the midst of the battle!

O Jonathan, thou wast slain in thine high places.
I am distressed for thee, my brother Jonathan:
very pleasant hast thou been unto me:
thy love to me was wonderful,
passing the love of women.
How are the mighty fallen,
and the weapons of war perished!

NOW WILL I SING TO MY WELLBELOVED

(8th cent. BC)

Now will I sing to my wellbeloved
a song of my wellbeloved touching his vineyard.
My wellbeloved hath a vineyard
in a very fruitful hill:
and he fenced it, and gathered out the stones thereof,
and planted it with the choicest vine,
and built a tower in the midst of it,
and also made a winepress therein:
and he looked that it should bring forth grapes,
and it brought forth wild grapes.

And now, O inhabitants of Jerusalem, and men of Judah,
judge, I pray you, betwixt me and my vineyard.
What could have been done more to my vineyard,
that I have not done in it?
wherefore, when I looked that it should bring forth grapes,
brought it forth wild grapes?

And now go to; I will tell you
what I will do to my vineyard:
I will take away the hedge thereof, and it shall be eaten up;
and break down the wall thereof, and it shall be trodden down:
and I will lay it waste: it shall not be pruned, nor digged;
but there shall come up briers and thorns:
I will also command the clouds
that they rain no rain upon it.
For the vineyard of the Lord of hosts is the house of Israel,
and the men of Judah his pleasant plant:
and he looked for judgment, but behold oppression;
for righteousness, but behold a cry.

COMFORT YE, COMFORT YE MY PEOPLE
(6th cent. BC)

Comfort ye, comfort ye my people,
  saith your God.
Speak ye comfortably to Jerusalem,
  and cry unto her,
that her warfare is accomplished,
  that her iniquity is pardoned:
for she hath received of the Lord's hand
  double for all her sins.

The voice of him that crieth in the wilderness,
Prepare ye the way of the Lord,
  make straight in the desert a highway for our God.
Every valley shall be exalted,
  and every mountain and hill shall be made low:
and the crooked shall be made straight,
  and the rough places plain:
and the glory of the Lord shall be revealed,
  and all flesh shall see it together:
  for the mouth of the Lord hath spoken it.

The voice said, Cry.
  And he said, What shall I cry?
All flesh is grass,
  and all the goodliness thereof is as the flower of the field:
the grass withereth, the flower fadeth:
  because the spirit of the Lord bloweth upon it:
surely the people is grass.
The grass withereth, the flower fadeth:
  but the word of our God shall stand for ever. . . .

Behold, the Lord God will come with strong hand,
  and his arm shall rule for him:
behold, his reward is with him,
  and his work before him.
He shall feed his flock like a shepherd:
  he shall gather the lambs with his arm,
and carry them in his bosom,
  and shall gently lead those that are with young.

THE HEAVENS AND THE LAW (*?7th cent. BC*)

The heavens declare the glory of God;
and the firmament sheweth his handywork.
Day unto day uttereth speech,
and night unto night sheweth knowledge.
There is no speech nor language,
where their voice is not heard.
Their line is gone out through all the earth,
and their words to the end of the world.
In them hath he set a tabernacle for the sun,
which is as a bridegroom coming out of his chamber,
and rejoiceth as a strong man to run a race.
His going forth is from the end of the heaven,
and his circuit unto the ends of it:
and there is nothing hid from the heat thereof.
The law of the Lord is perfect, converting the soul:
the testimony of the Lord is sure, making wise the simple.
The statutes of the Lord are right, rejoicing the heart:
the commandment of the Lord is pure, enlightening the eyes.
The fear of the Lord is clean, enduring for ever:
the judgments of the Lord are true and righteous altogether.
More to be desired are they than gold, yea, than much fine gold:
sweeter also than honey and the honeycomb.
Moreover by them is thy servant warned:
and in keeping of them there is great reward.
Who can understand his errors?
cleanse thou me from secret faults.
Keep back thy servant also from presumptuous sins;
let them not have dominion over me:
then shall I be upright,
and I shall be innocent from the great transgression.
Let the words of my mouth, and the meditation of my heart,
be acceptable in thy sight,
O Lord, my strength, and my redeemer.

HOW MANIFOLD ARE THY WORKS! (*?7th cent. BC*)

Bless the Lord, O my soul.
O Lord my God, thou art very great;
thou art clothed with honour and majesty.

Who coverest thyself with light as with a garment:
  who stretchest out the heavens like a curtain:
who layeth the beams of his chambers in the waters:
who maketh the clouds his chariot:
  who walketh upon the wings of the wind:
who maketh his angels spirits;
  his ministers a flaming fire:
who laid the foundations of the earth,
  that it should not be removed for ever.
Thou coveredst it with the deep as with a garment:
  the waters stood above the mountains.
At thy rebuke they fled;
  at the voice of thy thunder they hasted away.
They go up by the mountains; they go down by the valleys
  unto the place which thou hast founded for them.
Thou hast set a bound that they may not pass over;
  that they turn not again to cover the earth.
He sendeth the springs into the valleys,
  which run among the hills.
They give drink to every beast of the field:
  the wild asses quench their thirst.
By them shall the fowls of the heaven have their habitation,
  which sing among the branches.
He watereth the hills from his chambers:
  the earth is satisfied with the fruit of thy works.
He causeth the grass to grow for the cattle,
  and herb for the service of man:
that he may bring forth food out of the earth;
  and wine that maketh glad the heart of man,
and oil to make his face to shine,
  and bread which strengtheneth man's heart.
The trees of the Lord are full of sap;
  the cedars of Lebanon, which he hath planted;
where the birds make their nests:
  as for the stork, the fir trees are her house.
The high hills are a refuge for the wild goats;
  and the rocks for the conies.
He appointed the moon for seasons:
  the sun knoweth his going down.
Thou makest darkness, and it is night:
  wherein all the beasts of the forests do creep forth.
The young lions roar after their prey,
  and seek their meat from God.

The sun ariseth, they gather themselves together,
and lay them down in their dens.
Man goeth forth unto his work
and to his labour until the evening.
O Lord, how manifold are thy works!
in wisdom hast thou made them all:
the earth is full of thy riches.
So is this great and wide sea,
wherein are things creeping innumerable,
both small and great beasts.
There go the ships:
there is that leviathan, whom thou hast made to play therein.
These wait all upon thee;
that thou mayest give them their meat in due season.
That thou givest them they gather:
thou openest thine hand, they are filled with good.
Thou hidest thy face, they are troubled:
thou takest away their breath, they die,
and return to their dust.
Thou sendest forth thy spirit, they are created:
and thou renewest the face of the earth.
The glory of the Lord shall endure for ever:
the Lord shall rejoice in his works.
He looketh on the earth, and it trembleth:
he toucheth the hills, and they smoke.
I will sing unto the Lord as long as I live:
I will sing praise to my God while I have my being.
My meditation of him shall be sweet:
I will be glad in the Lord.
Let the sinners be consumed out of the earth,
and let the wicked be no more.
Bless thou the Lord, O my soul.
Praise ye the Lord.

A PILGRIM'S SONG. FOR DAVID

(?6th cent. BC)

When they said to me
'To the house of God we will go'
Gladly
In your gates, Jerusalem,
Our feet were standing.

Jerusalem, newly built,
Crafted
Together.

There came
The families,
The families of God,
Israel's witnesses;
To worship the name of God.

There were thrones,
Thrones,
For the house of David,
For Judgement.

The peace of Jerusalem,
Ask;
Serene be your lovers.

At peace in your wealth,
Tranquil in your palaces.

My friends and brothers
Through me
Wish you peace.

For the house of God,
How well
I wish you.

LOVE SONG (*?5th cent. BC*)

How beautiful your steps in sandals
    O prince's daughter!
The curves of your thighs
    are like the links of a chain
    a craftsman's handiwork
your navel is a round goblet
    with no lack of mingled wine
your belly is a pile of wheat
    surrounded by roses
your two breasts are like two fawns
    twins of a gazelle

your neck is like a tower of ivory
your eyes are pools in Heshbon
beside the gate of Bath-rabbim
your nose is like the tower of Lebanon
looking towards Damascus
your head on you is like Carmel
and the locks of your head like purple:
they keep a king prisoner.

How beautiful and how pleasant
is love among delights!
This figure of yours is slim as a palm-tree
and your breasts are as bunches of grapes.
I said: I will climb up the palm-tree
and take hold of its branches
and your breasts shall be
like bunches of the vine
and the sweet smell of your nose
like apples
and your palate
like the best wine
gliding as my caress
straight down
easing the lips of sleepers.

OUT OF THE WHIRLWIND (*?5th cent. BC*)

Then God answered Job out of the whirlwind:

Who is this whose ignorant words
smear my design with darkness?
Stand up now like a man;
I will question you: come, instruct me.

Where were you when I planned the earth?
Tell me, if you are wise.
Do you know who took its dimensions,
measuring its length with a cord?
What were its pillars built on?
Who laid down its cornerstone,
while the morning stars burst into singing
and the angels shouted for joy?

Were you there when I stopped the waters,
as they issued gushing from the womb;
when I wrapped the ocean in clouds
and swaddled the sea in shadows;
when I closed it in with barriers
and set its boundaries, saying:
'Here you may come, but no farther;
here shall your proud waves break'?

Have you ever commanded morning
or guided dawn to its place—
to hold the corners of the sky
and shake off the last few stars?
All things are touched with colour;
the whole world is changed.

Have you walked through the depths of the ocean
or dived to the floor of the sea?
Have you stood at the gates of death
or looked through the gates of doom?
Have you seen to the edge of the universe?
Speak up, if you have such knowledge. . . .

OLD AGE (*3rd cent. BC*)

Remember now thy Creator in the days of thy youth,
while the evil days come not,
nor the years draw nigh, when thou shalt say,
I have no pleasure in them;
while the sun, or the light,
or the moon, or the stars, be not darkened,
nor the clouds return after the rain:
in the day when the keepers of the house shall tremble,
and the strong men shall bow themselves,
and the grinders cease because they are few,
and those that look out of the windows be darkened,
and the doors shall be shut in the streets,
when the sound of the grinding is low,
and he shall rise up at the voice of the bird,
and all the daughters of musick shall be brought low;
also when they shall be afraid of that which is high,
and fears shall be in the way,

and the almond tree shall flourish,
  and the grasshopper shall be a burden,
  and desire shall fail:
because man goeth to his long home,
  and the mourners go about the streets:
or ever the silver cord be loosed,
  or the golden bowl be broken,
or the pitcher be broken at the fountain,
  or the wheel broken at the cistern.
Then shall the dust return to the earth as it was:
  and the spirit shall return unto God who gave it.

from the Prayer-Book

from the EIGHTEEN BLESSINGS (*1st cent. AD*)

You that feed the living in your kindness
Bring the dead to life in your great mercy
Support the fallen
And heal the sick
Free those who are bound
And keep faith with those who sleep in the dust—
Who is like you, Master of strong deeds,
And who can equal you,
King who kills and makes alive
And causes salvation to sprout?

from the BLESSINGS OF 'HEAR, O ISRAEL' (*1st cent. AD*)

Our Father,
Merciful Father,
The Merciful One,
Have mercy on us,
And put into our hearts
To understand and to discern,
To mark, learn and teach,
To heed, do and fulfil
All the words of the teaching of your Torah
With love.

Amittai ben Shephatiah (8th–9th cent.)

from THE DAY OF ATONEMENT SERVICE

Lord, I remember, and am sore amazed
  To see each city standing in her state,
And God's own city to the low grave razed;
  Yet in all time we look to Thee and wait.

Send us Thy mercy, O Redeemer! Make,
  O thou my soul, to Him thy mournful plaint;
And crave compassion for my people's sake;
  Each head is weary and each heart is faint.

O Thou who hearest weeping, healest woe,
  Our tears within Thy vase of crystal store;
Save us, and all Thy dread decrees forgo,
  For unto Thee our eyes turn evermore.

Solomon ibn Gabirol (1020–c. 1057)

from THE ROYAL CROWN

Thine is the existence from the shadow of whose light every being was created,
Of which we say, in His shadow we live.
Thine are the two worlds between which Thou hast set a boundary,
The first for deeds and the second for reward.
Thine is the reward which Thou for the righteous hast stored up and hidden,
Yea, Thou sawest it was goodly and didst hide it.

Thou existest, but hearing of ear cannot reach Thee, or vision of eye,
Nor shall the How have sway over Thee, nor the Wherefore and Whence.
Thou existest, but for Thyself and for none other with Thee.
Thou existest, and before Time began Thou wast,
And without place Thou didst abide.
Thou existest, and Thy secret is hidden and who shall attain to it?
'So deep, so deep, who can discover it?'

so deep: cf. Ecclesiastes 7: 24.

Thou art great, and compared with Thy greatness all greatness is
humbled and all excess diminished.
Incalculably great is Thy being,
Superber than the starry heaven,
Beyond and above all grandeur,
'And exalted beyond all blessing and praise.'

Thou art the God of gods, and the Lord of lords,
Ruler of beings celestial and terrestrial,
For all creatures are Thy witnesses
And by the glory of this Thy name, every creature is bound to
Thy service.
Thou art God, and all things formed are Thy servants and
worshippers.
Yet is not Thy glory diminished by reason of those that worship
aught beside Thee,
For the yearning of them all is to draw nigh Thee,
But they are like the blind,
Setting their faces forward on the King's highway,
Yet still wandering from the path.

Moses ibn Ezra (*c. 1055–1135*)

from TARSHISH

By friendship's waters, with a chosen few,
Noble of soul, of jocund heart and true,
Drink, to the sound of laughter, lute and song,
And joy to precious talk of old and new.

Come, friends, within—the cheerful cup to drain;
The world is bleak, without—November's rain
Beats on chill fields, of their green mantles stript,
And boughs are bare, and furrows void of grain.

Drink with me, till the magic of the wine
Makes this a palace-court, where we recline;
Yon sound of water is the fountain's plash—
And hark! The nightingale in song divine!

and exalted: cf. Nehemiah 9: 5.

Drink! Whilst the rain-drenched earth for summer yearns,
And shivering forests dream that spring returns,
The ruby wine glows in its crystal cup
Like flame of God, within the hail that burns.

Mark how the lightings of the cup leap forth
To smite my serried sorrows; floods of mirth
Beat down my troubles, as the floods of heaven
Level the ridges of the furrowed earth.

O spirit, ransomed of the bowl, burn bright
For these, my friends! Shine through the starless night,
A beacon to guide hitherward their joys
And put the shadows of their cares to flight!

Come, Ophrah, fill my cup—but not with wine.
The splendor of thine eyes therein let shine;
So shall the draught thou pour'st this night in Spain,
Bear to far lands and days, thy fame—and mine!

Drink, friends, the days of wintry chill are done;
Earth thrills to the embraces of the sun
And drops the mask of age. O'er hill and dale,
The green-clad hosts of youth march swiftly on.

*

A man should remember, from time to time,
That he is occupied with death,
That he is taken a little further
On a journey every day
Though he thinks he is at rest,
Like a ship's passenger lounging on deck,
Being carried on by the wings of the wind.

Judah ha-Levi (c. 1075–c. 1141)

ISRAEL'S COMPLAINT

My love, have you forgotten how you lay between my breasts?
Why have you now sold me for ever to those who enslave me?
Did I not follow you through an unsown land;

Witness Seir, Mount Paran, Sin and Sinai?
How can you share my glory among those who are not mine,
When my love was yours, and your delight was in me?
Expelled towards Seir, thrust back towards Kedar,
Tried in the furnace of Greece, subjected to Persian tyranny,
Since I shall give you my love, give of your strength to me.
There is no saviour but you; no prisoner of hope but I.

DIALOGUE BETWEEN ISRAEL AND GOD

My friend, the days of my affliction have compelled me
To dwell in the scorpion's and the viper's company,
In captivity.
Have mercy on me.

My soul despairs of the rise of the dawn,
To wait and hope more after morn.
What can I say, O my lover, when
Edom is in my citadel, born free,
And I am subject to the Arab and the Admoni,
Who oppress me,
Like the dregs of humanity?

My name which once stood supreme
Has become, in strangers' mouths, a mark of shame.
The Ammonite, the Moabite, and Hagar's line
Glorify themselves in visions because of me,
Despising the word of God and Palmoni,
Enticing me
By false prophecy.

Come let us return to the gardens, my friend,
To gather there both lilies and nard.
How can the doe live with the jackals' herd?
Awake to my harp, and my bells' harmony.
Yearn for my pomegranate, my wine that is spicy.
Gazelle, flee
Back to my sanctuary.

Seir, Edom, the Admoni: Christendom.
Kedar, Hagar's line: Islam.
Palmoni: 'that certain one' who gives the date of Israel's redemption (cf. Daniel 8: 13).

'Be ready for the end, even if it delays;
For I have not put another nation in your place.
You have chosen me. You also are my choice.
Which other people in the north, or the south, is to me
Like my son, bound as a sacrifice, my power's primacy,
Who loves me?
Which god is like me?'

Abraham ibn Ezra (1089–1164)

OUT OF LUCK

'Twas sure a luckless planet
  That ruled when I was born—
I hope for fame and fortune,
  I have but loss and scorn.

An evil fate pursues me
  With unrelenting spite;
If I sold lamps and candles,
  The sun would shine all night.

I cannot, cannot prosper
  No matter what I try—
Were selling shrouds my business,
  No man would ever die!

Anonymous (12th cent.)

ADON OLAM

Reigned the universe's Master, ere were earthly things begun;
When his mandate all created Ruler was the name He won;
And alone He'll rule tremendous when all things are past and gone.
He no equal has, nor consort, He, the singular and lone,
Has no end and no beginning; His the sceptre, might, and throne,
He's my God and living Saviour, rock to whom in need I run;
He's my banner and my refuge, fount of weal when called upon;
In his hand I place my spirit, at nightfall and rise of sun,
And therewith my body also; God's my God—I fear no one.

Adon olam: Lord of the universe.

Immanuel Frances (1618–1710)

EPITAPH ON A DWARF

This stone commemorates his name.
This grave received his tiny frame.
He's food for worms. To be precise,
One worm, one mouthful, would suffice.

Chaim Nachman Bialik (1873–1934)

WHEN THE DAYS GROW LONG

from the visions of the later prophets

When the days grow long, each one an eternity,
Each one as alike as yesterday and the day before it,
Just days, without much pleasure and filled with dullness,
And men and animals are seized by boredom,
A man will go out at sunset to walk on the seashore,
And see that the sea has not fled,
And he will yawn,
And go to the Jordan, and it will not flow back,
And he will yawn,
And see the Pleiades and Orion, not budging from their places,
And he will yawn;
And men and animals will sit, bored, together,
With their lives weighing heavily upon them,
And men will pluck the hairs of their head in distraction,
And cats will lose their whiskers.

Then the longings will rise,
Rise of themselves—like mushrooms raising a stench
In a decaying plank of wood.
The longings will fill all cracks and crevices,
As lice fill rags.
And when a man comes back to his hut for his supper,
And dips his crust and his salt herring in vinegar,
He will long,
He will drink his cup of murky, lukewarm water

the sea has not fled: cf. Psalm 114: 3 and Exodus 14: 21.

And he will long;
He will take off his shoes and socks by his bed,
And he will long;
Man and animal both will sit in longing:
The man will wail in his dreams from his vast longing,
While the cat, on the tin roof, yells and scratches.
Then the hunger will come,
Growing, increasing, like nothing before it,
Not hunger for bread or vision, but for the Messiah.

And early in the morning, with the sun not quite showing,
The man, exhausted, shaken, glutted with dreams and empty in spirit,
The webs of an angry sleep still on his eyelids,
The night's dread in his bones,
Will get up from his bed, from the darkness of his hut,
And with the cat still wailing, its nails
Still grating on his brain and his nerves,
He will hurry to his window and wipe off the steam,
Or he will get up and go to the entrance of his shack
And, shading his eyes with his hand, look out, blearily, fevered
And hungry for salvation, towards the little path behind his yard,
Towards the slope of the rubbish-tip opposite his home,
Looking for the Messiah;
And under the blanket, the woman will wake, uncovering herself,
Her hair all wild, her body chafed, and her spirit murky,
And, pulling her shrivelled nipple from her baby's mouth,
She will turn and listen very carefully:
Isn't the Messiah coming?
Hasn't anyone heard his donkey braying?
And the infant will look out of its cot,
And the mouse will peep out of its hole:
Isn't the Messiah coming?
Has no one heard his donkey's jingling bell?
And the maid, heating the kettle on the stove,
Will stick out her sooty face:
Isn't the Messiah coming?
Has no one heard the sound of his horn?

David Vogel (1891–1944)

TO HIS DAUGHTER

Through countless generations
You've come to stay with me.
You are very young
And just sleep all day.

From your half-lit past a world will grow for you,
With bears and lambs and fabulous creatures,
And laughter will light up your slumber.

Already in your flesh you are conceiving me,
And when you wake, my darling,
I shall go with you to the farthest shores of life,
I and my father and the first man.

Uri Zvi Greenberg (1894–)

WITH MY GOD THE BLACKSMITH

In all revelations my days flare like chapters of prophecy.
Mass of metal, my flesh between them awaits the fire.
Above looms my God the blacksmith, hammering terribly.
Each wound carved in me by Time splits into a fissure,
Sparking out inward fire in flashes of memory.

My fate controls me, till day has sunk in the west.
When this battered mass, thrown back on the bed, lies still,
With a gaping wound for a mouth, which none has dressed,
Naked I say to my God: Thou hast wrought thy will.
Now it is night: of thy goodness, let us rest.

S. Shalom (1904–)

Guard me, O God, from hating man my brother,
Guard me from recalling what, from my early youth, to me he did.
When all the stars in my sky are quenched, within me my soul's
voice grows mute—
When I am overcome by disaster, let me not lay bare his guilt.

For he is my hidden dwelling-place, in him am I reflected again,
Like a wayfarer from the planets, beholding his face in a pool.
What use is all my struggle, to whom shall I wail out the pain—
If hollow, blemished is my distant night's moon?

When the gates are locked, darkness over the city reclining,
And emptied of love, rejected, I am bound to my rock:
Permit me to see in him a spark, only a spark still shining,
That I may know that in myself, in me, all is not yet snuffed out.

Leah Goldberg (1911–)

Will there yet come days of forgiveness and grace,
When you walk in the field as the innocent wayfarer walks,
And the soles of your feet the clover leaves caress,
Though stubble will sting you, sweet will be their stalks.

Or rain will overtake you, its thronging drops tapping
On your shoulder, your chest, your throat, your gentle head bowed,
And you walk in the wet field, the quiet in you expanding
Like light in the hem of a cloud.

And you will breathe the odor of furrow, breathing and quiet,
And you will see mirrored in the gold puddle the sun above,
And simple will be these things and life, permitted to touch,
Permitted, permitted to love.

Slowly you will walk in the field. Alone. Unscorched by flame
Of conflagrations on roads that bristled with horror and blood.
Again
You will be peaceful in heart, humble and bending
Like one of the grasses, like one of man.

Yehuda Amichai (1924–)

from THREE SYNAGOGUES

Spring softness in the synagogue yard,
A tree in blossom and four little girls playing
In between their lessons in the holy tongue

In front of a memorial wall made of marble:
Levi, Sonnino, Cassuto and others
In straight lines as in a newspaper
Or Torah scroll.

And the tree isn't there in remembrance of anything
Except remembrance of this spring,
Arrivederci, Our Father,
Buona notte, Our King.

There are tears in the eyes
Like dry crumbs in the pocket
From a cake that once was.

Buona notte, Sonnino,
Arrivederci, six million,
And little girls, and tree, and crumbs.

Haim Be'er (1945–)

THE ORDER OF THE GENERATIONS

I here am a child
Of six generations
Under the sun of Southern Syria,
My mother and aunts
In the World War
Eat durra
And go around looking for a little
Colonial merchandise,
Girls lingering in poverty
And in hard want
Wait for General Allenby,
A leader more like Wellington
Than Napoleon,
An Englishman spending
His last ten years
In the study of bird life
And in long journeys,
Alights from his horse at the Jaffa Gate
And in the Street of the Patriarch
Gentiles say to them

Return, return, O Shulamite,
Eyes enough to trouble,
Return and let us look at you.
And they run away and reply
Why should you look at the Shulamite?
Girls starving in check dresses
Reminding them
Of Mistress Mary, oriental woman,
In Terra Israel,
And I a child
In the world of deeds build up little by little
A family tree,
Always like one going
In a joyful light.
There is nothing in life more fascinating than this,
To live in the Crusader East
And see the sheep scattered on the hills
And only the Lamb of God
Stands weeping,
Dominus flevit, the lord (Adonis,
Baal) master of the beauty of Byzantium
Stands weeping
On the Mount of Olives,
Coming from Bethany, House of Poverty
And in the threshingplace of Araunah the Jebusite
Already the mother of Zion hears
Words of a husband to a wife
And laughs,
Praise is comely.

Shulamite: cf. Song of Songs 6: 13 (AV).
Araunah: cf. 2 Samuel 24: 16.
praise is comely: cf. Psalm 147: 1.

Contributors

HARRY AVELING. Born in Sydney 1942; MA in Indonesian and Malayan Studies, Diploma in Anthropology. Has taught at Monash (Melbourne), Universiti Sains Malaysia (Penang); now Senior Lecturer in Southeast Asian Studies at Murdoch (Perth). Has translated extensively from modern Indonesian and Malay literature. Took *sannyas* from Bhagwan Shree Rajneesh 1977 and is now known as Swami Anand Haridas.

PETER AVERY. Born 1923; BA in Persian, London, MA Cambridge. Since 1957 University Lecturer in Persian, Cambridge; since 1965 Fellow of King's College. Visiting Scholar, Ann Arbor, Michigan, 1962; Visiting Professor, Harvard, 1965 and Chicago, 1968. Books: *Hafiz: Thirty Poems* with John Heath-Stubbs (1952); *Modern Iran* (1965, 1967); *Advanced Persian Reader* (1965); *The Ruba'iyat of Omar Khayyam* with John Heath-Stubbs (1979). Articles in journals and *Encyclopaedia Britannica.*

TANER BAYBARS. Born in Cyprus 1936 but has lived most of his life in England. *To Catch a Falling Man*, poems (1963); *Narcissus in a Dry Pool,* poems (1978); also a novel and an autobiography. Translations from Nazım Hikmet: *Selected Poems* (1967), *The Moscow Symphony* (1970), *The Day Before Tomorrow* (1972).

KEITH BOSLEY. Born 1937, read French at Reading and Caen. *The Possibility of Angels*, poems (1969); *Dark Summer*, poems (1976); *Stations*, poems (1979); many books of translations include *Finnish Folk Poetry: Epic* (1977—awarded Finnish State Prize 1978), *Mallarmé: The Poems* (1977); see also Vietnamese and Hebrew Sources.

PETER DENT. Born in London 1938, graduated in English and Education; schoolteacher. His poems have appeared widely in Europe and America: *Proxima Centauri* (1972); *The Time Between* (1974); *Surfaces* (1975); *Focus Germanus* (1978).

EDWIN GEROW. Born in Ohio 1931; early studies in Philosophy (BA Chicago), French, Linguistics. Read Sanskrit at Chicago, Paris, Madras; PhD Chicago 1962. Has taught Sanskrit at Chicago, Rochester, Columbia, Washington; since 1973 Frank L. Sulzberger Professor of Indic Civilization and Professor of Sanskrit at Chicago. Has published many articles on Sanskrit literature, poetics and teaching in leading journals, *Encyclopedia Americana*, *Encyclopaedia Britannica*, *The Penguin Companion to Literature*, *The Literatures of India: an Introduction* (1974) and elsewhere.

HARRY GUEST. Born 1932, read Modern Languages at Cambridge and the Sorbonne. Teaches French in England, lectured in English Literature at Yokohama. Books include *Arrangements*, *The Cutting-*

Room, *A House against the Night*, poems (1968, 1970, 1976); a novel, and *Post-War Japanese Poetry* (1972).

SYED SHAMSUL HAQ. Born in Rangpur, Bengal, 1935; has worked in the BBC Eastern Service. Has published six collections of poems, four of short stories, three plays and six novels in Bengali. Was the youngest recipient of the Bangla Academy Award. See also Bengali Sources.

JOHN HEATH-STUBBS. Born 1918, read English at Oxford. Gregory Fellow in Poetry at Leeds 1952–5, Visiting Professor of English at Alexandria 1955–8, at Michigan 1960–1; now lectures in English Literature at the College of St Mark and St John, Chelsea, London. Has published many books of verse, plays, translations and criticism, including *Selected Poems* (1965) and *Artorius* (1973–4). Received the Queen's Gold Medal for Poetry 1973.

GEORGE HEWITT. Born 1949, MA in Classics, Dip. Ling. Cambridge; specialist in Caucasian linguistics. Has been a British Council exchange student at Tbilisi State University, Georgia, and a Research Assistant at Cambridge; has a Wardrop Scholarship from Oxford for a contrastive study of Georgian and Abkhaz. Has published articles on Abkhaz, Adyghe and Armenian.

JUDITH JACOB. Author of a Khmer grammar and dictionary, and of various articles on Old and Modern Khmer, is Lecturer in Cambodian Studies at the School of Oriental and African Studies, London.

USA KANCHANAVATEE. Born in Bangkok 1953, read French at Lancaster; now doing research at University College, London. Has published poems and stories in Thai journals.

ZAIRA KHIBA. Born in Abkhazia, speaks several Caucasian languages as well as Russian and German. Has done postgraduate work at the Georgian Academy of Sciences, Tbilisi; is now married to George Hewitt and raising a family.

FRANCIS LANDY. Born in London 1947, read English at Cambridge; now doing research on *The Song of Songs* at Sussex. Has published poems here and there. See also Ugaritic Source.

PETER H. LEE. Born in Seoul, Korea; educated in United States and Europe; Professor of Korean and Comparative Literature at Hawaii; Guggenheim Fellow 1975. Latest books include *Songs of Flying Dragons* (1975). See also Korean Sources.

HYAM MACCOBY. Born 1924; Exhibitioner in Classics and MA in English, Balliol; a schoolteacher for many years, now Librarian of Leo Baeck College, London. Books: *Revolution in Judea: Jesus and the Jewish Resistance* (1973); *The Day God Laughed*, anthology of the Talmud (1978); *Jewish-Christian Medieval Disputations* (1978); a study of T. S. Eliot is forthcoming.

ALAN MARSHFIELD. Born 1933, read English at London; department head at a London comprehensive. *Mistress*, poems (1972); *Dragonfly*, poems (1972); work in many periodicals, anthologies, radio programmes; translates from Greek, Latin, French, Finnish.

DAVID MATTHEWS. Born in London 1942; BA London in Classics, PhD London in Urdu Literature; Lecturer in Urdu and Nepali at School of Oriental and African Studies, London. Publications: *Anthology of Classical Urdu Love Lyrics* with C. Shackle (1972) and articles on Urdu and Nepali literature. A biography of Sayid Ahmad Khan is forthcoming.

EDWIN MORGAN. Born in Glasgow 1920; Titular Professor of English at Glasgow. Books include *The Second Life*, poems (1968); *Instamatic Poems* (1972); *From Glasgow to Saturn*, poems (1973); *The New Divan*, poems (1977); a collection of essays, and many translations, of which *Rites of Passage* (1976) is a selection.

NGUYEN THI CHAN QUYNH. Born in Hanoi, graduated from the Ecole Supérieure des Industries Textiles, Lyon; left industry for health reasons and worked in the BBC Far Eastern Service for over five years, during which she collaborated anonymously in *The War Wife* (see Vietnamese Sources). Is now studying and teaching at the Sorbonne.

JOHN OKELL. Born 1934; MA Lit. Hum. Oxford; Lecturer in Burmese at the School of Oriental and African Studies, London. Books: *A Reference Grammar of Colloquial Burmese* (1969); *A Guide to the Romanization of Burmese* (1971); many articles. Working on a Burmese-English dictionary and a new beginners' course in the language.

A. K. RAMANUJAN. Born in Mysore, India; Professor of Dravidian Studies at Chicago. Has published two books of poems in Kannada, three in English—*The Striders*, *Relations*, *Selected Poems* (1966, 1971, 1976)—and three works of translation—*The Interior Landscape* from Tamil (see Tamil Sources), *Speaking of Śiva* from Kannada (1972) and a novel from Kannada; has contributed to *The Literatures of India: an Introduction* (1974).

DONALD RAYFIELD. Born 1942; Lecturer in Russian at Queen Mary College, London. Has studied Georgian in Georgia, which he visits regularly. He is concerned to arouse interest in Georgian literature, and is currently preparing further translations. Publications: *Chekhov: the Evolution of his Art* (1975), *The Dream of Lhasa: The Life of Nikolay Przhevalsky, Explorer of Central Asia* (1976), articles on Mandelstam.

PETER SHERWOOD. Born in Budapest 1948; BA, Dip. Ling. London; Lecturer in Hungarian at the School of Slavonic and East European Studies, London. Has published articles on Uralic culture and linguistics and translations of Hungarian literature in Hungarian, British and American journals.

SHUI CHIEN-TUNG. Born in China's far west 1921; has taught Chinese literature at Sinkiang, Shanghai and Hong Kong Universities; now works in the BBC Far Eastern Service. Has published poems, novels and other prose in Chinese with a Central Asian background; collaborated with Bernard Martin in *Makers of China* (1972) and contributed calligraphy to Arthur Cooper's *Li Po and Tu Fu* (see Chinese Sources).

ABDULLAH AL-UDHARI and G. B. H. WIGHTMAN. Co-translators of *Birds through a Ceiling of Alabaster* (see Arabic Sources) and co-editors of *TR*, an Anglo-Arab literary arts magazine. Abdullah al-Udhari is Lecturer in Arabic at the Central London Polytechnic.

GARBIS YESSAYAN. BA London; Armenian studies under Hagop Oshagan and Shahan R. Berberian at the Sorbonne. Former headmaster, Armenian Schools, Cyprus; now teaches at Stationers' Company's School, London, and lectures in Western Armenian at the Central London Polytechnic. London correspondent to many Armenian papers; writes and lectures on education and Western Armenian literature.

Sources

CHINESE

THE BOOK OF ODES: Arthur Cooper, 'From the Shi King' in *Agenda*, London, 1975; reprinted by permission of Arthur Cooper and the Editor of *Agenda*. Ezra Pound, *The Classic Anthology Defined by Confucius*, London, 1955; reprinted by permission of Faber & Faber Ltd; published in the USA by Harvard University Press; All Rights Reserved.

SONGS OF THE SOUTH: David Hawkes, *Ch'u Tz'u: The Songs of the South: an ancient Chinese anthology*, Oxford; © Oxford University Press 1959; reprinted by permission of Oxford University Press.

NINETEEN OLD POEMS: *Ku Shih Yuan* (*Fountain of Ancient Poems*), Shanghai, 1969.

T'ao Ch'ien: William Acker, *T'ao the Hermit*, Thames & Hudson, London, 1962.

Hsieh Ling-yün and Shen Yüeh: William McNaughton (ed.), *Chinese Literature: an anthology*, Rutland (Vermont) and Tokyo, 1974; reprinted by permission of Charles E. Tuttle Co., Inc.

Wang Wei: C. H. Kwôck and Vincent McHugh, *Why I Live on the Mountain*, San Francisco, 1958; reprinted by permission of Golden Mountain Press.

Li Po: Ezra Pound, *Personae*, Copyright 1926 by Ezra Pound/*The Translations of Ezra Pound*, 1953; reprinted by permission of New Directions Publishing Corporation, New York and Faber & Faber Ltd, London. *Li Po and Tu Fu*, trans. Arthur Cooper, Harmondsworth (Penguin Classics, 1973), pp. 143–45. Copyright © Arthur Cooper, 1973; reprinted by permission of Penguin Books Ltd.

Tu Fu: *Li Po and Tu Fu* (q.v.), pp. 167–68 and 231–33.

Han-shan: Gary Snyder, *Riprap & Cold Mountain Poems*, Four Seasons Foundation, San Francisco/*A Range of Poems*, Fulcrum Press, London; Copyright © 1966 Gary Snyder.

Han Yü: *Poems of the Late T'ang*, trans. A. C. Graham, Harmondsworth (Penguin Classics, 1965), p. 74; Copyright © A. C. Graham, 1965; reprinted by permission of Penguin Books Ltd.

Po Chü-i and Yüan Chen: *Translations from the Chinese*, trans. Arthur Waley, Copyright 1919 and renewed 1947 by Arthur Waley/Arthur Waley, *Chinese Poems*, 1946; reprinted by permission of Alfred A. Knopf, Inc., New York and George Allen & Unwin (Publishers) Ltd, London.

Li Ho: C. J. Chen and Michael Bullock (eds), *Poems of Solitude*, Abelard-Schuman, London and New York, 1960; Copyright © 1960 by Jerome Ch'en and Michael Bullock; reprinted by permission of Harper & Row, Publishers, Inc.

Li Shang-yin: *T'ang Sung Shih Chü Yao* (*Anthology of the T'ang and Sung Periods*), Shanghai, 1973.

Li Yü: *Chinese Literature: an anthology* (q.v.).

Li Ch'ing-chao: *Why I Live on the Cold Mountain* (q.v.).

Hsin Ch'i-chi: 'Seven Poems translated from the Chinese' in *Agenda*, London, 1974; reprinted by permission of Arthur Cooper and the Editor of *Agenda*.
Wang Shih-fu and Kuan Han-ch'ing: *The West Chamber: A Medieval Drama*, trans. Henry H. Hart, Stanford (Calif.), 1936; Copyright 1936 by the Board of Trustees of the Leland Stanford Junior University. Copyright renewed 1964 by Henry H. Hart; reprinted by permission of Stanford University Press.
T'ang Yin: John Scott and Graham Martin, *Love & Protest*, Rapp & Whiting, London and Harper & Row, New York, 1972; reprinted by permission of André Deutsch Ltd.
Mao Tse-tung: Alan Ayling and Duncan Mackintosh, *A Folding Screen*, Andoversford, 1974; reprinted by permission of the Whittington Press.
Wen I-to: *Red Candle: selected poems by Wen I-to*, trans. Tao Tao Sanders, London, 1972, distributed in the USA by Grossman Publishers; reprinted by permission of Jonathan Cape Ltd.
Sun Yü-t'ang: *Pao Ma* (*The Rare Horses*), Hong Kong, 1963.

JAPANESE

KO-FUDOKI: William I. Elliott and Noah S. Brannen, *Wind and Pines*, Image Gallery Press, Portland (Oregon), 1977; reprinted by permission of the copyright-holders, Messrs Elliott and Brannen, and the publishers.
KINKAFU: William I. Elliott and Noah S. Brannen, *Festive Wine*, Tokyo, 1969; reprinted by permission of John Weatherhill, Inc.
Kakinomoto no Hitomaro, Yamabe no Akahito, Ôe no Chisato, Fujiwara no Toshiyuki, Ki no Tsurayuki, Ôshikôchi no Mitsune, Nôin and Jakuren: Kenneth Rexroth, *100 Poems from the Japanese*, New York, 1957; All Rights Reserved; reprinted by permission of New Directions Publishing Corporation. 'A strange old man' and 'The colored leaves' by Kakinomoto no Hitomaro and 'I wish I were close' by Yamabe no Akahito also in Eric Mottram (ed.), *The Kenneth Rexroth Reader*, Jonathan Cape, London, 1972; reprinted by permission of Laurence Pollinger Ltd.
Ôtomo no Yakamochi, Sarumaru and Mononobe Hirotari: Kenneth K. Yasuda (ed.), *Land of the Reed Plains: lyrics from the Manyôshû*, Charles E. Tuttle, Rutland (Vermont) and Tokyo, 1972 [texts].
Lady Ono no Komachi, Lady Ise, Ki no Tomonori, Saigyô, Princess Shikushi and Chikamatsu Monzaemon: Donald Keene (ed.), *Anthology of Japanese Literature*, Grove Press, New York and George Allen & Unwin, London, 1955 (Monzaemon taken from the [slightly revised] Penguin edition, Harmondsworth, 1968); reprinted by permission of Donald Keene.
'If only, when one heard': Arthur Waley, *Japanese Poetry*, Oxford, 1919 and London, 1976; reprinted by permission of George Allen & Unwin Ltd.
Zeami Motokiyo: Ezra Pound, *Translations*; Copyright © 1926, 1954 by Ezra Pound; All Rights Reserved/*The Translations of Ezra Pound*, 1953; reprinted by permission of New Directions Publishing Corporation, New York and Faber & Faber Ltd, London.
Bashô, Kyoroku, Bonchô, Onitsura, Kikaku, Chiyo, Buson, Ryôta, Chora, Issa, Shiki and Katô Shûson: Kadokawa Motoyoshi (ed.), *Haiku Saijiki* (*Haiku Almanac*), Kadokawa, Tokyo, 1957; and Tomikura Tokujirô (ed.), *Waka. Haiku. Shi* (*Songs. Haiku. Poems*), Ôbunsha, Tokyo, 1956.
Shimazaki Tôson: *Shishû* (*Selected Poems*), Haku-ô, Tokyo, 1965.
Hagiwara Sakutarô: *Shishû*, Kadokawa, Tokyo, 1968.

AINU

Arthur Waley, *The Secret History of the Mongols and Other Pieces*, London and New York, 1963; reprinted by permission of George Allen & Unwin Ltd; distributed in the USA by Barnes & Noble.

KOREAN

All pre-modern poems: Peter H. Lee, *Poems from Korea: a historical anthology*, London and Honolulu, 1974; reprinted by permission of George Allen & Unwin Ltd and University Press of Hawaii.
Pak Tu-jin: *Susŏk yŏlchŏn* (*Connected Traditions of Stones*) and *Kosan singmul* (*High Mountain Plant*), Ilchisa, Seoul, 1973.
Pak Mogwŏl: *Sisŏnjip* (*Selected Poems*), vol. 2, Samjungdang, Seoul, 1973.
Shin Kyŏng-nim: *Nongmu* (*Farmer's Dance*), Wŏlgan munhaksa, Seoul, 1973.

VIETNAMESE

Keith Bosley, *The War Wife: Vietnamese poetry*, London, 1972; reprinted (with revisions) by permission of Allison & Busby Ltd.

KHMER

REAMKER: *Reamker*, Buddhist Institute, Phnom Penh, 1937.
THE CODE OF BEHAVIOUR FOR THE YOUNG: Ch. Corbet (ed.), *Roeung Preng*, Phnom Penh, c. 1940.

PHILIPPINE

HOUSEWARMING SONG: Teófilo del Castillo y Tuazón and Buenaventura S. Medina, Jr, *Philippine Literature from Ancient Times to the Present*, Quezon City, 1966.
José Rizal: *Noli me tangere*, Manila, 1950.
José García Villa: *The Essential Villa: José García Villa's poems 55*, Albert S. Florentino, Manila, 1965.

MALAY

PANTUNS: R. J. Wilkinson and R. O. Winstedt (eds), *Pantun Mĕlayu*, Malaya Publishing House, Singapore, 1961; A. W. Hamilton (ed.), *Malay Pantuns* [texts], Donald Moore for Eastern Universities Press, Singapore, 1959.
Amir Hamzah: *Njanji Sunji* (*Lonely Songs*), Pustaka Rakjat, Jakarta, 1959.
Chairil Anwar: *Deru Tjambur Debu* (*Dust and Pain*), Pustaka Rakjat, Jakarta, 1949.
Sitor Situmorang: *Surat Kertas Hidjau* (*Letter on Green Paper*), Pustaka Rakjat, Jakarta, 1953.
Rendra: *Ballads and Blues*, Kuala Lumpur, 1974; reprinted (with revisions) by permission of Oxford University Press.

Taufiq Ismail: Harry Aveling (ed.), *Contemporary Indonesian Poetry*, St Lucia (Queensland), 1975; reprinted (with revisions) by permission of University of Queensland Press.
Sutardji Calzoum Bachri: *Arjuna in Meditation*, Writers Workshop, Calcutta, 1976.
A. Ghafar Ibrahim: *Tan Sri Bulan* (*My Lord Moon-Kite*), Kuala Lumpur, 1976; reprinted by permission of Dewan Bahasa dan Pustaka.

BALINESE

J. H. Hooykaas-van Leeuwen Boomkamp, *De 'Goddelijke Gast' op Bali: I Bagoes Diarsa, Balisch Gedicht en Volksverhaal* (*The 'Divine Guest' on Bali: I Bagus Diarsa, a Balinese poem and folk tale*), Batavia (i.e. Jakarta), 1949.

THAI

Anon.: *Lilit Phra Lŏ* (*The Epic of Excellency Lŏ*), Kurusapa, Bangkok, 1951.
Si Prat and Phra Maha Montree Sub: P. Na Pramuanmak (ed.), *Sib-song Kawee* (*Twelve Poets*), Praepittaya, Bangkok, 1967.
Sunthŏn Phu: Trirat Rommani (ed.), *Phēt Khōng Sunthŏn Phū* (*Eleven Works of Sunthŏn Phu*), 2nd ed., Praepittaya, Bangkok, 1967.
Mŏm Rachothai: *Nirāt Lǫndǫn lae Chotmāi-Hēt khǫng Mǫm Rāchōthai: Records of the Thai Embassy to London in 1857*, Klang Vidhya, Bangkok, 1965.
Sujit Wongtes: Chonthira Klatyu (ed.), *Song Thai* (*Thai Studies*), Suksit Siam, Bangkok, 1975.
Wat Wanlayangkoon: *Prachachāt* (newspaper), Bangkok, 1976.
Nowarat Pongpaiboon: *Pieng Kwam Kluen Wai* (*Just a Stir*), Praphansarn, Bangkok, 1976.

BURMESE

Padei-tha-ya-za: U Kyaw Dun (ed.), *Myan-ma-za Nyun-baung Kyan* (*Anthology of Burmese Literature*), Government Press, Rangoon, 1927.
Sein-dakyaw-thu: Hsaya Pwa and Maung Nyun (eds), *Yadu-mya* (*'Yadu' Poems*), Burma Research Society, Rangoon, 1929.
Nu Yin: Ashin A-nan-da (ed.), *Gu-hkit Myan-ma Kabya Let-ywei-zin Shu-gin* (*A Glimpse of Contemporary Burmese Poetry*), *Rangoon Gazette*, Rangoon, 1968.
Thamein Thaung: *Ngwei-ta-yi* magazine, Rangoon, 1973.
Tin Mo: *Hlei tazin-hnin Thachin-the* (*A Boat and a Singer*), Kaba-hkit, Mandalay, 1965.

TIBETAN

Milarepa: Sir Humphrey Clarke Bt, *The Message of Milarepa*, London, 1958; reprinted by permission of John Murray (Publishers) Ltd.
Tsangyang Gyatso: *The Blue Winged Bee: love poems of the VIth Dalai Lama*, trans. Peter Whigham, copyright by Peter Whigham, London, 1969; reprinted by permission of Anvil Press Poetry.

SANSKRIT

RIGVEDA: F. Max Müller (ed.), *Ṛg Veda Saṃhitā*, vol. 4, London, 1892.
RAMAYANA: P. L. Vaidya (ed.), *The Ayodhyākāṇḍa, the second book of the Vālmīki Rāmāyaṇa*, Baroda, 1962.
Hala: Albrecht Weber (ed.), *Das Saptaśatakam des Hāla*, Leipzig, 1881.
Shudraka: N. R. Acharya (ed.), *Mṛcchakaṭikam* (*The Little Clay Cart*), Bombay, 1950.
Kalidasa: N. R. Acharya (ed.), *Meghadūta* (*The Cloud Messenger*), Bombay, 1953.
Bhartrihari: D. D. Kosambi (ed.), *Śatakatrayādisubhāṣitasaṃgraha*, Bombay, 1948.
Amaru: N. R. Acharya (ed.), *Amaruśatakam*, Bombay, 1954.
Vidyakara's Treasury: D. D. Kosambi and V. Gokhale (eds), *Subhāṣitaratnakoṣa*, Cambridge (Mass.), 1957.
Jayadeva: Barbara Stoler Miller (ed.), *Love Song of the Dark Lord: Jayadeva's Gītagovinda* [text], New York, 1977.

BENGALI

Three Vaishnava poets: *In Praise of Krishna: songs from the Bengali*, trans. Edward C. Dimock, Jr and Denise Levertov, New York, 1967 and London, 1968; Copyright © 1967 by The Asia Society, Inc.; reprinted by permission of Doubleday & Company, Inc. and Jonathan Cape Ltd.
Rabindranath Tagore: *Rachanavali* (*Collected Works*), vol. 26, Biswa-Bharati, Calcutta, 1959 [who publish their own English translations].
Jibanananda Das: *Srestha Kabita* (*Best Poems*), Bharabi, Calcutta, 1976.
Sudhindranath Datta: *Longmans Miscellany Number Four*, 1946; reprinted by permission of Orient Longman Limited, New Delhi, India.
Buddhadev Bose: *Morche-para Pereker-gan* (*Songs of a Rusty Nail*), Bharabi, Calcutta, 1966.
Shamsur Rahman: *Srestha Kabita* (*Best Poems*), Jatiyo Shahitya Prokashoni, Dacca, 1976.
Syed Shamsul Haq: *Protidhanigan* (*Echoes*), Sandhani Prokashoni, Dacca, 1974.

URDU

Dard: K. R. Daudī (ed.), *Dīvān-i Dard* (*Lyrics of Dard*), Majlis-e Taraqqi-e Adab, Lahore, 1962.
Mir: I. Brelvī (ed.), *Kulliyāt-i Mīr* (*Works of Mir*), Urdu Dunya, Karachi, 1958.
Insha: M. Askarī (ed.), *Kalām-i Inshā* (*Verse of Insha*), Allahabad, 1952.
Ghalib: G. R. Mihr (ed.), *Dīvān-i Ghālib*, Ghulam Ali, Lahore, 1967.
Momin: K. A. K. Fāiq (ed.), *Kulliyāt-i Momin*, vol. 1, Majlis-e Taraqqi-e Adab, Lahore, 1964.
Zafar: S. A. Khān (ed.), *Intikhāb-i Kalām-i Zafar* (*Selected Verse of Zafar*), Lahore, n.d.
Iqbal: *Bāng-i Darā* (*The Call of the Road*), Ghulam Ali, Lahore, 1963.

TAMIL

Eight Anthologies: *The Interior Landscape: poems from a classical Tamil anthology,*

trans. A. K. Ramanujan, Bloomington (Indiana), 1967 and London, 1970; copyright © 1967 by A. K. Ramanujan; reprinted by permission of Indiana University Press and Peter Owen Ltd.
Oreruṛavanar: A. K. Ramanujan, *Relations*, Oxford, 1971; © Oxford University Press, 1971; reprinted by permission of Oxford University Press. Poem also included in *The Interior Landscape*, Bloomington (Indiana; q.v.), reprinted by permission of Indiana University Press.
Ponmutiyar: A. C. Turaicamippillai (ed.), *Purananuru*, 2 vols, Madras, 1962, 1967.
Nammaṛvar: Annankaracariyar (ed.), *Tiruvaymoṛi*, Kanchipuram, 1953.
Kampaṇ: Kamil Zvelebil, *The Smile of Murugan*, E. J. Brill, Leiden, 1973; reprinted (with slight revision) by permission.
Subramanya Bharati: *Paratiyar Kavitaikal*, Maturai, n.d.
N. Piccamurti: Adil Jussawallah (ed.), *New Writing in India*, Penguin, Harmondsworth, 1973.

MONGOL

ERINDZEN MERGEN: G. J. Ramstedt, ed. Harry Halén, *Nordmongolische Volksdichtung*, vol. 1, Suomalais-Ugrilainen Seura, Helsinki, 1973.
Pajai: G. Kara, *Chants d'un Barde Mongol* in *Bibliotheca Orientalis Hungarica 12*, Akadémiai Kiadó, Budapest, 1970.

KIRGHIZ

Pertev Boratav, *Aventures merveilleuses sous terre et ailleurs d'Er-Töshtük, le géant des steppes* (Unesco Collection of Representative Works—Kirghiz), Gallimard, Paris, 1965; published by permission of Unesco.

KAMASSIAN

Péter Hajdú, *Chrestomathia Samoiedica*, Tankönyvkiadó, Budapest, 1968 (English translation of poem, © The Menard Press and Keith Bosley, 1976).

VOGUL

SONG MADE BY TUR MY GRANDFATHER and SONG OF CONVERSION: B. Munkácsi (ed.), *Vogul népköltési gyüjtenény* (*Anthology of Vogul Folk Poetry*), Hungarian Academy of Sciences, Budapest, 1892–1922.
SONG ABOUT MY VILLAGE: Béla Kálmán (ed.), *Chrestomathia Vogulica*, Tankönyvkiadó, Budapest, 1976 (in Hungarian, German and Vogul).

ABKHAZ

Sh. D. Inal-ipa, K. S. Shakrel and B. V. Shĕnkwba (eds), *Nart Sasrĕqw'ei Pshĕnywazhwi Zezhwywĕk' Iara Iashcwei: Apswa Zhwlar Repos* (*Nart Sasrĕqwa and his Ninety-nine Brothers: Abkhaz folk epic*), Sukhumi, 1962.

GEORGIAN

THE YOUTH AND THE LEOPARD: *K'ot'et'ishvili* (ed.), *Xalxuri P'oezia* (*Folk Poetry*), Tbilisi, 1961.
Shota Rustaveli: *Vepxist'q'aosani* (*The Knight in the Panther Skin*), Ganatleba, Tbilisi, 1966.
Vazha Pshavela: *Xuti P'oema* (*Five Poems*), Tbilisi University, Tbilisi, 1975.
Galaktion Tabidze and Titsian Tabidze: Donald Rayfield (trans.), *Modern Poetry in Translation*, London, 1974.

ARMENIAN

BIRTH OF THE FIRE-GOD: Moses of Khorene, *Badmoutyun Hayots* (*History of the Armenians*), Monastery of San Lazzaro, Venice, 1881.
St Gregory of Narek: *Madyan Voghbergoutyan* (*Book of Lamentations*), Monastery of San Lazzaro, Venice, 1926.
Nahabed Kouchag: *Haireni Garkav* (*Collected Stanzas*), Haibedhrad, Yerevan, 1957.
Vahan Tekeyan: *Ser* (*Love*), Araks Press, Paris, 1933.
Siamanto: *Hadĕndir* (*Selected Poems*), Edvan Press, Beirut, 1955.
Daniel Varouzhan: *Hetanos Yerker* (*Heathen Songs*), Shant Press, Istanbul, 1912.
Yeghishe Charents: *Panasdeghtsoutyunner* (*Poems*), vol. 1, Sevan Press, Beirut, 1955.

PERSIAN

Rudaki: Basil Bunting, *Collected Poems*, London, 1968 and Oxford, 1978; © Basil Bunting 1978; reprinted by permission of Oxford University Press. L. P. Elwell-Sutton, 'The Ruba'i in Early Persian Literature', in *The Cambridge History of Iran*, vol. 4: *From the Arab Invasion to the Saljuqs*, ed. R. N. Frye, London and Cambridge, 1975; reprinted by permission of Cambridge University Press.
Firdawsi: Beroukhim after Vullers (ed.), *Shahnama*, Tehran, 1934–5.
Farrokhi: Nizami 'Aruzi, ed. Mirza Muhammad Qazvini, *Chahar Maqala* (*Four 'Discourses'*), Cambridge and London, 1910.
'Unsuri, Abu Sa'id ibn Abi'l-Khair and Mu'izzi: as Rudaki (Elwell-Sutton).
Minuchihri: Muhammad Dabirsiyaghi (ed.), *Divan-i-Minuchihri*, Tehran, 1324/1945.
Omar Khayyam: Muhammad 'Ali Furughi and Dr Ghani (eds), *Ruba'iyat-i-Hakim Khayyam-i-Nishaburi*, Tehran, 1321/1943. Sadiq Hedayat, *Taranehha-ye-Khayyam*, Tehran, 1313/1934–5.
Rumi: Badi' al-Zaman Firuzanfar (ed.), *Kulliyat-i-Shams ya Divan-i-Kabir*, Tehran, 1957–68. R. A. Nicholson (ed.), *The Masnavi* [text], Leiden and London, 1925.
Amir Khusrow Dehlavi: *Kulliyat-i 'anasir-i dawawin-i Amir Khusrow* (*Collected Elements of the Diwans of Amir Khusrow*), Nawal Kishor, Lucknow/Cawnpore, 1328/1910.
Hafiz: Natil Parviz Khanlari (ed.), *Ghazalha-ye-Hafiz-i-Shirazi*, Sokhan, Tehran, 1959.
Abu Talib Kalim and Hatif of Isfahan: E. G. Browne, *A Literary History of Persia*, vol. 4 [text], Cambridge University Press, Cambridge, 1930.
Iraj: F. Machałski, *La Littérature de l'Iran contemporain*, vol. 1, Cracow, 1965.

ANCIENT EGYPTIAN

Pyramid texts, wisdom literature and religious poetry: Miriam Lichtheim, *Ancient Egyptian Literature: a book of readings*, 2 vols, Berkeley (Los Angeles) and New York; vol. 1 Copyright 1973 by The Regents of the University of California, vol. 2 Copyright 1976 by The Regents of the University of California; reprinted by permission of the University of California Press.
Love songs: John L. Foster, *Love Songs of the New Kingdom*, New York; copyright © 1974 John L. Foster; reprinted by permission of Charles Scribner's Sons.

UGARITIC

The Tale of Aqhat, London; © 1978 The Menard Press and Francis Landy.

MESOPOTAMIAN (SUMERIAN, AKKADIAN)

THE EPIC OF GILGAMESH: *The Epic of Gilgamesh*, trans. N. K. Sandars, Harmondsworth (Penguin Classics, Revised edition, 1972), pp. 114–17; © N. K. Sandars, 1960, 1964, 1972; reprinted by permission of Penguin Books Ltd.
THE BABYLONIAN CREATION EPIC and INANNA'S JOURNEY TO HELL: *Poems of Heaven and Hell from Ancient Mesopotamia*, trans. N. K. Sandars, Harmondsworth (Penguin Classics, 1971), pp 73, 155–57, 160, 164; © N. K. Sandars, 1971; reprinted by permission of Penguin Books Ltd.
THE MESSAGE OF LUDINGIRA TO HIS MOTHER: Jerrold S. Cooper, 'New Cuneiform Parallels to the Song of Songs' in *Journal of Biblical Literature*, Missoula (Montana) 1971.
A late Babylonian religious text: W. G. Lambert, 'The Problem of the Love Lyrics' in Goedicke and Roberts (eds), *Unity and Diversity: Essays in the History, Literature and Religion of the Ancient Near East*, Johns Hopkins University Press, Baltimore, 1975.
A LAMENT: Raphael Kutscher, *Oh Angry Sea*, Yale University Press, New Haven (Conn.); Copyright © 1975 by Yale University.
PROVERBS: E. I. Gordon, *Sumerian Proverbs*, University of Pennsylvania Press, Philadelphia, 1959; reprinted by permission of the University Museum, University of Pennsylvania.

TURKISH

THE BOOK OF DEDE KORKUT: *The Book of Dede Korkut*, trans. Geoffrey Lewis, London (Penguin Classics, 1974), pp. 95–96, 98; translation © Geoffrey Lewis, 1974; reprinted by permission of Penguin Books Ltd.
Yunus Emre, Eşrefoğlu, Nedim and Ahmet Haşim: *Başlangıcından Bugüne Türk Şiiri* (*Turkish Poetry from the Beginning to the Present Day*), Varlık, Istanbul, 1968.
Nazım Hikmet: *Selected Poems*, trans. Taner Baybars, London and New York, 1967; reprinted by permission of Jonathan Cape Ltd (distributed in the United States by Grossman Publishers).
Cahit Sıtkı Tarancı, Orhan Veli Kanik and Oktay Rifat: *Literature East and West* magazine, Austin (Texas), 1973.
Fazıl Hüsnü Dağlarca, İlhan Berk and Cahit Külebi: *Modern Poetry in Translation*, 1971; copyright in translations held by the translators.

Melih Cevdet Anday: *Göçebe Denizin Üstünde* (*On the Nomad Sea*), Cem Yayınları, Istanbul, 1970; translation © Nermin Menemencioğlu, 1979.
Behçet Necatigil, Attilâ İlhan and Cemal Süreya: *The Penguin Book of Turkish Verse*, ed. Nermin Menemencioğlu in collaboration with Fahir İz, London, 1978; copyright © Nermin Menemencioğlu and Fahir İz, 1978; reprinted by permission of Nermin Menemencioğlu.
Can Yücel: *Sevgi Duvarı* (*Wall of Love*), Sander Yahinları, Istanbul, 1973.

ARABIC

Find al-Zimmani: Abu Tammam, *Hamasa* (*Heroic Poetry*), Cairo, 1954.
Munakhal al-Yashkuri and Waddah al-Yaman: Abu al-Faraj al-Isfahani, *Kitab al-Aghani* (*The Book of Songs*), Cairo, 1935.
Urwa ibn al-Ward: *Diwan* (*Lyrics*), Damascus, 1966.
Abu Mihjan: *Diwan*, Beirut, 1970.
Majnun Laila: *Majnun Laila*, trans. A. Y. al-Udhari and G. B. H. Wightman, TR Press, London, 1976.
Jamil: *Diwan*, Cairo, 1960.
Umar ibn Abi Rabi'a: *Diwan*, Beirut, 1952.
Arji: *Diwan*, Baghdad, 1956.
Abu al-Shamaqmaq: Jahiz, *Kitab al-Hayawan* (*The Book of Animals*), Cairo, 1943.
Abu Nuwas: Adonis, *Diwan al-Shi'r al-Arabi* (*An Anthology of Arab Poetry*), Beirut, 1964.
Abbas ibn al-Ahnaf, Abdullah ibn al-Mu'tazz and Abu al-Ala al-Ma'arri: A. Y. al-Udhari and G. B. H. Wightman, *Birds through a Ceiling of Alabaster: three Abbasid poets*, Harmondsworth (Penguin Classics, 1975); Copyright © G. B. H. Wightman and A. Y. al-Udhari, 1975; reprinted by permission of Penguin Books Ltd.
Ibn al-Rumi: *Diwan*, Cairo, c. 1930.
Buhturi: *Diwan*, Cairo, 1964.
Mutanabbi: *Diwan*, Beirut, 1964.
Hafsa bint Hamdun, Wallada, Nazhun and Mariam bint Abu Ya'qub: Maqqari, *Nafh al-Tib min Ghusn al-Andalus al-Ratib* (*The Fragrant Branch of al-Andalus*), Beirut, 1968.
Hafsa bint al-Haj: Ibn Sa'id, *Al-Mughrib fi Hula al-Maghrib* (*Rare Gems from al-Maghrib and al-Andalus*), Cairo, 1955.
Yusuf al-Khal: *Al-A'mal al-Shi'riya al-Kamila* (*Collected Poems*), Al-Ta'awiniya al-Lubnaniya lil Tauzi wal Nashr, Beirut, 1973.
Nizar Qabbani, Mouin Besseiso, Shauqi Abu Shaqra and Unsi al-Haj: Abdullah al-Udhari, *A Mirror for Autumn*, Menard Press, London, 1974.
Abdul Wahab al-Bayati: *The Singer and the Moon*, trans. Abdullah al-Udhari, TR Press, London, 1976.
Buland al-Haidari: *Songs of the Tired Guard*, trans. Abdullah al-Udhari, TR Press, London, 1977.
Adonis: *Mirrors*, trans. Abdullah al-Udhari, TR Press, London, 1976.
Muhammad al-Maghut: *Al-A'mal al-Kamila* (*Collected Poems*), Dar al-Auda, Beirut, 1973.
Samih al-Qasim: *Al-Maut al-Kabir* (*The Great Death*), Dar al-Adab, Beirut, 1972.

HEBREW

Extracts from the Authorised Version of the Bible, which is Crown Copyright, are reprinted with permission.

A PILGRIM'S SONG: Hebrew Bible.

LOVE SONG: Keith Bosley, *The Song of Songs*, Andoversford, 1976; reprinted by permission of the Whittington Press.

OUT OF THE WHIRLWIND: Stephen Mitchell, *God Damn the Day I Was Born: a translation of the Book of Job*, New York, 1979; reprinted by permission of Doubleday & Company, Inc.

THE PRAYER-BOOK: *Authorised Daily Prayer-Book*, ed. S. Singer, many editions.

Amittai ben Shephatiah, Solomon ibn Gabirol and Moses ibn Ezra: A. E. Millgram (ed.), *An Anthology of Medieval Hebrew Literature*, Abelard Schuman, London and New York, 1961; Copyright © 1961 by Abraham E. Millgram; translations of Amittai ben Shephatiah and Solomon ibn Gabirol reprinted by permission of Harper & Row, Publishers, Inc.

Judah ha-Levi: David Goldstein, *The Jewish Poets of Spain*, Penguin, Harmondsworth, 1971.

Abraham ibn Ezra: H. Brody and M. Wiener, *Mivhar ha-Shirah ha-Ivrit* (*Anthology of Hebrew Poetry*), Insel Verlag, Leipzig, 1922.

ADON OLAM: G. A. Kohut (ed.), *A Hebrew Anthology*, S. Bacharach, Cincinnati, 1913.

Immanuel Frances: J. Schirmann (ed.), *Anthologie der hebräischen Dichtung in Italien*, Schocken Verlag, Berlin, 1934.

Chaim Nachman Bialik: *Kitvei* (*Writings*), Dvir, Tel Aviv, 1935.

David Vogel: A. C. Jacobs (tr.), *The Dark Gate: selected poems of David Vogel*, London, © 1976 The Menard Press and A. C. Jacobs.

Uri Zvi Greenberg: S. Y. Penueli and A. Ukhmani (eds), *Anthology of Modern Hebrew Poetry*, Institute for the Translation of Hebrew Literature, Jerusalem, 1966; copyright reserved by the author.

S. Shalom and Leah Goldberg: Ruth Finer Mintz (ed.), *Modern Hebrew Poetry: a bilingual anthology*, Berkeley (Los Angeles) and New York; Copyright 1966 by The Regents of the University of California; reprinted by permission of the University of California Press.

Yehuda Amichai: *Ha'aretz* (newspaper), Jerusalem, 1973.

Haim Be'er: *Sha'ashu'im Yom Yom* (*Delights Day by Day*), Am Oved, Tel Aviv, 1970.

Appendix

It is the wish of the publishers of the works of Rabindranath Tagore, Viśva-Bharati, Calcutta, that the translation by Amiya Chakravorty of Tagore's poem No. 15 from *Seshlekha* (included in *Rabindra-Rachanavali*, vol. 26, Viśva-Bharati) should be given here as the authorised English version of this poem, and for this reason the version they would have preferred to appear in this book. Dr Chakravorty's translation entitled 'The Last Poem' is included in Tagore, *Poems*, Viśva-Bharati.

Acknowledgement is made to Viśva-Bharati for their permission to print the three versions of Tagore appearing on pages 139–40. Viśva-Bharati record their preference for 'greet' rather than 'salute' in '*from* On a Sickbed' (page 140, line 4), and point out that the originals of this and the version entitled '*from* Birthday' are included in *Rabindra-Rachanavali*, vol. 25 (No. 27 from *Rogsayyay* and No. 9 from *Janmadine*).

Rabindranath Tagore

THE LAST POEM

Your creation's path you have covered
with a varied net of wiles,
Thou Guileful One
False belief's snare you have
laid with skilful hands
in simple lives.
With this deceit have you left a mark
on Greatness;
for him kept no secret night.
The path that is shown to him
by your star
is the path of his own heart
ever lucid,
which his simple faith
makes eternally shine.
Crooked outside yet it is straight within,
in this is his pride.
Futile he is called by men.
Truth he wins
in his inner heart washed
with his own light.
Nothing can deceive him,
the last reward he carries
to his treasure-house.
He who has easefully borne your wile
gets from your hands
the unwasting right to peace.